INfINITE

By Lyrra

无限之选

2019—2020
中国餐厅指南

THE CHOICE OF INFINITE OF CHINA CITIC BANK RESTAURANT GUIDE BOOK 2019—2020

李赛钛◎编

中信出版集团 | 北京

图书在版编目（CIP）数据

无限之选2019—2020中国餐厅指南 / 李赛铱编. -- 北京：中信出版社, 2019.6
ISBN 978-7-5217-0538-6

Ⅰ.①无… Ⅱ.①李… Ⅲ.①餐馆－中国－2019-2020－指南 Ⅳ.①F726.93-62

中国版本图书馆CIP数据核字(2019)第086142号

无限之选2019—2020中国餐厅指南

编　　者：李赛铱
出版发行：中信出版集团股份有限公司
（北京市朝阳区惠新东街甲4号富盛大厦2座 邮编 100029）
承 印 者：北京盛通印刷股份有限公司

开　　本：787mm×1092mm　1/16　　印　　张：17　　字　　数：220千字
版　　次：2019年6月第1版　　印　　次：2019年6月第1次印刷
广告经营许可证：京朝工商广字第8087号
书　　号：ISBN 978-7-5217-0538-6
定　　价：96.00元

美食不仅是一个被物化的载体，它还让人心情愉悦，在美食的影响下，所有阴霾都可以被甩在脑后。调研显示，大部分受访者认为享受美食是生活中的重要组成部分，希望能在有限的时间和行程里找到美味又舒适的餐厅，但相对的，有近 80% 的人认为，简单、快捷地找到环境优雅、菜品优良的餐厅仍然比较困难。

曾经，很多中信银行信用卡客户为了寻找到好的餐厅而劳心费力，一部分客户为此还特地寻求我们的帮助，而我们总能很快为客户寻找到环境佳、菜品好的餐厅，让他们能够节省更多时间精力来畅快地享受美食盛宴。在多次满足客户的需求后，我们渐渐萌生了把好餐厅与热爱美食的人联结在一起的想法，让更多的人去发现美食，分享美食带来的愉悦。

因为责任，我们精益求精；因为热爱，我们乐此不疲。希望在未来的岁月里，大家可以带上这本指南和中信银行信用卡，迎接每一个享用美食的美好日子。

Tasty food is not only a real object but also mental enjoyment that can bring in recreation and pleasure for human. Under the influence of it, all upset and blue mood could be left behind. As shown by the research, most of the interviewees regarded that the delicious were the most important part of life and hoped to find out a cozy restaurant to taste good food in the limited time and certain distance. However, nearly 80% of the interviewees thought that it was still pretty difficult to easily and quickly find out an elegant restaurant providing delicious food.

Many CITIC credit card users had ever paid a lot of effort to find out a great restaurant and even some of them would turn to us for help. And we could always satisfy them by introducing a comfortable restaurant with good food and helping them enjoy a feast in an easy way and save time and energy for them. After many times of such trials, an idea came to us. That is, to become a bridge connecting the good restaurants and the food lovers, helping more people to discover tasty food and sharing the pleasure from delicious food with more people.

We are always on the way for perfecting because of the sense of responsibility; we never get tired of our dedication because of love. We hope that everyone can welcome numerous nice days that are full of tasty food with our restaurant guidebooks and CITIC credit card in hand in future.

中信银行信用卡中心
Credit Card Center of China CITIC Bank

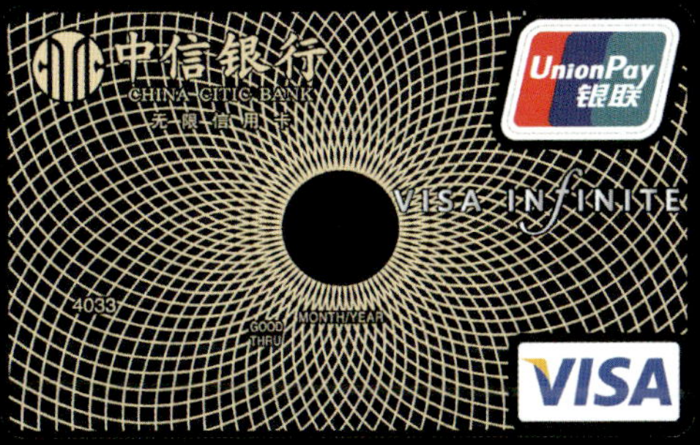

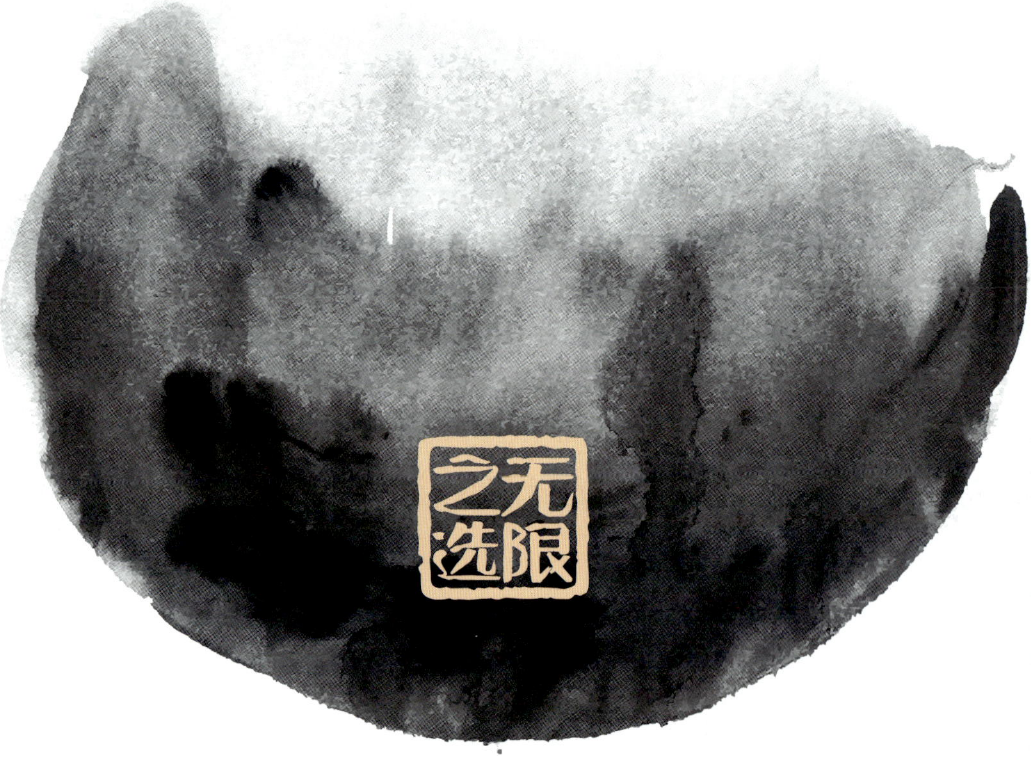
无限之选

目 录
CONTENTS

所列信息截止日期为 2018 年 12 月 31 日，难免会有更新变化，最后请以相关餐厅的官网信息为准

编者的话
FROM THE EDITOR

李赛铱
Angelina Saiyi Lee
无限之选创始人
Founder
The Choice of Infinite

餐饮行业发展到了今天，延伸出了多重功能，但无论是哪种功能，最终也是最重要的一步依然和千百年前没有变化，就是将食物放入口中的那一刻，让食物原始的味道充盈于口中。所以评价一家餐厅好与坏的标准始终是：好不好吃？

涉及餐厅指南，这就意味着，一本好的指南需要尽可能地多涵盖好吃的餐厅。然而评价一家餐厅好吃与否，是需要一个多么复杂的评审体系来得出，我们生活在信息经济时代，本身就依赖于迅速更新的复杂体系，比如，我们现在的餐饮数据在10年前我做第一本餐饮指南的时候根本是不存在的，而且有可能在10年后也会过时，即使是20世纪90年代，餐饮从业者根本想不到今天还需要掌握数字分析能力。所以想要在餐饮指南中保持价值，必须快速学习复杂的统计艺术及不断更新评价项目，如果不进行更新，很有可能随着大众消费的更迭而被淘汰。

中国的好餐厅千千万，想要把好餐厅都囊括进一本纸质的餐厅指南是相当困难的。今年的餐厅指南，与之前的相比不但餐厅数量增加了一倍，更是用了一年半的时间来观察它们在市场上稳定的经营能力，同时我们继续与微软必应搜索引擎合作，从原来的全国全网数据抓取，延伸到全球全网数据抓取，我们用数据展示了国人的消费及喜好习惯。同时根据这几年餐饮风向的改变，增加了最具性价比餐厅、健康餐厅、约会胜地等选项，意图延续无限之选餐厅指南的初衷：把最好的美食经验分享出去。

我们希望食客们能捕捉到关于美食变化的这些细节，让自己的每一顿饭都变成人生中难忘的记忆。

With the development of today's catering industry, the restaurants have extended multiple functions, but no matter what, the most important function has no changed for thousands of years, that is releasing the original tastes of food in the mouth after eating. So the criterion used to evaluate whether a restaurant is good or bad is always: Does it delicious?

For a restaurant guide, it means that an excellent guide needs to provide as many good restaurants as possible. However, the evaluation of whether a restaurant is delicious or not passes through a complex review system. We are living in the era of information economy, and depend on the rapid updating of complex systems. For example, the catering data we now have does not exist 10 years ago when I was preparing the first restaurant guide, and it may also become obsolete after 10 years, even the food and beverage practitioners in the 90s would not expect that they should grasp the digital analysis ability today. Therefore, in order to maintain the value among catering guides, it is necessary to learn the complex statistical methods quickly and keep the evaluation projects up to date. Without updating, it is likely to be eliminated as the mass consumption changes.

There are so many good restaurants in China; therefore it is difficult to cover them all in a paper restaurant guide. Compared with the former, this restaurant guide not only includes more restaurants, but also assess their business ability during stable market for one and a half years; at the same time, we continue to work with Microsoft's Bing to collect data expanded from the entire national network to the entire global network, we demonstrate the consumption habits and preferences of our people through data. Besides, according to the changes in the direction of catering in recent years, we add some new options, such as the most cost-effective restaurants, healthy restaurants, the best dating places, with the original intention of Infinite Restaurant Guide Book: share the best food experience.

We hope that diners can discover the details of food changes and leave an unforgettable memory of each meal in their life.

使用方法
HOW TO USE

扫二维码可查看餐厅信息
Scan QR Code for More Restaurant Information

餐厅菜系
Cuisine

餐厅信息
Restaurant Description

餐厅星级
Stars of Restaurant

无限卡特权
Unlimited Card Privilege

必应搜索指数
Bing Search Index

最受欢迎餐厅
The Most Popular Restaurants

地区分类
Regional Classification

迪卡博意大利餐厅
Daccapo

意大利菜
Italian Cuisine

必应 搜索热度 Search priority 5.8

电话 /Tel
+86 10 8522 1888-3826

地址 /Address
北京市东城区金宝街 99 号丽晶酒店 2 层
2F, Regent Hotel, No.99, Jinbao Street, Dongcheng District, Beijing

营业时间 Opening Hours
午餐 Lunch 11:30 - 14:30
晚餐 Dinner 18:00 - 22:30
着装要求 Dress Code
商务休闲 Business Casual
人均消费
Per Capita Consumption
283 元 283 RMB

迪卡博的环境透着浓郁的意大利风情，服务也充满意大利式的热情。餐厅以轻松的方式延续意式美食的精髓，午餐时间氛围自在活泼，入夜后则洋溢着惬意悠闲的气息。
It is decorated in Italian styles with Italian-style considerate services. It provides delicacies in a relaxing way, and creates delightful lunch period and cozy dinner atmosphere.

长安壹号
Made in China

无限卡特权

中餐
Chinese Cuisine

必应 搜索热度 Search priority 9.1

电话 /Tel
+86 10 6510 9024

地址 /Address
北京市东长安街 1 号东方君悦大酒店大堂层
Lobby, Grand Hyatt Hotel Beijing, No.1, Chang' an East Street, Beijing

营业时间 Opening Hours
早餐 Breakfast 06:30 - 10:00
午餐 Lunch 11:30 - 14:30
晚餐 Dinner 17:30 - 22:30
着装要求 Dress Code
商务休闲 Business Casual
人均消费 Per Capita Consumption
300 元 300 RMB

长安壹号风格独特，走的是摩登中国风，就餐环境优美，开放式厨房还可以令食客现场目睹美味佳肴的制作过程。菜肴精选了不少深入人心的中国传统美味，中西合璧，别有意境。
With a unique style, Made in China is an awesome modern Chinese restaurant with beautiful space and open kitchen where the diners can enjoy the culinary show. It features many popular specialties from northern China,and touch of western flavor with Chinese characteristics.

BEIJING 北京 · 11

无线网络
Wi-Fi

需订位
Reservations Required

有包房
Private Room

残疾人通道
Passage for the Disabled

有露台
Terrace Dining

有景观
With a View

可刷卡
POS

新上榜
New Entrant

最佳约会餐厅
Best Dating Restaurant

代客停车
Valet Parking

有停车位
Car Park

新店开业
Newly Opened

有优良酒单
Excellent Wine List

餐厅星级
Stars of Restaurant

最佳健康餐
Optimal Health Diet

最具性价比
Most Cost-effective

中信银行 Visa 无限卡用户餐前小食
Snacks for Infinite Cardholders

中信银行 Visa 无限卡用户优先订位
Priority Reservation for Infinite Cardholders

郑永麒
Vicky Cheng

VEA Restaurant and Lounge 主厨
VEA Restaurant and Lounge Chef

中国最佳青年厨师 China's Best Emerging Chefs

郑永麒虽然在西方文化下长大，但是不忘他的亚洲血统与传统，他综合了中国菜与法国菜的特色，结合了法国烹饪技术的精确性和技巧，并始终强调使用新鲜、正宗和季节性的食材，其中餐厅的食材选自世界各地，尤其是亚洲地区。在 VEA 餐厅，精心制作的品尝菜单围绕着一种独特的烹饪理念，就是当食材对香港本地食客散发出怀旧的吸引力时，对于外国食客可能是一种口味上的新发现。

Vicky Cheng grew up in Western culture, but he did not forget his Asian descent and traditions. He combines the characteristics of Chinese cuisine with French food, adopts the accuracy and skills of French culinary arts, and always selects fresh, authentic and seasonal food materials. The ingredients of this restaurant come from all over the world, especially from Asia. At VEA, the elaborate menu displays a unique culinary concept: the ingredients attracts local Hong Kong diners because of nostalgic atmosphere, and may be new flavors for foreign diners.

HONG KONG 香港 · 257

厨师姓名
Chef Name

厨师所在餐厅
Current Restaurant

厨师奖项分类
Chef Awards Classification

厨师介绍
Chef Introduction

厨师所在地区
Current Regional

星级餐厅
STAR RESTAURANTS

三星餐厅
3-Star Restaurants

福和慧（上海）
Fu He Hui(Shanghai)

Ultraviolet by Paul Pairet（上海）
Ultraviolet by Paul Pairet(Shanghai)

8½ Otto e Mezzo BOMBANA（香港）
8½ Otto e Mezzo BOMBANA(Hong Kong)

Amber（香港）
Amber(Hong Kong)

Bo Innovation（香港）
Bo Innovation(Hong Kong)

Caprice（香港）
Caprice(Hong Kong)

乔尔 · 卢布松美食坊（香港）
L'Atelier de Joël Robuchon(Hong Kong)

龙景轩 （香港）
Lung King Heen(Hong Kong)

二星餐厅
2-Star Restaurants

官也街澳门火锅（北京新源里店）
Guanyejie Macao Hotpot(Beijing Xinyuanli)

京华阁（北京）
The Capital(Beijing)

Mio（北京）
Mio(Beijing)

海天阁中餐厅（北京）
The Horizon Chinese Restaurant(Beijing)

Opera BOMBANA（北京）
Opera BOMBANA(Beijing)

夏宫（北京）
Summer Palace(Beijing)

小红门港式海鲜火锅（北京永安里店）
Red Door(Beijing Yonganli)

鮨魯山（香港）
Rozan(Hong Kong)

乔尔 · 卢布松美食坊（上海）
L'Atelier de Joël Robuchon(Shanghai)

Mr & Mrs Bund – Modern Eatery by Paul Pairet（上海
Mr & Mrs Bund – Modern Eatery by Paul Pairet(Shanghai)

喜粤 8 号（上海）
Canton 8(Shanghai)

兰庭厉家菜（上海）
Family Li Imperial Cuisine(Shanghai)

Felix（香港）
Felix(Hong Kong)

吉地士餐厅（香港）
Gaddi's (Hong Kong)

Tosca（香港）
Tosca(Hong Kong)

天龙轩（香港）
Tin Lung Heen(Hong Kong)

Wagyu Takumi（香港）
Wagyu Takumi(Hong Kong)

柏屋香港（香港）
Kashiwaya Hong Kong(Hong Kong)

欣图轩 （香港）
Yan Toh Heen(Hong Kong)

御苑餐厅（成都）
Royal Court Restaurant(Chengdu)

湖滨 28 （杭州）
28Hubin Road(Hangzhou)

金沙厅 （杭州）
Jin Sha(Hangzhou)

钱湖渔港 （宁波）
Seafood House(Ningbo)

一星餐厅
1-Star Restaurants

采逸轩（北京）
Cai Yi Xuan(Beijing)

长安壹号（北京）
Made in China (Beijing)

大董（北京团结湖店）
Da Dong(Tuanjiehu)

京雅堂（北京）
Jing Yaa Tang(Beijing)

瓢嘻日本料理（北京）
Hyoki(Beijing)

玉（北京）
Yu(Beijing)

艾利爵士（上海）
Sir Elly's Restaurant & Terrace(Shanghai)

大董（上海环贸店）
Da Dong(iapm mall)

大蔬无界 · 外滩和美馆（上海）
WUJIE The Bund(Shanghai)

鹿园（上海）
Moose(Shanghai)

苏浙总会（上海）
Jade Mansion(Shanghai)

唐阁 （上海）
T'ang Court(Shanghai)

逸龙阁（上海）
Yi Long Court(Shanghai)

雍福会（上海）
The Yong Foo Elite(Shanghai)

雍颐庭（上海）
Yong Yi Ting(Shanghai)

玉堂春暖餐厅 （广州）
Jade River(Guangzhou)

炳胜公馆（广州）
Bing Sheng(Guangzhou)

江 - 由辉师傅主理（广州）
Jiang By Chef Fei(Guangzhou)

1949 全鸭季 （深圳）
Duck de Chine by 1949(Shenzhen)

蚝门九式（深圳海上世界店）
Oyster King (Shenzhen Sea World)

嘉麟楼 （香港）
Spring Moon(Hong Kong)

唐阁（香港）
T'ang Court(Hong Kong)

牛焱潮汕火锅（杭州）
Niu Yan Chaoshan Beef Hotpot(Hangzhou)

文华扒房 & 酒吧（香港）
Mandarin Grill & Bar(Hong Kong)

星级餐厅由持卡人、美食评审团、媒体、必应 搜索数据综合选出

The stars of the restaurants are figured out according to the evaluation by the credit cardholders, gourmet jury, media and 必应 Search Index

最受欢迎餐厅
THE MOST POPULAR RESTAURANTS

梧桐（北京）
Wish(Beijing)

琥禄（北京）
Hulu(Beijing)

晴空（深圳）
Seiku(Shenzhen)

玉（北京）
Yu(Beijing)

Mercato（上海）
Mercato(Shanghai)

串场（北京）
LINK(Beijing)

Mio（北京）
Mio(Beijing)

POP 美式餐厅与酒吧（上海）
POP American Bresserie(Shanghai)

绚景楼（上海）
Aurora(Shanghai)

On（香港）
On(Hong Kong)

樱馆（海宁）
Sakura(Haining)

长安壹号（北京）
Made in China(Beijing)

佰鲜汇（广州）
Catch(Guangzhou)

阿丽雅（北京）
Aria(Beijing)

廊桥（成都）
The Bridge(Chengdu)

TRB Hutong（北京）
TRB Hutong(Beijing)

刃扒房 （北京）
The Cut(Beijing)

意廬（广州）
Alfresco(Guangzhou)

宝丽轩中餐厅（上海）
Bvlgari(Shanghai)

最受欢迎餐厅根据 必应 全网大数据选出
The most popular restaurants are selected by the big data from 必应 Search

北京

BEIJING

Aye by Meeting Someone
Aye by Meeting Someone

西餐
Western Cuisine

3.7 必应搜索热度 Search priority

电话 /Tel
+86 10 8589 0377

地址 /Address
北京市建国路郎家园 6 号郎园 Vintage15 号楼
Building No.15, Vintage, No.6, Langjiayuan, Jianguo Road, Beijing

营业时间 Opening Hours
午餐 Lunch 11:30 – 14:30
晚餐 Dinner 17:30 – 24:00
着装要求 Dress Code
优雅便服 Smart Casual
人均消费 Per Capita Consumption
380 元 380 RMB

餐厅希望为食客塑造一个“梦境”，所以其布置充满了梦幻的色彩与元素。餐厅一层环境接近禁酒令时期的美式地下酒吧风格，二层则倾向于超现实主义风格。特色多汁龙虾饭、肉眼牛排、蒜香辣鲜虾是餐厅的招牌菜。
It is decorated in full of dreamy colors and elements in order to create a "dream" for diners. The first floor is close to the American speakeasy style in the Prohibition-era, while the second floor presents a feeling of super-realism. Its signature dishes include Featured Juicy Lobster Rice, Rib-Eye Steak and Spicy Garlic Shrimps.

阿丽雅
Aria

西餐
Western Cuisine

8.9 必应搜索热度 Search priority

电话 /Tel
+86 10 6505 2266 – 5743

地址 /Address
北京市朝阳区建国门外大街 1 号
中国大饭店大堂层
Lobby, China World Hotel, No.1, Jianguomen Outer Street, Chaoyang District, Beijing

营业时间 Opening Hours
午餐 Lunch 11:30 – 14:30
晚餐 Dinner 17:30 – 22:00
着装要求 Dress Code
优雅便服 / 商务正装
Smart Casual / Business Attire
人均消费 Per Capita Consumption
300 ~ 400 元 300 ~ 400 RMB

阿丽雅餐厅环境高雅舒适，提供全新的西班牙美食，并有品类齐全的佐餐葡萄酒。其商务午餐菜单和晚餐零点菜单展现了主厨迈克传统西班牙菜式的烹制方法。
Aria offers brand new Spanish food and an extensive wine selection in an elegant and comfortable dining environment. The set lunch and a la carte dinner menus that reflect Chef Maiker's traditional Spanish cooking technique and his passion.

Blue Note Beijing
Blue Note Beijing

西餐
Western Cuisine

必应 搜索热度 Search priority 6.3

电话 /Tel
+86 170 0000 0288

地址 /Address
北京市东城区前门东大街前门 23 号院
No.23, Qianmen East Street, Dongcheng District, Beijing

营业时间 Opening Hours
晚餐 Dinner 18:00 – 21:00
着装要求 Dress Code
正装 Formal Clothes
人均消费 Per Capita Consumption
350 元 350 RMB

Blue Note Beijing 不同于常规餐厅的用餐体验，结合了音乐与美食。餐厅坚守美食无国界的理念，主打欧陆菜系，在菜品的制作上，采用分子料理、低温烹制等多种方法，坚持在传统的基础上不断融合创新。

Differing from the dining experiences in conventional restaurants, this restaurant provides delicacies under music environment. It holds on the concept of borderless food and focuses on the Continental cuisine. In terms of the food production, it adopts molecular cuisine techniques, low-temperature cooking and other methods, and insists on the integration and innovation based on the traditions.

Bad Farmers & Our Bakery
Bad Farmers & Our Bakery

西餐
Western Cuisine

必应 搜索热度 Search priority 2.8

电话 /Tel
+86 10 8447 2821

地址 /Address
北京市三里屯路太古里北区 N8 楼 1 层
1F, Building N8, Taikoo Li North, Sanlitun Road, Beijing

营业时间 Opening Hours
10:00 – 22:00
着装要求 Dress Code
无特别着装要求 Non-specified
人均消费 Per Capita Consumption
60 元 60 RMB

Bad Farmers & Our Bakery 分别是以健康饮食为特色的潮流沙拉专卖店和以新鲜美味为特色的潮流烘焙店。Bad Farmers 为年轻人量身打造，提供减少加工成分的天然食物，而 Our Bakery 拥有技法纯熟的烘焙师和咖啡师，为食客打造新鲜的食物和饮品。

It is a fashionable salad shop featured with healthy diets and a fresh and delicious cake shop. Bad Farmers is tailored for young people by its natural foods with less processing ingredients, while Our Bakery has skilled bakers and baristas making fresh foods and drinks for diners.

北京亮
China Grill

西餐
Western Cuisine

5.9 必应搜索热度
Search priority

电话 /Tel
+86 10 8567 1099
+86 10 8567 1840

地址 /Address
北京市朝阳区建国门外大街 2 号
柏悦酒店 66 层
66F, Park Hyatt Hotel, No. 2 Jianguomen Outer Street, Chaoyang District, Beijing

营业时间 Opening Hours
午餐 Lunch 11:30 – 15:00
晚餐 Dinner 18:00 – 22:45
着装要求 Dress Code
优雅便服 Smart Casual
人均消费 Per Capita Consumption
300 元 300 RMB

北京亮拥有令人惊艳的 360 度视野，每个角落都将古城北京的韵致和现代化大都市的风情尽收眼底。喜爱西式烧烤的食客可不能错过这个经典扒房。

China Grill has a breathtaking view in each seat to overlook the historical and dazzling Beijing. Any western-grill lover won't miss this classic steak house.

吧嗒饼
Biteapitta

中东菜
Middle Eastern Cuisine

2.8 必应搜索热度
Search priority

电话 /Tel
+86 10 6467 2961

地址 /Address
北京市三里屯后街同里 2 层
2F, Tongli, Sanlitun Houjie, Beijing

营业时间 Opening Hours
11:00 – 23:30
着装要求 Dress Code
无特别着装要求 Non-specified
人均消费 Per Capita Consumption
120 元 120RMB

吧嗒饼是京城少有的主营中东菜的餐厅。餐厅面积虽然不大，但是有着浓郁的异国风情，令人流连。餐厅的鹰嘴豆泥配合着吧嗒饼，香气四溢，软糯可口。还有餐厅招牌菜夹馅鸡，烤制得恰到好处，外酥里嫩。

It specializes in Middle Eastern cuisine which is rare in Beijing. Although it is not large, there is a rich exotic atmosphere, making diners linger. The restaurant's Hummus with Bite Pitta is not only fragrant, but also soft and delicious; and the signature dish, Stuffed Chicken, is crispy outside and tender inside after baking perfectly.

博璨（官舍店）
Brotzeit(The Grand Summit)

德国菜
German Cuisine

必应 搜索热度 Search priority 2.6

电话 /Tel
+86 10 8531 5166

地址 /Address
北京市朝阳区东方东路 19 号
外交公寓官舍南区 1 层 F109
F109, 1F, Diplomatic Apartment South, No.19, Dongfang East Road, Chaoyang District, Beijing

营业时间 Opening Hours
11:00 – 24:00
着装要求 Dress Code
无特别着装要求 Non-specified
人均消费 Per Capita Consumption
200 元 200 RMB

博璨作为一家德国啤酒屋，永远洋溢着轻松休闲的气氛，走过博璨官舍店的门口，食客很难忽略扑面而来的亲切召唤。麦芽混合啤酒花的清爽，穿插着烤猪肘的焦酥气味，不时还有混合香肠的炖肉味道，让人忍不住大快朵颐。

As a German beer house, it is always brimming with relaxing and leisure atmosphere. It is hard for diners to ignore the warm call coming from the gate of this restaurant. The malt mixed with refreshing hops, the crispy smell of roasted pork elbow and sometimes the stewed meat mixed with sausage make diners can't help enjoying them.

博璨（国贸店）
Brotzeit(China World)

德国菜
German Cuisine

必应 搜索热度 Search priority 2.6

电话 /Tel
+86 10 6505 6068

地址 /Address
北京市朝阳区建国门外大街 1 号
国贸商城北区 7 层 NL7006
NL7006, 7F, China World North, No.1, Jianguomen Outer Street, Chaoyang District, Beijing

营业时间 Opening Hours
11:00 – 24:00
着装要求 Dress Code
无特别着装要求 Non-specified
人均消费 Per Capita Consumption
200 元 200 RMB

博璨是一家经营德式菜肴的餐厅，旨在为食客带来一段美味慢时光。餐厅位置极佳，可在座位上欣赏北京繁华的景色。博璨餐厅有许多德式特色菜，其中博璨特色香肠拼盘、经典德式猪肘、牛肉土豆汤极受食客欢迎。

As a German cuisine restaurant, it aims to bring diners to enjoy a delicious and slow dining time. This restaurant is in an excellent location where can enjoy a Beijing view watching from the seats. There are many German specialties, among which the Featured Sausage Platter, Classic German Pork Elbow and Beef Potato Soup are very popular among diners.

巴西烤肉餐厅
Brazilian Churrascos

自助餐
Buffet

2.6 必应搜索热度 Search priority

电话 /Tel
+86 10 8498 2288/6178

地址 /Address
北京市朝阳区北四环中路 8 号
北辰五洲皇冠国际酒店 1 层大堂
1F, Lobby, V-Continent Wuzhou Hotel,
No.8, North 4th Circle, Middle Road,
Chaoyang District, Beijing

营业时间 Opening Hours
午餐 Lunch 11:30 – 14:30
晚餐 Dinner 17:30 – 22:30
着装要求 Dress Code
优雅便服 Smart Casual
人均消费 Per Capita Consumption
150 ~ 250 元 150 ~ 250 RMB

在这里可以感受到热烈奔放的南美风情，手艺精湛的厨师可根据你的喜好现场烘烤数十种美味烤肉、香肠及海鲜，简直是肉食主义者的天堂。餐厅环境宜人，服务到位，是小聚、约会的好地方。

Diners can feel the enthusiastic and exuberance of South America here. Its chefs with excellent culinary arts will bake all kinds of delicious BBQ, sausage and seafood at the scene according to diners' preferences. It is a heaven for meat lovers, and a good place for gathering and dating as it has a pleasant environment and satisfying services.

宝屋日料
Bao House Japanese Restaurant

日本料理
Japanese Cuisine

3.3 必应搜索热度 Search priority

电话 /Tel
+86 10 5972 4070

地址 /Address
北京市三里屯南路通盈中心 3 层
3F, InterContinental Sanlitun Beijing,
Sanlitun South Road, Beijing

营业时间 Opening Hours
18:00 – 22:30
着装要求 Dress Code
无特别着装要求 Non-specified
人均消费 Per Capita Consumption
900 元 900 RMB

作为京城轻奢日料的代表品牌，宝屋日料是众多日料爱好者不得不来的餐厅之一。餐厅的装修风格充满着日式的简约清雅，用餐氛围闹中有静，这里的所有食材都是由日本当天冷冻空运而来的，保证为食客提供最新鲜的口感。

As a representative brand of affordable luxury Japanese cuisine in Beijing, it is one of the must-try restaurants for many Japanese food lovers. With Japanese simple and elegant decoration style and quiet dining atmosphere, it provides the freshest taste for diners through transporting all frozen ingredients from Japan by air on the same day.

无限卡特权

本垒美式烤肉
Home Plate BBQ

美式西餐
American Western Cuisine

必应 搜索热度 Search priority 4.1

电话 /Tel
+86 400 0967 670

地址 /Address
北京市朝阳区南三里屯路
北京机电院 10 号 1 层
1F, No.10, Beijing Mechanical and Electrical Institute, Sanlitun South Road, Chaoyang District, Beijing

营业时间 Opening Hours
10:30 – 24:00
着装要求 Dress Code
优雅便服 Smart Casual
人均消费 Per Capita Consumption
150 元 150 RMB

本垒美式烤肉是京城颇具格调的传统美式烤肉餐厅，在北京饮食界独树一帜。狂野不羁的空间风格，灵感来源于美国烤肉街区并融合了传统和现代设计之美。
This is a traditional unique style American grill restaurant, which is rather extraordinary among Beijing restaurants. Inspired by the American BBQ block, Home Plate BBQ presents a bold style, blending the aesthetics of traditional and modern designs.

COVA
COVA

西餐
Western Cuisine

必应 搜索热度 Search priority 7.7

电话 /Tel
+86 10 6622 0221

地址 /Address
北京市西城区金融街购物中心 1 层 L113-116
L113-116, 1F, Financial Street Shopping Center, Xicheng District, Beijing

营业时间 Opening Hours
午餐 Lunch 11:00 – 13:30
晚餐 Dinner 18:00 – 21:30
下午茶 Afternoon Tea 14:00 – 17:30
着装要求 Dress Code
优雅便服 Smart Casual
人均消费 Per Capita Consumption
600 元 600 RMB

COVA 餐厅源于欧洲，其创立之初，店内出品各类甜品，巧克力的诱人香气吸引了整个欧洲的王公贵胄。位于金融街购物中心的 COVA 是该品牌在北京开的第一家咖啡餐厅，餐厅典雅华贵，力图呈现原汁原味的米兰总店形象。
Born in Europe, COVA 's dessert and chocolate captured the favors of numerous European notables and celebrities since its founding. COVA in Seasons Place is its first café shop in Beijing. This COVA has an elegant and dignified environment in order to bring the authentic COVA Milan flavors to Beijing.

采逸轩
Cai Yi Xuan

无限卡特权

中餐
Chinese Cuisine

3.6 必应搜索热度 Search priority

电话 /Tel
+86 10 5695 8520

地址 /Address
北京市朝阳区亮马桥路 48 号四季酒店 2 层
2F, Four Seasons Hotel, No.48 Liangmaqiao Road, Chaoyang District, Beijing

营业时间 Opening Hours
午餐 Lunch 11:30 – 14:30
晚餐 Dinner 17:30 – 22:30
着装要求 Dress Code
商务休闲 Business Casual
人均消费 Per Capita Consumption
500 元 500 RMB

采逸轩以“美食艺术体验”为主要理念，其粤菜佳肴琳琅满目，除了生猛海鲜（如鲍鱼、海参）之外，也少不了乳猪、烧鹅等特色烧味，还有多款广式滋补煲汤等，能够让来到这里的人大快朵颐。

Carrying the belief of "the Art of Dining", Cai Yi Xuan offers an impressive and extensive list of Cantonese cuisine, from live seafood—including abalone and sea cucumber—to barbecue specialties like suckling pig and roast goose, and a wide range of nourishing soups.

彩海轩
Choy's Seafood

无限卡特权

中餐
Chinese Cuisine

3.4 必应搜索热度 Search priority

电话 /Tel
+86 10 5927 8320

地址 /Address
北京市朝阳区霄云路甲 26 号
北京海航大厦万豪酒店 2 层
2F, Beijing Marriott Hotel Northeast, No.26A, Xiaoyun Road, Chaoyang District, Beijing

营业时间 Opening Hours
午餐 Lunch 11:30 – 14:30
晚餐 Dinner 17:30 – 22:30
着装要求 Dress Code
无特别着装要求 Non-specified
人均消费 Per Capita Consumption
160 元 160 RMB

北京海航大厦万豪酒店彩海轩是一个以海鲜为主题的时尚潮流中餐厅，门面大气，落地玻璃散发着低调的奢华。餐厅主打正宗粤港风味的精致菜品，是北京为数不多的正宗粤菜馆。

Located in Beijing Marriott Hotel Northeast, Choy's Seafood is a stylish Chinese restaurant featuring seafood dishes. Its massive French windows seem understatedly elegant. With its authentic regional flavor, it is one of the few authentic Cantonese restaurants around Beijing.

串场 LINK

烧烤
Broil

必应 搜索热度 Search priority 9.5

电话 /Tel
+86 182 0142 3526

地址 /Address
北京市朝阳区曙光西里甲 5 号院
No.5A, Shuguang Xili, Chaoyang District, Beijing

营业时间 Opening Hours
17:30 – 02:00
着装要求 Dress Code
无特别着装要求 Non-specified
人均消费 Per Capita Consumption
220 元 220 RMB

串场是一个充满了吃串氛围又不失优雅闲适的地方，餐厅在串的种类和食材选择上颇下功夫，最为招牌的羊肉小串选取小尾寒羊的羊肋排肉，当天送来，当天制作上桌，保证肉质鲜嫩，脂香而不腻，口感最佳。

It is a place full of atmosphere of eating strings without losing elegance and leisure. This restaurant makes great efforts in the types of strings and selection of food materials. The most famous mutton strings are made with the lamb ribs meats from small-tailed sheep which is delivered and cooked on the same day to ensure the meat freshness, flavors and fragrance without greasy for diners.

赤火锅 Red Bowl

火锅
Hotpot

必应 搜索热度 Search priority 7.4

电话 /Tel
+86 10 6536 0066

地址 /Address
北京市朝阳区呼家楼京广中心北京瑰丽酒店 1 层
1F, Rosewood Hotel Beijing, Jing Guang Centre, Hujialou, Chaoyang District, Beijing

营业时间 Opening Hours
17:30 – 01:00
着装要求 Dress Code
优雅便服 Smart Casual
人均消费 Per Capita Consumption
300 元 300 RMB

在这里，你可以优雅地享用具有时髦感的火锅大餐。赤火锅打破传统火锅概念，在保留传统火锅特色的基础上，加以改良与创新，菜单设计与餐厅轻松前卫的环境相得益彰。

This restaurant allows diners to elegantly enjoy the fashionable hotpot feast. Breaking the traditional concept of hotpot and remaining the characteristics of traditional hotpot, it also brings in improvement and innovation. Menu design echoes the restaurant environment.

大董（团结湖店）
Da Dong(Tuanjiehu)

中餐
Chinese Cuisine

3.5 必应搜索热度 Search priority

电话 /Tel
+86 10 6582 4003
+86 10 6582 2892

地址 /Address
北京市朝阳区团结湖北口 3 号楼
Building 3, Tuanjiehu Park North Gate, Chaoyang District, Beijing

营业时间 Opening Hours
11:00 - 22:00
着装要求 Dress Code
优雅便服 Smart Casual
人均消费 Per Capita Consumption
300 ~ 600 元 300 ~ 600 RMB

在大董餐厅里，既能吃到地道的北京风味菜品，如“酥不腻”烤鸭、董氏烧海参等，也能品尝到体现高端厨艺的“一品冰花玫瑰燕”等美味。

This restaurant provides authentic Beijing cuisine, such as "Super Lean" Suckling Duck, Chef Dong's Braised Sea Cucumber and Boiled Bird's Nest with Rose Jelly which is highly demanded for masterful culinary arts.

东田的厨房
Dong Tian

私房菜
Private Cuisine

7.4 必应搜索热度 Search priority

电话 /Tel
+86 10 5367 9276

地址 /Address
北京市南三里屯路通盈中心 5 层
5F, InterContinental Sanlitun Beijing, Sanlitun South Road, Beijing

营业时间 Opening Hours
周一至周五 Mon. - Fri.
11:30 - 14:00 17:00 - 22:00
周六、周日 Sat. - Sun. 11:30 - 22:00
着装要求 Dress Code
无特别着装要求 Non-specified
人均消费 Per Capita Consumption
130 元 130 RMB

东田的厨房是由知名造型师李东田倾力打造的，旨在与食客分享自己的私房菜。餐厅环境精致，适合朋友聚会或情侣约会。餐厅最出名的就是一道正宗的京味烙饼卷带鱼，此外，私房仔姜鸡、芝士焗红薯、拔丝豆腐也是店里的招牌菜品。

It is established by a famous stylist Tony Lee to share his private home cuisine with diners. This restaurant has an exquisite environment which is suitable for friends gathering or lovers dating. The most famous dish in this restaurant is an authentic Beijing Pancake with Belt Fish. In addition, the signature dishes include Private Home Ginger Chicken, Cheese Baked Sweet Potato and Candied Floss Bean Curd.

迪卡博意大利餐厅
Daccapo

意大利菜
Italian Cuisine

必应 搜索热度 Search priority 5.8

电话 /Tel
+86 10 8522 1888-3826

地址 /Address
北京市东城区金宝街 99 号丽晶酒店 2 层
2F, Regent Hotel, No.99, Jinbao Street, Dongcheng District, Beijing

营业时间 Opening Hours
午餐 Lunch 11:30 - 14:30
晚餐 Dinner 18:00 - 22:30
着装要求 Dress Code
商务休闲 Business Casual
人均消费 Per Capita Consumption
283 元 283 RMB

迪卡博的环境透着浓郁的意大利风情，服务也充满意大利式的热情。餐厅以轻松的方式延续意式美食的精髓，午餐时间氛围自在活泼，入夜后则洋溢着惬意悠闲的气息。
It is decorated in Italian styles with Italian-style considerate services. It provides delicacies in a relaxing way, and creates delightful lunch period and cozy dinner atmosphere.

无限卡特权

长安壹号
Made in China

中餐
Chinese Cuisine

必应 搜索热度 Search priority 9.1

电话 /Tel
+86 10 6510 9024

地址 /Address
北京市东长安街 1 号东方君悦大酒店大堂
Lobby, Grand Hyatt Hotel Beijing, No.1, Chang'an East Street, Beijing

营业时间 Opening Hours
早餐 Breakfast 06:30 - 10:00
午餐 Lunch 11:30 - 14:30
晚餐 Dinner 17:30 - 22:30
着装要求 Dress Code
商务休闲 Business Casual
人均消费 Per Capita Consumption
300 元 300 RMB

长安壹号风格独特，走的是摩登中国风，就餐环境优美，开放式厨房还可以令食客现场目睹美味佳肴的制作过程。菜肴精选了不少深入人心的中国传统美味，中西合璧，别有意境。
With a unique style, Made in China is an awesome modern Chinese restaurant with beautiful space and open kitchen where the diners can enjoy the culinary show. It features many popular specialties from northern China,and touch of western flavor with Chinese characteristics.

鼎泰丰
Din Tai Fun

淮扬菜
Huaiyang Cuisine

7.0 必应搜索热度
Search priority

电话 /Tel
+86 10 8562 6583

地址 /Address
北京市朝阳区东大桥路 9 号侨福芳草地 LG2-20
LG2-20, Parkview Green, No.9, Dongdaqiao Road, Chaoyang District, Beijing

营业时间 Opening Hours
午餐 Lunch 11:00 – 14:30
晚餐 Dinner 17:00 – 21:30
着装要求 Dress Code
无特别着装要求 Non-specified
人均消费 Per Capita Consumption
150 元 150 RMB

小笼包几乎是到店客人必点的，每个小笼包都按照 5 克的皮、16 克的馅、18 个褶的标准出品，为的就是达到极佳的口感。其他点心和小菜也很丰富，食客们可以多尝试一下。

The Steamed Buns should not be missed. Each Steamed Bun must meet the quantity standard of 5 grams of wrapper, 16 grams of stuffing with 18 wrinkles. Besides, many other dim sums and side dishes are also good choices.

Feast
Feast

西餐
Western Cuisine

7.5 必应搜索热度
Search priority

电话 /Tel
+86 10 8414 9820

地址 /Address
北京市朝阳区酒仙桥路 22 号东隅酒店 2 层
2F, East Hotel, No.22, Jiuxianqiao Road, Chaoyang District, Beijing

营业时间 Opening Hours
午餐 Lunch 11:30 – 14:30
晚餐 Dinner 17:30 – 22:00
着装要求 Dress Code
优雅便服 Smart Casual
人均消费 Per Capita Consumption
180 ~ 300 元 180 ~ 300 RMB

“将简单的事情做到最好”是北京东隅酒店的全天候餐厅 Feast 的美食理念。这里有富有动感的开放式厨房，厨师们每天使用最新鲜的食材现场烹制精选国际美食。

The East Beijing's all-day dining restaurant Feast (Food by EAST) carries its food philosophy of achieving the best for simple things. With an interesting open kitchen as a feature, Feast focuses on using the freshest ingredients to cook every dish on site.

无限卡特权

FIUME 精品意大利葡萄酒餐厅
FIUME

意大利菜
Italian Cuisine

必应 搜索热度 Search priority 7.5

电话 /Tel
+86 10 6501 9878

地址 /Address
北京市朝阳区麦子店西街 39 号
No.39, Maizidian West Street, Chaoyang District, Beijing

营业时间 Opening Hours
午餐 Lunch 12:00 – 14:30
晚餐 Dinner 18:00 – 22:30
着装要求 Dress Code
商务休闲 Business Casual
人均消费 Per Capita Consumption
165 元 165 RMB

驴肉三角饼、鸽子肉大饺子搭配精选意大利红酒、白酒、啤酒、果渣白兰地和餐前酒，意趣十足。既然是葡萄酒餐厅，餐厅老板对葡萄酒的挑选自然非常用心，酒单中不乏京城罕有的意大利佳酿。

Donkey-meat triangle pie and pigeon-meat big tortellini match with Italian red wine, white wine, beer, grappa and apéritif, bringing in so interesting taste. FIUME is picky about wine and provides some Italian vintage wines that are rare in Beijing.

峰山家烤肉
Feng Shan Jia

烤肉
Barbecue

必应 搜索热度 Search priority 2.6

电话 /Tel
+86 10 5136 5198

地址 /Address
北京市三里屯路 3.3 大厦 5 层
5F, Tower 3.3, Sanlitun Road, Beijing

营业时间 Opening Hours
11:00 – 22:00
着装要求 Dress Code
无特别着装要求 Non-specified
人均消费 Per Capita Consumption
120 元 120 RMB

峰山家烤肉主营韩式烤肉，以其新鲜丰富的菜品赢得了诸多新老食客的心。餐厅的五花肉、洛杉矶牛排和雪夜秘制牛排，肉质新鲜，搭配餐厅特色烤肉酱，令食客食欲大开。此外，餐厅环境温馨，适合家人或者朋友聚餐。

It mainly provides Korean barbecue, and has won the hearts of numerous diners with its rich and fresh dishes. It serves fresh Pork Belly, Los Angeles Steak and Snowy Secret Steak with featured barbecue sauce, giving diners a good appetite. In addition, this restaurant has a warm and comfortable environment, which is suitable for family or friends gatherings.

官也街澳门火锅（新源里店）
Guanyejie Macao Hotpot(Xinyuanli)

无限卡特权

火锅
Hotpot

2.6 必应搜索热度 Search priority

电话 /Tel
+86 10 8451 2520

地址 /Address
北京市朝阳区新源里 45 号
No.45, Xinyuanli, Chaoyang District, Beijing

营业时间 Opening Hours
11:00 – 04:00
着装要求 Dress Code
优雅便服 Smart Casual
人均消费 Per Capita Consumption
550 元 550 RMB

在官也街澳门火锅餐厅，你能吃到空运来的最新鲜的进口牛肉以及虾滑、鱼滑等好食材。用心制作的浓汤令官也街成为京城老饕食客及时尚明星的聚集地。
It provides the freshest beef imports, mashed shrimp paste and mashed fish paste which are delivered by air. With such top ingredients and carefully-made soup, it has become a popular restaurant among Beijing gourmets and stars.

官也街澳门火锅（国贸店）
Guanyejie Macao Hotpot(China World)

火锅
Hotpot

2.6 必应搜索热度 Search priority

电话 /Tel
+86 10 8595 0538

地址 /Address
北京建国门外大街 1 号
国贸商城北区顶 7 层 NL7001
NL7001, 7F, China World North, No.1, Jianguomen Outer Street, Beijing

营业时间 Opening Hours
11:00 – 04:00
着装要求 Dress Code
优雅便服 Smart Casual
人均消费 Per Capita Consumption
550 元 550 RMB

官也街澳门火锅国贸店地理位置绝佳，全景落地窗 270 度一览国贸好风景。在数种材料基础上加入新鲜鸡脚、猪软骨的招牌澳门鸡脚猪骨煲，肉香中更添鲜甜，满一锅胶原蛋白，美味又美容，更有满足不同食客口味的多种选择。
With the best location and panoramic windows providing 270 degrees vie of China World Trade Center scenery, it has a signature Macao Chick Feet and Pig Bone Pot adding fresh chicken feet and pig cartilages as w as dozens of materials, which is full of meat fresh and sweet flavors. T signature is not only full of collagen, but also delicious and nourishing, as w as provides a variety of choices to meet different tastes of diners.

官也街澳门火锅（东直门店）
Guanyejie Macao Hotpot(Dongzhimen)

无限卡特权

火锅
Hotpot

必应 搜索热度 Search priority 2.6

电话 /Tel
+86 10 8407 8842

地址 /Address
北京市东城区东直门内大街 9 号
NAGA 上院公寓
NAGA LOHAS Apartment, No.9 Dongzhimen Inner Street, Dongcheng District, Beijing

定位高端火锅餐厅的官也街澳门火锅，得名于澳门著名食街。老板自小在这条食街长大，也将家乡的好味道带到北京，以十余载时间将其打造成京城知名的火锅品牌。

Oriented as a high-end hotpot restaurant, Guanyejie Macao Hotpot names after Guanyejie, a well-known food street where the owner spent his childhood. He managed to bring his hometown flavor to Beijing, using more than ten years to list this restaurant as one of the best hotpots in Beijing.

营业时间 Opening Hours
11:00 – 04:00
着装要求 Dress Code
优雅便服 Smart Casual
人均消费 Per Capita Consumption
550 元 550 RMB

桂寿司
Gui Sushi

日本料理
Japanese Cuisine

必应 搜索热度 Search priority 3.7

电话 /Tel
+86 139 1062 4096
+86 10 8589 2237

地址 /Address
北京市建国路 SOHO 现代城
A 座 26 层 2610 号
Room 2610, 26F, Building A, SOHO Modern City, Jianguo Road, Beijing

“桂”来自于桂离宫一处皇家庭院，象征着高贵、吉祥。北京的桂寿司内设 5 个独立私密包厢，保证食客的清静用餐环境。此外，这里的食材均来自北海道和加拿大等地，让您的每一道菜都吃得新鲜、安心、放心。

"Gui" comes from a royal courtyard of Katsura Imperial Villa, symbolizing nobility and auspiciousness. This restaurant has 5 independent private boxes to ensure the quiet dining environment for diners. In addition, the ingredients here are all from Hokkaido, Canada and other places, so as to ensure the freshness, assurance and safety of dishes for each diner.

营业时间 Opening Hours
18:00 – 23:00
着装要求 Dress Code
无特别着装要求 Non-specified
人均消费 Per Capita Consumption
600 元 600 RMB

国贸 79
Grill 79

无限卡特权

西餐
Western Cuisine

3.6 必应搜索热度
Search priority

电话 /Tel
+86 10 8571 6459

地址 /Address
北京市建国门外大街一号 北京国贸大酒店 79 层
79F, China World Summit Wing Hotel, No.1, Jianguomen Outer Street, Beijing

营业时间 Opening Hours
午餐 Lunch 11:30 – 14:00
晚餐 Dinner 17:30 – 22:00
着装要求 Dress Code
时尚优雅正装 Fashion and Elegant Dress
人均消费 Per Capita Consumption
午餐 300 ~ 500 元
Lunch 300 ~ 500 RMB
晚餐 1000 ~ 2000 元
Dinner 1000 ~ 2000 RMB

在高居于国贸大厦 79 层的国贸 79 餐厅，你可以欣赏到令人惊叹的城市天际线，并纵览故宫壮丽的景象。和绝佳视野相呼应的，是这里令人印象深刻的用餐体验，厨师团队擅长对每个季节特供的新鲜食材进行完美的搭配。

With breathtaking views of urban skyline and the Forbidden City, Grill 79, located on Floor 79 of China World Towers, a chic, modern western restaurant, is a captivating destination for those in search of a memorable, sensory dining experience. The delicate flavors in dishes have been made with fresh seasonal ingredients by chef team.

海天阁中餐厅
The Horizon Chinese Restaurant

中餐
Chinese Cuisine

2.8 必应搜索热度
Search priority

电话 /Tel
+86 10 8565 2188

地址 /Address
北京市朝阳区光华路 1 号
北京嘉里大酒店商场 1 层
1F, Carry Center Hotel Mall, No.1. Guanghua Road, Chaoyang District, Beijing

营业时间 Opening Hours
午餐 Lunch 11:30 – 14:30
晚餐 Dinner 17:30 – 22:30
着装要求 Dress Code
优雅便服 Smart Casual
人均消费 Per Capita Consumption
200 ~ 300 元 200 ~ 300 RMB

海天阁凭借精致粤菜和北京烤鸭在饕客心中占有一席之地。开放式的厨房各具特色，其中一间用于制作以传统古法燃百年枣木而闻名的京鸭缘烤鸭，另一间则专门用于准备各式醇厚的老火靓汤。

The Horizon is famous for its refined Cantonese cuisine and Peking Roast Duck. Each open kitchen has its own style. One features the traditionally jujube wood-fired Beijing Duck; while the other for various kinds of double-stewed soup.

好酒好蔡
Howard's Gourmet

中餐
Chinese Cuisine

必应 搜索热度 Search priority 2.9

电话 /Tel
+86 10 6522 1297

地址 /Address
北京市东城区王府井大街 269 号院
王府中环 1 号楼 3 层 307 号
Room 307, 3F, Building 1, Wangfu Central, No.269, Wangfujing Street, Dongcheng District, Beijing

营业时间 Opening Hours
午餐 Lunch 11:30 – 14:30
晚餐 Dinner 17:30 – 22:00
着装要求 Dress Code
无特别着装要求 Non-specified
人均消费 Per Capita Consumption
2200 元 2200 RMB

好酒好蔡一贯坚持“中国菜的国际化表达”的美食理念，在博大精深的中国菜基础上，融入了更多合理和富有创造力的食材搭配组合，以及中国菜配威士忌的极致味蕾体验，独树一帜地完美实现了好酒好蔡餐饮理念的国际化表达。

It always insists on the food concept of “Make Chinese food international”, integrates more reasonable and creative food combinations into the extensive and profound Chinese cuisine, and matches Chinese dishes with whiskey to provide ultimate taste buds experience and innovatively present the catering concept of international expression.

禾家
JIA

粤菜
Cantonese Cuisine

必应 搜索热度 Search priority 7.9

电话 /Tel
+86 10 5926 8281

地址 /Address
北京市朝阳区将台路甲 2 号北京诺金酒店 1 层
1F, NUO Hotel Beijing, No.2A, Jiangtai Road, Chaoyang District, Beijing

营业时间 Opening Hours
午餐 Lunch
周一至周五 Mon. – Fri. 11:30 – 14:00
周六、周日 Sat. – Sun. 11:00 – 14:30
晚餐 Dinner 17:30 – 22:00
着装要求 Dress Code
优雅便服 Smart Casual
人均消费 Per Capita Consumption
400 元 400 RMB

餐厅环境雅致，除了绝美的院子，还有灵感源自明代徐渭作品的诸多装饰元素。禾家以新式粤菜为主，秉承使用当季鲜美食材烹制地道美食的理念，并根据时节变换、调整菜单。

It is chic and delicate. Besides the fabulous courtyard, there are many decorative elements inspired by Xu Wei of Ming Dynasty. It features new Cantonese cuisine, insists on using local seasonal food materials and updates its menu according to different seasons.

和木私厨（达美中心店）
The Home(Damei Center)

中餐
Chinese Cuisine

4.9 必应搜索热度 Search priority

电话 /Tel
+86 10 8892 9669

地址 /Address
北京市青年路 7 号院达美中心 5 号楼 5 层
5F, No.5, Damei Center, No.7, Qingnian Road, Beijing

营业时间 Opening Hours
11:30 – 21:30
着装要求 Dress Code
优雅便服 Smart Causal
人均消费 Per Capita Consumption
720 元 720RMB

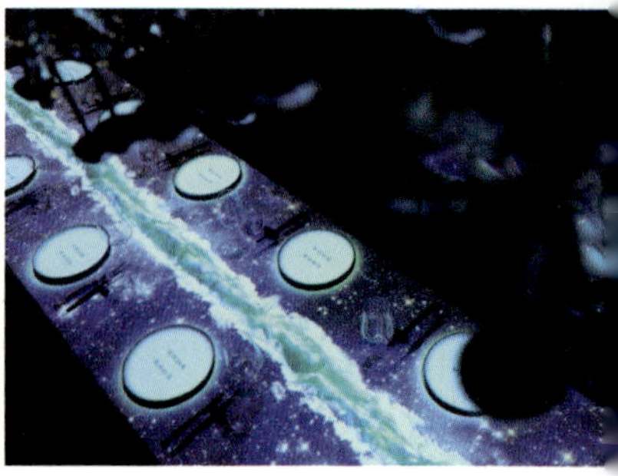

和木私厨团队携裸眼 3D 技术，打造中式感官体验餐桌，突破原先的用餐模式，将活灵活现的齐天大圣、栩栩如生的烹饪场景带到和木私厨（达美中心店）的餐桌。中式感官体验餐桌定制了一套专属菜单，给食客不同的用餐体验。

It adopts the glasses-free 3D technique to create a Chinese-style sensory experience on the table, breaking through the original dining pattern and presenting the vivid Monkey King and cooking process to diners here (Damei Center). There is a customized exclusive menu for Chinese sensory experience table to give diners a different dining experience.

和木私厨（北土城店）
The Home (Beitucheng)

无限卡特权

北京菜
Beijing Cuisine

4.9 必应搜索热度 Search priority

电话 /Tel
+86 10 6237 7681

地址 /Address
北京市海淀区北土城西路瑞洁加油站西侧
West of Ruijie Gas Station, Beitucheng West Road, Haidian District, Beijing

营业时间 Opening Hours
午餐 Lunch 11:30 – 14:00
晚餐 Dinner 17:30 – 21:00
着装要求 Dress Code
无特别着装要求 Non-specified
人均消费 Per Capita Consumption
500 元 500 RMB

和木私厨菜品精雕细琢，为每一位到店的客人提供优质餐食。同时坚持国宴级别的高规格就餐服务，每道菜按照一人份摆盘，以冷菜、汤、主菜、主食、甜品的顺序依次上桌，颇为隆重却不会让人感觉不自在。

The Home pursues upmost delicacy. It sticks to serving in the way of state banquet with each dish for one diner and following the order of cold dish, soup, main dish, staple food and dessert. By these, it gives the diner a sense of ritual and coziness.

和木私厨（鼓楼店）
The Home(Drum Tower)

创意中餐
Creative Chinese Cuisine

必应 搜索热度 Search priority 4.9

电话 /Tel
+86 134 2118 6001

地址 /Address
北京市东城区钟楼湾胡同广场草厂北巷 13 号
No.13.Caochang North Alley, Zhonglouwan Alley, Dongcheng District, Beijing

营业时间 Opening Hours
午餐 Lunch 11:00 – 14:30
晚餐 Dinner 17:00 – 22:00
着装要求 Dress Code
干净整洁 Clean and Tidy
人均消费 Per Capita Consumption
650 元 650 RMB

它隐身于北京鼓楼后面的一个小四合院里，整体环境体现了浓郁的传统中国风，所有的家具都是原木风格，呈现出有棱有角的厚重，桌上的花草和窗外小段的石头路则柔化了空间的线条。

The Home hides in a small courtyard behind Drum Tower of Beijing, presenting classical Chinese ambience. The timber furniture expresses hardness and grandness by its linear and corner features; the flowers on the table and the pebble path outside the window give the space a gentle touch.

琥禄
Hulu

西餐
Western Cuisine

必应 搜索热度 Search priority 9.9

电话 /Tel
+86 10 6512 5701

地址 /Address
北京市朝阳区三里屯北路 19 号
三里屯太古里南区 3 层 S4-32
S4-32, 3F, Taikoo Li Sanlitun South, No.19, Sanlitun North Road, Chaoyang District, Beijing

营业时间 Opening Hours
周一至周四及周日 Mon. – Thur. Sun.
11:00 – 23:00
周五、周六 Fri. – Sat. 11:00 – 24:00
着装要求 Dress Code
无特别着装要求 Non-specified
人均消费 Per Capita Consumption
212 元 212 RMB

琥禄为食客带来一个全新的餐饮概念：虽然提供高端餐饮服务，但是没有高级法餐的仪式感，轻松和分享才是这里的主旨。在菜单上你会看到体现了琥禄座右铭的菜品：森林蘑菇沙拉、烤乳猪、波士顿龙虾烩饭，丰盛感十足。

It introduces a new concept of dining for diners: it provides high-end catering services without ritual sense of fine French cuisine, and focuses on relaxing and sharing. The menu reflects its motto, such as: Forest Mushroom Salad, Roasted Suckling Pig, and Boston Lobster Risotto, which are sumptuous.

花厨（三里屯店）
Tomacado(Sanlitun)

西餐
Western Cuisine

3.2 必应搜索热度
Search priority

电话 /Tel
+86 186 1002 3354

地址 /Address
北京市东三环北路 27 号嘉铭中心 B 座 B1 层
B1, Building B, Jiaming Center, No.27, East 3rd Circle, North Road, Beijing

营业时间 Opening Hours
周一至周五 Mon. – Fri. 11:00 – 21:30
周六、周日 Sat. – Sun. 10:30 – 22:00
着装要求 Dress Code
优雅便服 Smart Casual
人均消费 Per Capita Consumption
200 元 200 RMB

花厨是一家餐厅，也是一家花店。餐厅环境美好，处处都有大量鲜花作为装饰，再加上暖色的灯光，使餐厅富有浪漫情调，适合情侣约会，或者三五好友小聚。香草烤三黄鸡、花厨特色班尼迪克蛋、花厨特色沙拉是餐厅的特色菜品。
It is a restaurant and a flower shop. This restaurant has a beautiful environment with a large number of flowers as adornment everywhere, together with the warm lighting, creating a rich romantic atmosphere, which is suitable for lovers datings and friends gathering. Its signature dishes include Herbs San Huang Chicken, Tomacado Featured Eggs Benedict, and Tomacado Featured Salad.

花样罗马
Via Roma

西餐
Western Cuisine

6.4 必应搜索热度
Search priority

电话 /Tel
+86 6465 3388-4215

地址 /Address
北京市朝阳区亮马桥路 50 号凯宾斯基饭店 1 层
1F, Kempinski Hotel, No. 50, Liangmaqiao Road, Chaoyang District, Beijing

营业时间 Opening Hours
11:00 – 22:00
着装要求 Dress Code
优雅便服 Smart Causal
人均消费 Per Capita Consumption
150 ~ 200 元 150 ~ 200 RMB

花样罗马为您呈现融合了现代元素的经典意大利美食。菜品新颖多样，服务细致，无论商务用餐还是家庭欢聚，这里都将给您带来宾至如归的温馨氛围。意大利主厨手工自制意面及披萨带来最地道的意大利味道，周末更有选择丰富的家庭自助午餐。
Via Roma redefines Italian cuisine with opulent modernity. Reinventing itself as a pizza and pasta powerhouse, the homemade creations all feature premium ingredients that are sustainably sourced. Creativity meets simplicity; the approach and philosophy of the dishes served creatively combine the classic Italy with the new in an intimate atmosphere.

凰庭
Huang Ting

中餐
Chinese Cuisine

必应 搜索热度 Search priority 3.6

电话 /Tel
+86 10 8516 2888-6707

地址 /Address
北京市东城区金鱼胡同 8 号
王府半岛酒店 B2 层
B2, Peninsula Hotel Beijing, No. 8, Jinyu Hutong, Dongcheng District, Beijing

凰庭的新餐单以粤菜为主，招牌菜首选高级烧味，冠绝京城的烤鸭与半岛集团点心大师叶永华师傅秘方炮制的夹饼相得益彰。

Huang Ting renews its menu by featuring Cantonese cuisine. The signature must be the upscale grill dishes, including the impressive Roast Duck which gets elevated by the pie made by the dim-sum master Ye Yonghua from Peninsula Corporation.

营业时间 Opening Hours
午餐 Lunch 11:30 - 14:30
晚餐 Dinner 18:00 - 22:00
着装要求 Dress Code
优雅便服 Smart Casual
人均消费 Per Capita Consumption
300 ~ 400 元 300 ~ 400 RMB

IL Ristorante Niko Romito
IL Ristorante Niko Romito

西餐
Western Cuisine

必应 搜索热度 Search priority 4.0

电话 /Tel
+86 10 8555 8585
+86 10 8555 8555

地址 /Address
北京市新源南路 8 号院 2 号楼
北京宝格丽酒店 1 层
1F, Bvlgari Hotel Beijing, Building 2, No.8, Xinyuan South Road, Beijing

餐厅坐拥怡人花园景观和雅致氛围，整体设计时尚现代，每一处元素都是为了确保宾客获得温馨的用餐体验而精心设计。餐厅严格挑选食材，通过注重探索食材本味的方法，为食材赋予全新的意义，并不断融入创意与灵感。

With a pleasant garden landscape and elegant environment, it has a fashionable and modern decoration which is carefully designed to bring diners a warm and comfortable dining experience. This restaurant strictly selects food materials, and presents them in an innovative form with brand new meaning through the method of exploring their original tastes and constantly integrating into creativity and inspiration.

营业时间 Opening Hours
早餐 Breakfast 06:30 - 10:30
午餐 Lunch 11:30 - 14:30
晚餐 Dinner 18:00 - 22:00
着装要求 Dress Code
优雅便服 Smart Casual
人均消费 Per Capita Consumption
1250 元 1250 RMB

JW Kitchen
JW Kitchen

无限卡特权

自助餐
Buffet

3.6 必应搜索热度
Search priority

电话 /Tel
+86 10 6391 6391

地址 /Address
北京市西城区宣武门外大街 18 号
北京粤财 JW 万豪酒店 4 层
4F, JW Marriott Hotel Beijing Central, No. 18, Xuanwumen Outer Street, Xicheng District, Beijing

营业时间 Opening Hours
早餐 Breakfast
周一至周五 Mon.-Fri. 06:00 - 10:30
周六、周日 Sat. - Sun. 06:00 - 11:00
午餐 Lunch 11:30 - 14:30
晚餐 Dinner 17:30 - 21:30
着装要求 Dress Code
无特别着装要求 Non-specified
人均消费 Per Capita Consumption
228 元 228 RMB

餐厅内设独特的“健康果蔬吧”，受过专门训练的厨师采用蔬菜根茎及各式果蔬精心调制各款特饮、鲜榨果汁、蔬菜汁和思慕雪，宾客还可按照个人喜好调制自己的健康饮品。
The "Healthy Garden Stuff Bar "inside the restaurant serves special drinks, freshly squeezed fruit, vegetable juices and smoothies made with vegetable rootstock and garden stuff by trained special chefs. Guests can even tailor their own blends according to personal preference.

江户前寿司（盈坤世纪店）
Edomae Sushi (Yingkun Century)

日本料理
Japanese Cuisine

4.0 必应搜索热度
Search priority

电话 /Tel
+86 10 8360 2162

地址 /Address
北京市汽车博物馆东路盈坤世纪 H 座
Building H, Yingkun Century, Motor Museum East Road, Beijing

营业时间 Opening Hours
早餐 Breakfast 06:30 - 10:30
11:00 - 22:00
着装要求 Dress Code
商务休闲 Business Casual
人均消费 Per Capita Consumption
300 元 300 RMB

江户前寿司始终坚持让食客吃到原汁原味日料的理念，整体环境为典型的日式风格，木质装饰与榻榻米让你仿佛置身于京都的料理店内。各类寿司和刺身拼盘是店里的招牌菜。
Insisting on the concept of providing original Japanese cuisine for diners, it has a typical Japanese style environment with wooden decoration and tatami, making diners feel like in the restaurant of Kyoto. Sushi and Sashimi Platter are the signature dishes of the restaurant.

健壹景园
JE MANSION

中餐
Chinese Cuisine

必应 搜索热度 Search priority 3.9

电话 /Tel
+86 10 8259 6669

地址 /Address
北京海淀区青龙桥西洼果园 18 号
No.18, Xiwa Orchard, Qinglongqiao, Haidian District, Beijing

营业时间 Opening Hours
午餐 Lunch 11:00 – 14:00
晚餐 Dinner 17:00 – 22:00
着装要求 Dress Code
商务休闲 Business casual
人均消费 Per Capita Consumption
1000 元 1000 RMB

健壹景园设有 20 间中式顶级风格包房，有北京烤鸭和各种宫廷菜肴，并复现以古法制作的宫廷菜肴。净咖啡位于一层，将中式风格与现代健康生活方式相结合。

JE MANSION has 20 exclusive VIP rooms in top Chinese style and provides Beijing Roast Duck as well as gives a recurrence of various royal dishes. Jing Coffee, located on Floor 1, is a combination of Chinese style and modern healthy life.

健壹公馆
JE MANSION

中餐
Chinese Cuisine

必应 搜索热度 Search priority 3.7

电话 /Tel
+86 10 5139 8739

地址 /Address
北京市朝阳区道家园甲 16 号
No.16A, Daojiayuan, Chaoyang District, Beijing

营业时间 Opening Hours
早餐 Breakfast 06:00 – 10:00
午餐 Lunch 11:00 – 14:00
晚餐 Dinner 17:00 – 22:00
着装要求 Dress Code
商务休闲 Business Casual
人均消费 Per Capita Consumption
1000 元 1000 RMB

坐落于繁华都市的健壹公馆可谓闹市之中的一方净土，这里的高级中餐厅呈现的是精美的中华美食，涵盖中国四大菜系。客人们在享受美食的同时，还可饱览大自然的美景。

It is an oasis of serenity in Beijing, and its high-end Chinese restaurant provides Chinese delicacies covering four major Chinese cuisines. It is the best place for enjoying delicious food and beautiful natural view.

京华阁

The Capital

私房菜
Private Home Cuisine

7.5 必应搜索热度 Search priority

电话 /Tel
+86 10 5911 8888-28

地址 /Address
北京市东城区金宝街 68 号
北京香港马会会所 1 层
1F, Beijing Hong Kong Jockey Club Clubhouse, No. 68, Jinbao Street, Dongcheng District, Beijing

营业时间 Opening Hours
午餐 Lunch 11:00 – 14:00
晚餐 Dinner 17:30 – 22:30
着装要求 Dress Code
优雅便服 Smart Casual
人均消费 Per Capita Consumption
500 元起 Starting from 500 RMB

"研味美馔荟萃，尽揽京华气韵"。京华阁长久以来凭借其向宾客提供的专业细致的私人伺餐服务以及精致如艺术的佳肴美馔而立足京城。

With an extensive collection of delicacies, special and meticulous custom service and artwork-like dishes, the Capital always has a high reputation in Beijing.

京雅堂

Jing Yaa Tang

中餐
Chinese Cuisine

3.7 必应搜索热度 Search priority

电话 /Tel
+86 10 6410 5230

地址 /Address
北京市朝阳区三里屯路 11 号
三里屯太古里北区瑜舍 LG 层
LG, Opposite House, Taikoo Li Sanlitun North, No.11, Sanlitun Road, Chaoyang District, Beijing

营业时间 Opening Hours
午餐 Lunch
周一至周五 Mon. – Fri. 12:00 – 14:30
周六、周日 Sat. – Sun. 11:00 – 14:30
晚餐 Dinner 18:00 – 22:30
着装要求 Dress Code
优雅便服 Smart Casual
人均消费 Per Capita Consumption
300 ~ 400 元 300 ~ 400 RMB

京雅堂中的"堂"取自"厅堂"，食客步入餐厅便会被强烈的中式剧院风格环绕，内部紫红色与深橘色的细节和装饰也颇具特色，公用简食餐区由烤鸭炉组成的中央舞台十分引人注目。

The word "Tang" in Jing Yaa Tang is taken from the literal Chinese translation of hall. It is designed with strong Chinese theatre style. The aubergine and deep orange detailing and ornamentals highlight the interior and the center area comprising duck ovens which attract all eyes.

京兆尹
King's Joy

素菜
vegetarian Cuisine

必应 搜索热度 Search priority 6.0

电话 /Tel
+86 10 8404 9191
+86 10 8404 8885

地址 /Address
北京市东城区五道营胡同 2 号
No.2, Wudaoying Hutong, Dongcheng District, Beijing

营业时间 Opening Hours
午餐 Lunch 11:30 – 14:00
下午茶 Afternoon Tea 14:00 – 17:00
晚餐 Dinner 17:30 – 22:00
着装要求 Dress Code
优雅便服 Smart Casual
人均消费 Per Capita Consumption
500 元 500 RMB

颇具文化内涵的京兆尹餐厅，位于北京旧城内重要的人文建筑集中街区，毗邻雍和宫，由著名建筑设计大师张永和参与整体设计，环境舒适雅致。

With strong culture connotation, King's Joy is located in the most important culture block of Beijing old town and adjoins The Lama Temple. The integrated design was made by architectural design master Zhang Yonghe, presenting a comfortable and elegant environment.

九十九顶毡房（清河店）
Ninety Nine Yurts(Qinghe)

西北菜
Northwest cuisine

必应 搜索热度 Search priority 3.4

电话 /Tel
+86 10 6299 1888
+86 10 6299 5888

地址 /Address
北京市东升乡马坊村永泰庄北路 9 号
No. 9, Yongtaizhuang North Road, Mafang Town, Dongsheng County, Beijing

营业时间 Opening Hours
午餐 Lunch 11:00 – 14:00
晚餐 Dinner 17:00 – 21:00
着装要求 Dress Code
无特别着装要求 Non-specified
人均消费 Per Capita Consumption
300 元 300 RMB

九十九顶毡房属于烤羊特色主题餐厅，餐厅有许多极富特色的蒙古包，是家庭聚会、亲朋欢庆的绝佳场所。作为餐厅特色招牌的烤全羊，更是每桌客人的必点菜品。

It is a restaurant characterized by roasted lambs. This restaurant has many special Mongolian yurts, which is the best place for family and relatives gatherings, and celebrations. The signature Roasted Lamb is a must-try dish for each table.

聚餐厅
Azur

法餐
French Cuisine

7.7 必应搜索热度 Search priority

电话 /Tel
+86 10 6841 2211-6727

地址 /Address
北京香格里拉饭店新阁 1 层
1F, New Pavilion of Shangri-La Hotel, Beijing

营业时间 Opening Hours
午餐 Lunch 11:30
晚餐 Dinner 17:30
着装要求 Dress Code
商务休闲 Business Casual
人均消费 Per Capita Consumption
900 元 900 RMB

聚作为全新的高端法餐厅由知名厨师主理，为食客带来法国南部蔚蓝海岸的正宗创意美馔，以“诠释味道，突显本味”为烹制理念，让食客们在美好梦幻的环境及精心烹调的菜品的引导下，开启对法餐的全新认知。

As a new high-end French restaurant and managed by the star chef , it provides authentic and creative dishes originated from the Cote d' Azur in the south of France for diners, and illustrates the cooking concept of natural flavors with significant mixture of tastes. It guides the diners to understand a new French food through elaborate cooking dishes under the beautiful dreaming environment.

库迈墨西哥餐厅（乐成中心 Space 3）
Q Mex Bar & Grill(Yue Cheng Centre Space 3)

美式墨西哥菜
American Mexican Cuisine

2.6 必应搜索热度 Search priority

电话 /Tel
+86 10 8770 0668

地址 /Address
北京市朝阳区东三环中路乐成中心
商场 1 层 06 号
No.06, 1F, Yue Cheng Centre Space 3 , East 3rd Circle, Central Road, Chaoyang District, Beijing

营业时间 Opening Hours
早餐 Breakfast 11:00
午餐 Lunch 11:30 - 14:30
晚餐 Dinner 17:00 - 1:00
着装要求 Dress Code
优雅便服 Smart Casual
人均消费 Per Capita Consumption
130 元 130 RMB

京城著名墨西哥餐吧库迈乐成中心分店不仅占尽地理优势，在布置上也尽显墨西哥风情。食客可尽情享受正宗的美式墨西哥热辣舌尖风情。墨西哥美味在京城拥趸众多，美食、美酒与异域风情的氛围使得餐厅闻名全城。

It is a famous Mexican restaurant with geographical advantage and Mexican style layout in Beijing. Diners can enjoy authentic American-Mexican hot flavors. Beijing has a lot of Mexican cuisine fans, therefore it is known for its cuisine, wine and exotic atmosphere around the city.

无限卡特权

库迈墨西哥餐厅（三里屯店）
Q Mex Bar & Grill(Sanlitun)

素菜
vegetarian Cuisine

必应 搜索热度 Search priority 2.6

电话 /Tel
+86 10 6585 3828

地址 /Address
北京市朝阳区工体北路 4 号院
机电研究院餐饮街内
Catering Street, Electrical and Mechanical Institute, No.4, Gongti North Road, Chaoyang District, Beijing

库迈墨西哥餐厅位于北京潮流聚集地三里屯南街，为顾客提供室内外用餐的双重选择：室内活力洋溢，室外怡情舒适——墨西哥的美食之旅由此启程。
Q Mex Bar & Grill, located at the popular south street of Beijing Sanlitun, provides dynamic indoor space and cozy outdoor space for dining. Start gourmet trip from here.

营业时间 Opening Hours
11:00 – 03:00
着装要求 Dress Code
优雅便服 Smart Casual
人均消费 Per Capita Consumption
150 元 150 RMB

库迈墨西哥餐厅（新源里店）
Q Mex Bar & Grill(Xinyuanli)

西餐
Western Cuisine

必应 搜索热度 Search priority 2.6

电话 /Tel
+86 10 8435 3601

地址 /Address
北京市朝阳区新源里西 20 号金尚 1 层 106 室
Room 106, 1F, Jinshang, No.20, Xinyuanli West Street, Chaoyang District, Beijing

餐厅环境方面着重展现墨西哥风情，菜肴方面除了自制玉米饼卷成的各类墨西哥塔可外，各种墨西哥街头的经典小吃也融入了库迈的菜单，这些美味又经典的墨西哥菜肴在食客中大受好评。
It presents the Mexican style in terms of environment and provides various Mexican tacos made by homemade tortilla, and many traditional Mexican street snacks on its menu. These delicious and typical Mexican dishes are very popular among diners.

营业时间 Opening Hours
早餐 Breakfast 11:00
午餐 Lunch 11:30 – 14:30
晚餐 Dinner 17:00 – 2:00
着装要求 Dress Code
无特别着装要求 Non-specified
人均消费 Per Capita Consumption
150 元 150 RMB

Living Room
Living Room

7.6 必应搜索热度 Search priority

西餐
Western Cuisine

电话 /Tel
+86 180 1012 5998
+86 10 5871 5515

地址 /Address
北京市工体东路 4 号
北京三里屯 CHAO 1 层
1F, Sanlitun CHAO, No.4, Gongti East Road, Beijing

营业时间 Opening Hours
11:30 - 22:00
着装要求 Dress Code
优雅便服 Smart Casual
人均消费 Per Capita Consumption
400 元 400RMB

餐厅占地 400 平方米，设有多人卡座、木质台球桌与皮质座椅，搭配绝妙灯光，旨在营造轻松的用餐氛围。餐厅的厨师团队结合中西餐饮文化，创造出适合与家人、朋友分享的独特菜单，并甄选应季的新鲜食材，精心炮制地道美味。

Covering an area of 400 square meters, it has booths, wooden billiard tables and leather seats, together with excellent lighting, aiming to create a relaxing dining atmosphere. This restaurant's chef team integrates the Chinese and Western catering culture to create a unique menu suitable for family and friends to share, and selects seasonal fresh food materials to cook authentic delicacies.

辣府
La Fu

4.4 必应搜索热度 Search priority

火锅
Hotpot

电话 /Tel
+86 10 5135 5576

地址 /Address
北京市三里屯路 33 号 3.3 大厦 3006 商铺
Shop 3006, Tower 3.3, No.33, Sanlitun Road, Beijing

营业时间 Opening Hours
11:00 - 00:30
着装要求 Dress Code
无特别着装要求 Non-specified
人均消费 Per Capita Consumption
160 元 160 RMB

辣府火锅致力于让食客获得安全、健康、舒心的食物，自开业以来，吸引了诸多资深食客的光临。餐厅将传统与现代文化相结合，为食客创造舒适温馨的就餐环境和浓郁的用餐氛围，其中辣府特级肥牛和辣府鲜毛肚最受食客欢迎。

It insists in serving diners with safe, healthy and comfortable dishes, and has attracted many senior diners since its opening. This restaurant combines traditional culture with modern culture to create a comfortable and cozy dining environment with rich atmosphere for diners. Its Spicy Superior Beef Fat and Spicy Fresh Tripes are the most popular among diners.

乐三里屯面馆
Le Noodle

中餐
Chinese Cuisine

必应搜索热度 Search priority 2.6

电话 /Tel
+86 156 1198 7000

地址 /Address
北京市三里屯北路 3.3 商场 5 层 5007 室
Room 5007, 5F, Tower 3.3, Sanlitun North Road, Beijing

营业时间 Opening Hours
午餐 Lunch 11:30 – 14:30
晚餐 Dinner 17:00 – 21:30
着装要求 Dress Code
无特别着装要求 Non-specified
人均消费 Per Capita Consumption
60 元 60 RMB

乐三里屯面馆始终坚持用心做好每一碗面，用心服务每一位客人，为食客带来最纯正的美味。餐厅位于时尚地段，时常排队火爆，其中辣爆小公鸡拌面和茄子肉丁鸡蛋拌面最受食客欢迎。

This restaurant insists on making the best noodles, serves all diners with heart, and brings the most authentic delicious food to diners. Located at a fashionable area, it is very hot and often requires to queue. The Spicy Chicken Noodles and Eggplant Meat Egg Noodles are the most popular among diners.

莲花空间（国贸店）
Louts Space(China World)

素菜
vegetarian Cuisine

必应搜索热度 Search priority 3.0

电话 /Tel
+86 10 8527 4868

地址 /Address
北京市朝阳区建国门外大街
国贸商城北区 4 层 NL4006
NL4006, 4F, China World North, Jianguomen Outer Street, Chaoyang District, Beijing

营业时间 Opening Hours
11:00 – 21:30
着装要求 Dress Code
优雅便服 Smart Casual
人均消费 Per Capita Consumption
174 元 174 RMB

花空间倡导“蔬食主义”，食材选择注重“天时地利人和”，坚持味、香、色、的出品理念，注重菜品的营养搭配和人体的消化吸收。莲花空间极力营造简洁、、不做作的禅境感受，与素雅的饮食相得益彰。

advocates "vegetable food doctrine", selects food materials based on principle of "Good timing, geographical convenience and good human ations", insists on the taste, fragrance, color, and appearance cooking ncepts, as well as focuses on the nutrition arrangement of dishes and estion and absorption of human. This restaurant tries to create a simple, axing and natural Zen style, matching with its simple and elegant cuisine.

绿川寿司屋
Midorikawa Sushi

日本料理
Japanese Cuisine

2.6 必应搜索热度 Search priority

电话 /Tel
+86 10 6416 4861

地址 /Address
北京市朝阳区工体北路 4 号
机电研究院内滚石西门对面
Opposite of Rolling Stone, Electrical and Mechanical Institute, No.4, Gongti North Road, Chaoyang District, Beijing

营业时间 Opening Hours
午餐 Lunch 11:30 – 14:00
晚餐 Dinner 17:00 – 22:00
着装要求 Dress Code
优雅便服 / 商务正装
Smart Casual / Business Attire
人均消费 Per Capita Consumption
500 元 500 RMB

主厨绿川义辉拥有 30 多年寿司制作及五星级酒店工作经验，本店更是以厨师长的名字命名。这家餐厅坚持还原最基本的日本寿司烹饪技术，坚持用蒸馏水来煮饭，以手的热度来保持寿司饭的热度。

The restaurant is named after its Executive Chef Midorikawa Yoshiteru who has over 30 years of experience of sushi making and 5-star hotel working experience. The restaurant sticks to the most traditional sushi culinary skills, using distilled water to cook rice and hand making to keep rice hot.

陆羽
Lu Yu

无限卡特权

中餐
Chinese Cuisine

5.9 必应搜索热度 Search priority

电话 /Tel
+86 10 6584 6290

地址 /Address
北京市朝阳区东三环北路 29 号
北京康莱德酒店 1 层
1F, Conrad Beijing, No. 29, East 3rd Circle, North Road, Chaoyang District, Beijing

营业时间 Opening Hours
午餐 Lunch
周一至周五 Mon. – Fri. 11:30 – 14:00
周六、周日 Sat. – Sun. 11:30 – 14:30
晚餐 Dinner 17:30 – 22:00
着装要求 Dress Code
商务休闲 Business Casual
人均消费 Per Capita Consumption
大厅 140 ~ 200 元
Public Hall 140 ~ 200 RMB
包厢 300 ~ 500 元
Box 300 ~ 500 RMB

餐厅聘请北京一流厨师打造纯正的本地特色菜式，不仅风味独特、令人垂涎，更有着宛如艺术品一般、充满创意的呈现方式。

Beijing's top chefs here create authentic local specialties, bringing in a feast of palate, fragrance and creative artwork.

龙庭
The House of Dynasties

淮扬菜
Huaiyang Cuisine

必应 搜索热度 Search priority 3.6

电话 /Tel
+86 10 6536 0066

地址 /Address
北京市朝阳区呼家楼京广中心
北京瑰丽酒店 4 层
4F, Beijing Rosewood Hotel, Jing Guang Center, Hujialou, Chaoyang District, Beijing

营业时间 Opening Hours
午餐 Lunch 11:30 – 14:30
晚餐 Dinner 17:30 – 22:30
着装要求 Dress Code
优雅便服 Smart Casual
人均消费 Per Capita Consumption
零点 300 ~ 400 元
A La Carte 300 ~ 400 RMB
套餐 680 ~ 1680 元
Set Course 680 ~ 1680 RMB

龙庭主打精致淮扬菜，厨师将流传几百年的传统宫廷菜式加以改良，制作出符合现代人口味的经典菜肴，用料讲究，令人回味无穷。

The restaurant features exquisite Huaiyang cuisine. The chef improves the traditional palace dishes of hundreds-years history to create a modern taste. It devotes particular care to ingredients and presents a deep impression.

无限卡特权

Mio Mio

意大利菜
Italian Cuisine

必应 搜索热度 Search priority 9.4

电话 /Tel
+86 10 5695 8522

地址 /Address
北京市朝阳区亮马桥路 48 号四季酒店 3 层
3F, Four Seasons Hotel, No. 48, Liangmaqiao Road, Chaoyang District, Beijing

营业时间 Opening Hours
午餐 Lunch 11:30 – 14:00
晚餐 Dinner 17:30 – 22:00
着装要求 Dress Code
商务休闲 Business Casual
人均消费 Per Capita Consumption
600 元 600 RMB

餐厅亮点为品质上乘的地中海美食，前菜包括生和牛塔塔、蓝鳍金枪鱼和鹅肝巴菲等，精选主菜则有澳洲和牛里脊 9 级、布列塔尼蓝龙虾、阿拉斯加黑鳕鱼和 T 骨和牛 M6/7 等。

Mediterranean cuisine of superior quality makes a starred appearance on the menu. Appetizers like Wagyu Beef Tartare, Blue Fin Tuna and Foie Gras Parfait, to main courses such as Australian Beef Tenderloin Grade 9, Brittany Blue Lobster to Alaska Black Cod and Wagyu T-Bone M6/7.

满寿司
Sushi Man

日本料理
Japanese Cuisine

5.2 必应搜索热度
Search priority

电话 /Tel
+86 10 6571 7631

地址 /Address
北京市东坝中路金隅嘉品 B1 层
B1, BBMG Mall, Dongba Central Road, Beijing

营业时间 Opening Hours
午餐 Lunch 11:00 – 14:00
晚餐 Dinner 17:00 – 21:00
着装要求 Dress Code
无特别着装要求 Non-specified
人均消费 Per Capita Consumption
120 元 120 RMB

满寿司将高标准的日式风格一以贯之，无论是日料老饕还是食尚潮人，都能在这里品尝到精致而丰盛的美食。餐厅装修由日本设计师操刀，融合日式与西式风格，餐厅菜品将传统与创意融合，只为食客打造精致日料。

It carries out the high standard of Japanese cuisine, and provides delicate and sumptuous food for both Japanese cuisine gormandizers and fashionable diners. The restaurant is decorated by Japanese designers with a mixture of Japanese and Western style. Its dishes combine traditional and creative concepts to produce exquisite Japanese food for diners.

美食图书馆
Chapter

无限卡特权

创意菜
Creative Cuisine

7.7 必应搜索热度
Search priority

电话 /Tel
+86 10 6584 6270

地址 /Address
北京市朝阳区东三环北路 29 号
北京康莱德酒店 1 层
1F, Conrad Beijing, No.29, East 3rd Circle, North Road, Chaoyang District, Beijing

营业时间 Opening Hours
早餐 Breakfast 06:00 – 10:00
午餐 Lunch 12:00 – 14:30
晚餐 Dinner 18:00 – 22:00
着装要求 Dress Code
商务休闲 Business Casual
人均消费 Per Capita Consumption
200 ~ 300 元 200 ~ 300 RMB

步入美食图书馆餐厅，犹如置身于充满欧洲气息的图书馆中，又如来到了充满神秘气息的古堡，沿着镂空旋转楼梯徐徐而上，走过一整面的书墙，可以感受到旧日时光的温暖。

As entering the Chapter, you may feel like in an European library, or a mysterious castle. Strolling along the hollow staircase and passing a book wall, you can feel the warm old days coming back to you.

米家思（国贸店）
Migas Mercado(China World)

地中海菜
Mediterranean Cuisine

必应 搜索热度 Search priority 7.7

电话 /Tel
+86 10 6500 7579

地址 /Address
北京市朝阳区建国门外大街 1 号
国贸商城北区 7 层
7F, China World North, No.1, Jianguomen Outer Street, Chaoyang District, Beijing

餐厅的菜式推崇健康和原味，在地中海风味的基础上，根据中国人的口味进行调整，让人们在北京也能感受到浓郁的地中海式生活方式。

The menu emphasizes health and pureness. Based on the Mediterran - ean flavor and adjusted to the Chinese taste, it brings in a vibrant Mediterranean life style.

营业时间 Opening Hours
11:30 – 02:00
着装要求 Dress Code
优雅便服 Smart Casual
人均消费 Per Capita Consumption
330 元 330 RMB

无限卡特权

名轩楼
Noble House Restaurant

中餐
Chinese Cuisine

必应 搜索热度 Search priority 4.9

电话 /Tel
+86 10 6849 1357
+86 10 6849 1358

地址 /Address
北京市海淀区首体南路 6 号
新世纪日航饭店 32 层
32F, Hotel Nikko New Century Beijing, No.6, Shouti South Road, Haidian District, Beijing

名轩楼以高雅、高质、高标、高端的“四高”为经营理念，为对美食有独到见解的客人提供高雅的用餐环境、高质量的食材、高标准的菜肴，以及高端的贴身服务。

Noble House Restaurant dedicates to provide graceful environment, high-quality ingredients, top dishes and high-end services for each diner who has insightful view of delicious foods.

营业时间 Opening Hours
午餐 Lunch 11:00 – 14:00
晚餐 Dinner 17:00 – 22:00
着装要求 Dress Code
干净整洁 Clean and Tidy
人均消费 Per Capita Consumption
350 元 350 RMB

明阁
Ming Court

无限卡特权

粤菜
Cantonese Cuisine

5.5 必应搜索热度
Search priority

电话 /Tel
+86 10 6450 4312

地址 /Address
北京市首都机场朗豪酒店 2 层
2F, Langham Place Beijing Capital Airport, Beijing

营业时间 Opening Hours
午餐 Lunch 11:30 – 14:00
晚餐 Dinner 17:30 – 22:00
着装要求 Dress Code
时尚休闲 Fashion leisure
人均消费 Per Capita Consumption
360 元 360 RMB

菜品是衡量一家餐厅水平的核心标准。明阁每季度更换菜单，餐厅的回头客众多。上等的新鲜食材、严谨的操作程序加上每位厨师的匠人之心和创新精神，为客人打造专属明阁的醇厚味道。

As the quality of cuisine is the key to judging a restaurant, Ming Court's seasonal menu and unduplicated dishes attract guests to come time and time again. It provides Ming Court's unique flavors with top-level and fresh ingredients, strict cooking process and ingenuity of chefs.

摸石头
Mosto

无限卡特权

南美式西餐
South American Cuisine

6.8 必应搜索热度
Search priority

电话 /Tel
+86 10 5208 6030

地址 /Address
北京市朝阳区三里屯北街 81 号
1 幢 D308 那里花园 3 层
3F, Nali Patio, D308, Building 1, No.81, Sanlitun North Street, Chaoyang District, Beijing

营业时间 Opening Hours
午餐 Lunch 11:30 – 15:00
晚餐 Dinner 17:30 – 22:00
着装要求 Dress Code
舒适 Comfortable
人均消费 Per Capita Consumption
215 元 215 RMB

餐厅提供超值的商务午餐，亦有浪漫的晚餐，摸石头独有的地道红酒也值得一试。周末更有特别的早午餐，让用餐者感觉十分放松和愉快。

Both reasonable business lunch and romantic dinner are available here. And you cannot miss its special authentic red wine. On weekends, there are available special brunches, refreshing the diners with leisure and joy.

摩卡站（三里屯店）
MOKA Bros(Sanlitun)

西餐
Western Cuisine

必应 搜索热度 Search priority 5.7

电话 /Tel
+86 10 5208 6079

地址 /Address
北京市朝阳区三里屯北街 81 号
2 号楼 1 层 B101b
B101b, 1F, Building 2, No.81, Sanlitun North Street, Chaoyang District, Beijing

营业时间 Opening Hours
早餐 Breakfast 08:00 – 10:30
午餐 Lunch 10:30 – 16:00
晚餐 Dinner 16:00 – 22:30
着装要求 Dress Code
舒适 Comfortable
人均消费 Per Capita Consumption
120 元 120 RMB

餐厅多采用富含能量的食材，如富含蛋白质的全谷物（红米和藜麦）以及能抗氧化的蔬菜。以此制作而成的美味沙拉和果昔，营养均衡，十分美味。

MOKA Bros uses more energy-rich ingredients, such as protein-rich whole grains (red rice and quinoa), and anti-oxidation vegetables. The salad and juice are delicious and nutritionally balanced.

莫尔顿牛排坊（北京）
Morton's Steakhouse(Beijing)

西餐
Western Cuisine

必应 搜索热度 Search priority 3.3

电话 /Tel
+86 10 6523 7777

地址 /Address
北京市东城区金宝街 99 号丽晶酒店 2 层
2F, Regent Hotel, No.99, Jinbao Street, Dongcheng District, Beijing

营业时间 Opening Hours
17:30 – 23:00
着装要求 Dress Code
优雅便服 Smart Casual
人均消费 Per Capita Consumption
800 ~ 1000 元 800 ~ 1000 RMB

北京莫尔顿牛排坊坐落于繁华的金宝街地段，为食客和商务精英们又增添了一个好去处。餐厅拥有 8 间私人宴会厅，以及专为美酒鉴赏家而设的宽敞私人酒廊。莫尔顿的牛排以肉质鲜嫩多汁而闻名。

Beijing Morton's Steakhouse lies in the busy Jinbao Street and becomes a good place for gourmets and elites. It has 8 private banquet rooms and a grand private wine lounge for wine connoisseurs. Morton's steak is famous for its tenderness and juiciness.

墨圈儿
El Barrio

墨西哥菜
Mexican Cuisine

5.7 必应搜索热度
Search priority

电话 /Tel
+86 10 6416 1716

地址 /Address
北京市朝阳区三里屯那里花园 2 层
2F, Nali Patio, Sanlitun, Chaoyang District, Beijing

营业时间 Opening Hours
周一至周四、周日 Mon. - Thu. Sun.
12:00 - 01:00
周五、周六 Fir. - Sat. 12:00 - 03:00
着装要求 Dress Code
无特别着装要求 Non-specified
人均消费 Per Capita Consumption
160 元 160 RMB

要说到北京城里正宗的墨西哥餐厅，墨圈儿绝对算得上一家。热情的墨西哥本土音乐以及地道的墨西哥风情美食，让食客像是置身于墨西哥的欢乐小镇。餐厅的炭烧和牛沙拉、墨圈儿辣肠芝士玉米片和各式酒品都十分值得一试。

When it comes to authentic Mexican restaurants in Beijing, this restaurant is definitely count one. The enthusiastic music and authentic Mexican cuisine make diners feel like they are in a happy town of Mexico. The Charcoal Wagon-beef Salad, El Barrio Pepperoni Cheese Corn Chips and various wines are all well worth a try.

那家小馆（酒仙桥店）
Na Jia Restaurant(Jiuxianqiao)

官府菜
Official Cuisine

5.2 必应搜索热度
Search priority

电话 /Tel
+86 10 5978 9333-9999

地址 /Address
北京市朝阳区酒仙桥路 2 号
No.2, Jiuxianqiao Road, Chaoyang District, Beijing

营业时间 Opening Hours
11:00 - 21:00
着装要求 Dress Code
优雅便服 Smart Casual
人均消费 Per Capita Consumption
160 元 160 RMB

那家小馆酒仙桥店位于朝阳区酒仙桥 798 艺术区北门，是一座古朴庄重的中式宅院。那家小馆以清代官府精品北京菜为主线，汲取其他菜系的优点，力求形成自己的特色。

Located near the northern gate of 798 Park of Jiuxianqiao in Chaoyang District of Beijing, Na Jia Restaurant embeds in a classical and magnificent Chinese courtyard. It dedicates to form its own style by featuring the classical official cuisine of Qing Dynasty and extracting the essence of other cuisines.

无限卡特权

廿九阁
29 Grill

西餐
Western Cuisine

必应 搜索热度 Search priority 3.4

电话 /Tel
+86 10 6584 6300

地址 /Address
北京市朝阳区东三环北路 29 号
北京康莱德酒店 2 层
2F, Conrad Beijing, No.29, East 3rd Circle, North Road, Chaoyang District, Beijing

营业时间 Opening Hours
午餐 Lunch 11:30 – 14:30
晚餐 Dinner 18:00 – 22:00
周日不营业 Closed on Sunday
着装要求 Dress Code
商务休闲 Business Casual
人均消费 Per Capita Consumption
300 元 300 RMB

步入廿九阁，时尚而奢华的风格营造出了一个令人愉悦的用餐空间。餐厅汇聚众多优质海鲜、炭烤美味和风味肉食；庞大的酒窖珍藏着来自世界各地的各色美酒，让美食爱好者备感尽兴。

The sophisticated and stylish 29 Grill is a perfect place to enjoy delicious food in a relaxed setting. Here you can find superior seafood, regional grilled delicacies, and various flavor meats as well as a well-stocked wine cellar with a great variety of wines across the world.

牛排家（安贞店）
Steak House(Anzhen)

西餐
Western Cuisine

必应 搜索热度 Search priority 5.2

电话 /Tel
+86 10 5628 6728
+86 136 7112 9359

地址 /Address
北京市朝阳区安定路 5 号院 6 号楼
中海环宇荟购物中心 4 层 401
401, 4F, Zhonghai Huanyu Shopping Mall, Building 6, No.5, Anding Road, Chaoyang District, Beijing

营业时间 Opening Hours
11:00 – 22:00
着装要求 Dress Code
优雅便服 Smart Casual
人均消费 Per Capita Consumption
350 元 350 RMB

牛排家（安贞店）在环境方面拥有得天独厚的优势，餐厅精心打造高雅环境，而菜品方面，牛排家利用独家研发的高温瞬间锁水技术，可锁住牛排的水分，充分保留牛排的肉汁和营养成分，使牛排滋味更加诱人。

With elaborately designed decoration, its elegant and graceful environment has a unique advantage. This restaurant adopts the high temperature instant water-locking technique which is exclusive researched and developed to lock the water of steaks and fully retains the gravy and nutrients, making the flavor of steaks more attractive.

牛排家（王府井店）
Steak House(Wangfujing)

西餐
Western Cuisine

2.6 必应搜索热度
Search priority

电话 /Tel
+86 10 5840 5488
+86 187 0157 5316

地址 /Address
北京市东城区王府井东街 8 号澳门中心商场 L118
L118, Macao Center Mall, No.8, Wangfujing East Street, Dongcheng District, Beijing

营业时间 Opening Hours
11:00 – 22:00
着装要求 Dress Code
优雅便服 Smart Casual
人均消费 Per Capita Consumption
350 元 350 RMB

店内布置皆由专业团队精心打造，营造出高端时尚的用餐氛围。餐厅在烤制牛排时采用果木炭炙烤方法，其特制的果木牛排炉，炉内温度高达 800 ℉，可使牛排充分吸收果木炙烤带来的香气。

Its decoration is elaborately designed by a team to create a high-end and fashionable dining atmosphere. Its steaks are baked in a special fruit carbon steak oven with fruit carbons, the oven temperature is as high as 800 ℉ and can make the steaks absorb the aroma of fruit carbon.

牛排家（建国门店）
Steak House(Jianguomen)

西餐
Western Cuisine

5.2 必应搜索热度
Search priority

电话 /Tel
+86 10 5846 4388
+86 170 0113 5555

地址 /Address
北京市朝阳区建国门外大街丁 12 号
英皇集团中心 2 层 209
Room 209, 2F, Emperor Group Centre, No.12D, Jianguomen Outer Street, Chaoyang District, Beijing

营业时间 Opening Hours
11:00 – 22:00
着装要求 Dress Code
优雅便服 Smart Casual
人均消费 Per Capita Consumption
500 元 500 RMB

对于一个资深的牛排食客来说，品尝一份好的干式熟成牛排绝对是一种享受。在这里，所有的牛肉食材都经过 21 ~ 45 天的熟成，再加上特选的果木精心烤制，使得牛排满是肉汁，肉香四溢。

A piece of dry-aged steak must be a good gift for any experienced steak lover. Here every piece of beef must get through a dry-aged treatment over 21 ~ 45 days, and then roasted by selected fruit wood. Such procedure makes the steak juicy and full of appealing fragrance.

牛排家（三里屯店）
Steak House(Sanlitun)

西餐
Western Cuisine

必应 搜索热度 Search priority 3.1

电话 /Tel
+86 10 5780 9040
+86 10 5780 9041

地址 /Address
北京市朝阳区南三里屯路 1 号通盈中心 3-8
3-8, InterContinental Sanlitun Beijing, No.1, Sanlitun South Road, Chaoyang District, Beijing

营业时间 Opening Hours
11:00 – 22:00

着装要求 Dress Code
优雅便服 Smart Casual

人均消费 Per Capita Consumption
350 元 350 RMB

牛排家（三里屯店）属于三里屯地段的高端西餐厅，服务于高端食客以及商务精英，可满足食客的多种需要。餐厅的所有牛肉食材均采用美国安格斯进口牛肉与澳洲进口和牛，口感一流。

Located at Sanlitun area, it is a high-end Western restaurant, provides services for high-level diners and business elites, and can meet various needs of numerous diners. All beef ingredients of this restaurant are selected the imported United States Angus beef and Australian wagyu beef to provide the best taste for diners.

牛排家（双井店）
Steak House(Shuangjing)

西餐
Western Cuisine

必应 搜索热度 Search priority 5.2

电话 /Tel
+86 10 5703 7288
+86 185 1093 9100

地址 /Address
北京市朝阳区东三环中路 20 号
乐成中心 2 层 208
Room 208, 2F, Yue Cheng Centre Space 3 , No.20, East 3rd Circle, Central Road, Chaoyang District, Beijing

营业时间 Opening Hours
11:00 – 22:00

着装要求 Dress Code
优雅便服 Smart Casual

人均消费 Per Capita Consumption
350 元 350 RMB

牛排家（双井店）在口味上追求原味，并且针对中国食客进行了调整，既满足了中国食客的口味又符合西方友人的饮食标准。餐厅环境高雅且品位十足，适合商务宴请、朋友聚餐、情侣约会等。

It pursues original flavors, and has adjusted the flavors of dishes for catering to Chinese diners, which not only meets the dietary standards of Chinese diners but also meets those of western friends. The restaurant has an elegant and exquisite environment, which is suitable for business banquets, friends gathering, dating and other occasions.

Opera BOMBANA
Opera BOMBANA

无限卡特权

意大利菜
Italian Cuisine

4.8 必应搜索热度 Search priority

电话 /Tel
+86 10 5690 7177

地址 /Address
北京市朝阳区东大桥路 9 号侨福芳草地 LG2-21
LG2-21, Parkview Green, No.9, Dongdaqiao Road, Chaoyang District, Beijing

营业时间 Opening Hours
午餐 Lunch 12:00 – 14:30
晚餐 Dinner 18:00 – 22:30
着装要求 Dress Code
商务休闲 Business Casual
人均消费 Per Capita Consumption
午餐 300 元
Lunch 300 RMB
晚餐 1000 元
Dinner 1000 RMB

菜单由名厨 Umberto Bombana 设计，菜式由行政主厨用在当地找到的上佳食材加以诠释。酒单以意大利产区为主，精选世界各地的葡萄酒，储存于先进的玻璃恒温酒窖中。

The menu is designed by the famous Chef Umberto Bombana, and the cuisine is made with the best local ingredients and is fulfilled by Executive Chef. It offers an extensive selection of wines across the world, while most from Italy, stored in the advanced glass thermostatic wine cellar.

PHO 东田越南粉
PHO

越南菜
Vietnamese Cuisine

7.4 必应搜索热度 Search priority

电话 /Tel
+86 10 8535 1086

地址 /Address
北京市建国门外大街 1 号
国贸商城北区 6 层 NL6003
NL6003, 6F, China World North, No.1, Jianguomen Outer Street, Beijing

营业时间 Opening Hours
11:30 – 21:30
着装要求 Dress Code
无特别着装要求 Non-specified
人均消费 Per Capita Consumption
100 元 100 RMB

越南河粉以其酸辣鲜香的口味受到无数食客的欢迎，而在众多经营越南河粉的餐厅中，PHO 东田越南粉餐厅凭借正宗的火车头越南牛肉河粉脱颖而出，得到众多食客的青睐。这碗牛肉河粉汤底鲜浓，牛肉鲜嫩，令人意犹未尽。

The Vietnam pho is favored by numerous diners with its sour, hot and spicy tastes. This restaurant stands out among many restaurants that serve Vietnam pho because of its authentic locomotive Vietnamese beef pho which is praised by many diners. The soup base of this beef pho is fresh and thick with tender beef, making diners want to eat more.

无限卡特权

瓢嘻日本料理（北京）
Hyoki(Beijing)

日本料理
Japanese Cuisine

必应 搜索热度 Search priority 2.6

电话 /Tel
+86 10 6581 0072

地址 /Address
北京市朝阳区建国路 93 号
万达索菲特大酒店 6 层
6F, Sofitel Wanda Hotel, No. 93, Jianguo Road, Chaoyang District, Beijing

营业时间 Opening Hours
午餐 Lunch 11:30 – 14:30
晚餐 Dinner 17:30 – 22:30
着装要求 Dress Code
优雅便服 Smart Casual
人均消费 Per Capita Consumption
600 元 600 RMB

北京瓢嘻日本料理位于万达索菲特酒店 6 层，以高汤火锅为主打品，同时提供寿司、天妇罗、寿喜烧、铁板烧、怀石料理套餐等传统日本料理。

Standing on the 6th floor of Sofitel Wanda Hotel, it features soup-stock pot with other traditional Japanese cuisine such as sushi, tempura, sukiyaki, teppanyaki and kaiseki.

无限卡特权

莆田（王府井店）
PuTien(Wangfujing)

福建菜
Fujian Cuisine

必应 搜索热度 Search priority 7.5

电话 /Tel
+86 10 6525 7707

地址 /Address
北京市王府井大街 269 号
王府中环东座 4 层 403b
403b, 4F, East Building, Wangfu Central, No.269, Wangfujing Street, Beijing

营业时间 Opening Hours
午餐 Lunch 11:00 – 14:00
晚餐 Dinner 17:00 – 21:30
着装要求 Dress Code
优雅便服 Smart Casual
人均消费
Per Capita Consumption
130 元 130 RMB

莆田是一家成立于新加坡的福建餐厅，以其独具特色的福建菜俘获了食客的心。餐厅凭借着对食材品质的坚守和传统烹饪精髓的传承，成为备受欢迎的中餐品牌。百秒黄花鱼、莆田扁肉汤、莆田卤面是店内的招牌菜。

As a Fujian restaurant established in Singapore, it has captured the hearts of diners with its featured Fujian cuisine. This restaurant has become a popular Chinese food brand by adhering to the quality of ingredients and inheriting the essences of traditional culinary arts. Its signature dishes include Hundred Seconds Yellow Croaker, Putian Broth, and Putian Noodles.

恰牛扒房
Char Dining Room & Lounge

西餐
Western Cuisine

2.8 必应搜索热度
Search priority

电话 /Tel
+86 10 8516 0065

地址 /Address
北京市三里屯通盈中心洲际酒店 3 层
3F, InterContinental Sanlitun Beijing, Beijing

营业时间 Opening Hours
17:30 - 22:00
着装要求 Dress Code
优雅便服 Smart Casual
人均消费 Per Capita Consumption
700 ~ 800 元 700 ~ 800 RMB

恰牛扒房是一家现代扒房餐厅，环境既现代摩登又舒适惬意。宾客可通过开放式厨房观赏厨师承袭传统烹饪技法雕琢食材。餐厅严选各地优质食材提炼美味，为京城饕客带来前所未有的顶级牛排体验。

It is a modern steakhouse restaurant with a fashionable and comfortable environment. Diners can watch chef cooking ingredients with traditional cooking techniques through the open kitchen. It strictly selects high-quality ingredients to bring unprecedented top steak experience to Beijing diners.

曲廊院
Ten House in Hutong

西餐
Western Cuisine

3.8 必应搜索热度
Search priority

电话 /Tel
+86 10 8403 8229

地址 /Address
北京市东四十条 25 号
No.25, Dongsishitiao, Beijing

营业时间 Opening Hours
午餐 Lunch 12:00 - 17:00
晚餐 Dinner 18:00 - 21:30
着装要求 Dress Code
优雅便服 Smart Casual
人均消费 Per Capita Consumption
560 元 560 RMB

曲廊院餐厅自创立至今初心始终未变，就是用心创建一处温雅的环境，并对珍稀的中国本土食材进行发掘与创作。曲廊院把大自然最美好的食材传递给每一位食客，如国内优质的甜虾、蝴蝶虾以及有“高级红鱼”之称的赤鯥鱼。

The original mind of this restaurant has never changed since its opening, which is to create a comfortable and elegant environment, and to explore and present Chinese rare local food materials. It provides the best natural food to diners, such as domestic high-quality sweet shrimps, butterfly shrimps and doederleinia berycoides, a senior red fish.

曲宴中餐厅
Quyan Chinese Restaurant

鲁菜
Shandong Cuisine

必应 搜索热度 Search priority 2.6

电话 /Tel
+86 10 8599 6666-7094

地址 /Address
北京市万达文华酒店 6 层
6F, Wanda Vista Hotel, Beijing

营业时间 Opening Hours
午餐 Lunch 11:30 – 14:00
晚餐 Dinner 17:30 – 22:00
着装要求 Dress Code
得体 Decent
人均消费 Per Capita Consumption
350 元 350 RMB

来自山东的主厨赵法红师从国内著名鲁菜大师，不仅精通葱烧、油焖、芫爆、汤爆等各种鲁菜烹饪手法，对鲁菜渊源及文化典故也了如指掌。

The Executive Chef Zhao Fahong learnt from a well-known Shandong cuisine master. Besides the traditional Shandong culinary skills, such as braising with scallion, braising, stewed Chinese coriander and boiling soup, Zhao knows well about the essence and the culture of Shandong cuisine.

Restaurant Y
Restaurant Y

西餐
Western Cuisine

必应 搜索热度 Search priority 2.7

电话 /Tel
+86 10 8405 9938

地址 /Address
北京市三里屯北路 19 号
三里屯太古里北区 N8 号楼 2 层
2F, Building N8, Taikoo Li Sanlitun North,
No.19, Sanlitun North Road, Beijing

营业时间 Opening Hours
10:00 – 24:00
着装要求 Dress Code
优雅便服 Smart Casual
人均消费 Per Capita Consumption
260 元 260 RMB

作为京城热门的西餐厅之一，餐厅环境富有格调且充满了浪漫的氛围，适合朋友聚会、情侣约会。餐厅的招牌菜为 Y 先生烤鸡、海鲜饭、酸奶碗，其中，餐厅的鸡尾酒以其超高的颜值，受到了许多女食客的欢迎。

As one of the most popular western restaurants in Beijing, it has a romantic environment with particular styles, which is suitable for friend gatherings and lovers dating. This restaurant's signature dishes include Mr. Y's Roast Chicken, Seafood Paella and Yogurt Bowls, among which the Yogurt Bowls are popular among many female diners because of their beautiful appearance.

然寿司（钱粮胡同店）
Sushi Gaku(Qianlianghutong)

日本料理
Japanese Cuisine

2.6 必应搜索热度
Search priority

电话 /Tel
+86 10 6403 7680

地址 /Address
北京市钱粮胡同东口 16-2 号
No.16-2, East Entrance, Qianliang Hutong, Beijing

营业时间 Opening Hours
周二至周日 Thu. – Sun. 18:00 – 22:00
着装要求 Dress Code
无特别着装要求 Non-specified
人均消费 Per Capita Consumption
1500 元 1500 RMB

然寿司开在一条不大的胡同内，店内一次最多容纳 8 个人，整体环境简朴优雅。餐厅用餐实行套餐制，厨师会根据当季的食材为食客做搭配，让食客品尝到最接近日本本土的美食。

Located at a small alley, it has a simple and elegant environment and can just accommodate up to eight diners at a time. This restaurant provides packages which are matched by chefs based on the seasonal ingredients, so that diners can feel the most authentic and local Japanese cuisine.

荣尊 1893
Brasserie 1893

西餐
Western Cuisine

7.5 必应搜索热度
Search priority

电话 /Tel
+86 10 8520 8989

地址 /Address
北京市东城区金鱼胡同 5-15 号
北京华尔道夫酒店 1 层
1F, Waldorf Astoria Beijing, No.5-15, Jinyu Hutong, Dongcheng District, Beijing

营业时间 Opening Hours
午餐 Lunch 11:30 – 14:00
晚餐 Dinner 17:30 – 22:30
着装要求 Dress Code
优雅便服 Smart Casual
人均消费 Per Capita Consumption
500 元 500 RMB

位于中央开放式厨房内的两台手工打造的梦泰尼炉具，是烹饪炉中的顶级精品。在这里可以品尝到纽约华尔道夫酒店的经典美食，如华尔道夫沙拉、本尼迪克特蛋等，并包含各类经典欧陆式佳肴及特色北京菜品。

The open kitchen is in the center of the restaurant. Two hand-built stoves of Molteni are top-of-the-range cooking stoves. The classic food of Waldorf Astoria New York can be found here, such as Waldorf salad and Eggs Benedict, as well as all kinds of classic European delicacies and special Beijing dishes.

无限卡特权

刃扒房
The Cut

西餐
Western Cuisine

必应 搜索热度 Search priority 8.8

电话 /Tel
+86 10 8507 3617

地址 /Address
北京市朝阳区建国门外大街永安东里 8 号
No.8, Yongandongli, Jianguomen Outer Street, Chaoyang District, Beijing

营业时间 Opening Hours
午餐 Lunch 11:30 – 14:00
晚餐 Dinner 18:00 – 22:30
着装要求 Dress Code
无特别着装要求 Non-specified
人均消费 Per Capita Consumption
500 元 500 RMB

作为京城首家供应百分百血统草饲安格斯牛肉和 500 天谷饲 AACO 级牛排的餐厅，这里提供优选的牛肉食材、多款优质香醇的葡萄酒。海鲜爱好者还可在此享用海鲜盛宴。

The Cut offers the sophisticated cuisine with the pure grass-fed Angus beef and 500-day grain-fed AACO steak in this restaurant in Beijing, going well with various mellow wines. Besides, the seafood banquet is tailored for seafood addicts.

三克映画
CINKER Pictures

西餐
Western Cuisine

必应 搜索热度 Search priority 3.6

电话 /Tel
+86 10 6409 4577

地址 /Address
北京市三里屯北路 19 号
三里屯太古里北区 4 层 N4-40b
N4-40b, 4F, Taikoo Li Sanlitun North, No.19, Sanlitun North Road, Beijing

营业时间 Opening Hours
11:30 – 01:00
着装要求 Dress Code
优雅便服 Smart Casual
人均消费 Per Capita Consumption
260 元 260 RMB

三克映画是三里屯的一家影院餐厅，餐厅环境优雅现代，每日播放文艺老电影，适合情侣约会或者朋友小聚。餐厅不仅拥有文艺的环境，在菜品方面也是用心经营，餐厅的套餐每天根据食材进行搭配，只为给食客带来美食享受。

It is a theatre restaurant located at Sanlitun, and has an elegant and modern environment with old and artistic movies playing every day, which is suitable for couple dating or friend gatherings. This restaurant not only has an artistic environment, but also provides sincere dishes. The set meals are matched according to ingredients every day, in order to bring diners to enjoy delicacies.

三五堂
San Wu Tang

自助餐
Buffet

3.7 必应搜索热度 Search priority

电话 /Tel
+86 10 8647 1035
+86 10 6505 2277

地址 /Address
北京市建国门外大街 1 号新国贸饭店 2 层
2F, Hotel Jen Beijing, No.1, Jianguomen Outer Street, Beijing

营业时间 Opening Hours
早餐 Breakfast
周一至周五 Mon. – Fri. 6:30 – 10:00
周六、周日 Sat. – Sun. 6:30 – 10:30
午餐 Lunch 11:30 – 14:30
晚餐 Dinner 17:30 – 21:30
着装要求 Dress Code
商务休闲 Business casual
人均消费 Per Capita Consumption
170 元 170 RMB

主打北京本地风味和北方美食的三五堂是北京最受欢迎的自助餐厅之一。食客在享用美味的同时可以欣赏北京天际线的唯美景致。三五堂餐厅注重供应营养均衡的菜肴，致力于打造真正的“农场到餐桌”的体验。

As one of Beijing's most popular buffets, it mainly serves Beijing local cuisine and northern Chinese dishes. Diners can enjoy the beautiful view of Beijing skyline while tasting delicacies. It pays attention to providing balanced and nutritious dishes and is committed to creating a true farm-to-table dining experience.

四方三川
By Mercedes Me

中餐
Chinese Cuisine

2.8 必应搜索热度 Search priority

电话 /Tel
+86 10 8588 7150

地址 /Address
北京市南三里屯一号
Mercedes me 三里屯体验店 2 层
2F, Sanlitun Mercedes Me Store, No.1, Sanlitun South Road, Beijing

营业时间 Opening Hours
11:00 – 14:30 17:00 – 21:30
着装要求 Dress Code
无特别着装要求 Non-specified
人均消费 Per Capita Consumption
250 元 250 RMB

四方三川是一家新潮的川菜餐厅，寓意为“走四方，越三川”。店内环境温馨，四处都布满了热气球模样的吊灯，营造出浪漫的氛围。餐厅招牌菜三川青椒鱼，鱼肉鲜嫩，味道鲜辣，回味鲜香，喜爱川菜又注重用餐环境的食客一定要来尝试。

It is a fashionable Sichuan cuisine restaurant, meaning "Travel around and walk everywhere". It has a comfortable environment with many fire balloon lights everywhere, creating a romantic atmosphere. Its signature dish Sanchuan Green Pepper Fish is fresh and tender with spicy tastes, which is a must-try dish for diners who love Sichuan cuisine and strict in dining environment.

四叶寿司（中关村店）
Sushi Yotsuba(Zhongguancun)

日本料理
Japanese Cuisine

必应 搜索热度 2.7
Search priority

电话 /Tel
+86 10 6256 4330
+86 131 4113 6970

地址 /Address
北京市科学院南路 2 号
融科资讯中心 A 座 1 层 103
Room 103, 1F, Building A, Raycom Infortech Park, No.2, Kexueyuan South Road, Beijing

营业时间 Opening Hours
午餐 Lunch 11:30 – 14:00
晚餐 Dinner 17:30 – 22:00
着装要求 Dress Code
商务休闲 Business Casual
人均消费 Per Capita Consumption
1000 元 1000 RMB

作为北京城内历史比较久的寿司店，四叶寿司非常有日本小酒屋的感觉。食客可围坐于吧台边，边欣赏料理的制作，边享受美食。四叶的寿司很地道，米粒的软硬和温度都恰到好处，口感清爽细腻，满足感妙不可言。

As one of the oldest sushi restaurants in Beijing, it gives a feeling of small Japanese wine house. Diners can sit around the bar and enjoy food while watching the cooking processes. Its sushi is very typical with perfect rice softness and temperature, provides a fresh and delicate taste, which leaves diners a sense of satisfaction beyond words.

思·全日餐厅
Cordis Market

自助餐
Buffet

必应 搜索热度 2.6
Search priority

电话 /Tel
+86 10 6457 5555

地址 /Address
北京市一经路首都机场东海康得思酒店
Cordis Beijing Capital Airport, Yijing Road, Beijing

营业时间 Opening Hours
06:30 – 23:00
着装要求 Dress Code
优雅便服 Smart Casual
人均消费 Per Capita Consumption
250 元 250 RMB

思·全日餐厅汇聚中西式美食和创新经典菜品，带领食客展开难忘的美食之旅。思·全日餐厅每日开放，来自世界各地的厨师在开放式厨房大显身手，施展出众厨艺，为食客打造不一样的餐饮体验。

It integrates Chinese and Western cuisine with innovative classical dishes to bring diners step on an unforgettable delicacies journey. This restaurant opens every day, and chefs from all over the world are displaying their skills in the open kitchen to bring diners a different dining experience.

TRB Hutong
TRB Hutong

西餐
Western Cuisine

8.8 必应搜索热度
Search priority

电话 /Tel
+86 10 8400 2232

地址 /Address
北京市东城区沙滩北街 23 号
No.23, Shatan North Street, Dongcheng District, Beijing

营业时间 Opening Hours
午餐 Lunch 11:30 – 14:30
晚餐 Dinner 17:30 – 22:30
着装要求 Dress Code
优雅便服 Smart Casual
人均消费 Per Capita Consumption
600 ~ 700 元 600 ~ 700 RMB

餐厅主打的是新式的欧陆菜系，来自法国的总厨善用地道食材，每一道菜品都以色彩缤纷的摆盘来呈现。龙虾和鹅肝是这里的特色，配以自制酱汁，口感醇厚又清爽。

TRB features new Continental cuisine, and its French Chef makes good use of the local ingredients and presents each dish in a colorful way. Lobsters and foie gras are the features here and their flavors are mellow and refreshing after dressing TRB's sauce.

TRB Forbidden City
TRB Forbidden City

西餐
Western Cuisine

3.8 必应搜索热度
Search priority

电话 /Tel
+86 10 6401 6676

地址 /Address
北京市东城区东华门大街 95 号
No. 95, Donghuamen Street, Dongcheng District, Beijing

营业时间 Opening Hours
午餐 Lunch 11:30 – 14:30
晚餐 Dinner 17:00 – 23:30
着装要求 Dress Code
优雅便服 Smart Casual
人均消费 Per Capita Consumption
300 ~ 400 元 300 ~ 400 RMB

这家餐厅旨在营造一个既精致又让人放松的环境。菜单由国际化团队设计打造，口味丰富，用餐者们能够在这里获得高雅却又不高冷的美味体验。

TRB Forbidden City aims to create a "Casual and Modern Eatery"—a relaxing and chic space. The menu is designed by an international chef team, offering a wide range of tastes. And it gives every diner an elegant gourmet trip in a nice and casual way.

墨西哥菜
Mexican Cuisine

The Taco Bar
The Taco Bar

必应 搜索热度 Search priority 3.0

电话 /Tel
+86 10 6501 6026

地址 /Address
北京市工体北路
机电工程院中国银行正对面
Opposite of BOC, Mechanical and Electrical Institute, Gongti North Road, Beijing

这家墨西哥餐厅面积虽然不大，但是却以氛围取胜。浓郁的墨西哥小餐馆氛围，吸引了无数慕名而来的食客。餐厅的玉米片牛油果、炸鱿鱼和多种多样的卷饼具有正宗的墨西哥风味，让食客仿佛置身于异国他乡。

This Mexican restaurant is small but wins with its atmosphere and decoration. The strong Mexican small restaurant style has attracted numerous diners. It provides Corn Flakes Avocado, Fried Squid and various Tacos with authentic Mexican flavors, making diners feel as if they are in a foreign country.

营业时间 Opening Hours
周二至周五 Tue. - Fri. 17:00 - 23:00
周六、周日 Sat. - Sun. 11:30 - 23:00
着装要求 Dress Code
无特别着装要求 Non-specified
人均消费 Per Capita Consumption
140 元 140 RMB

无限卡特权

西餐
Western Cuisine

The Georg
The Georg

必应 搜索热度 Search priority 3.9

电话 /Tel
+86 10 8408 5300

地址 /Address
北京市东城区地安门东大街
东不压桥胡同 45 号院
No.45, Dongbuyaqiao Hutong, Di'anmen East Street, Dongcheng District, Beijing

在这里，你可以一边品味北欧风格的创意菜式，一边欣赏融入北京传统四合院中的简约装潢风格。The Georg 匠心独运，缔造出了一个理念简约的生活空间。

In the Georg, diners can enjoy the creative Northern European cuisine and appreciate traditional Beijing courtyard with simple decorations. The Georg exercises its inventive mind to make a cozy life space based on a belief that less is more.

营业时间 Opening Hours
晚餐 Dinner 18:00 - 22:30
着装要求 Dress Code
优雅便服 Smart Casual
人均消费 Per Capita Consumption
400 ~ 500 元 400 ~ 500 RMB

桐寿司
Sushi Tong

日本料理
Japanese Cuisine

3.8 必应搜索热度
Search priority

电话 /Tel
+86 133 1111 0150

地址 /Address
北京市朝阳区工人体育场东门外辅路向南 150 米
150m South, Auxiliary Road, East Entrance Workers' Stadium, Chaoyang District, Beijing

营业时间 Opening Hours
午餐 Lunch 11:00 – 14:00
晚餐 Dinner 17:30 – 22:00
着装要求 Dress Code
商务休闲 Business casual
人均消费 Per Capita Consumption
2680 元 2680 RMB

新鲜、应季的食材，永远是日料最核心的部分。为了提供高品质的手握寿司，店
鱼鲜皆由日本经急速冷藏空运而来，这样才能保持食材的新鲜。为了确保货源稳
并维持与鱼商的良好关系，餐厅厨师长经常往返于中日两地。

Japanese cuisine always pays attention to the fresh and seaso ingredients. In order to provide high-quality hand-hold sushi, the seafoo this restaurant is transported from Japan through rapid refrigeration by so as to keep the ingredients fresh. In order to ensure the stable supply ingredients and maintain good relations with fish sellers, the head chef of t restaurant often travels between China and Japan.

塔沃拉意大利餐厅
Tavola Italian Dining

无限卡特权

意大利菜
Italian Cuisine

3.6 必应搜索热度
Search priority

电话 /Tel
+86 10 8532 5068

地址 /Address
北京市朝阳区东方东路 19 号
亮马桥外交公寓 B 区会所 2 层
2F, Block B, Liangmaqiao Diplomatic Apartment, No.19, Dongfang East Road, Chaoyang District, Beijing

营业时间 Opening Hours
午餐 Lunch 11:30 – 14:30
晚餐 Dinner
周日至周四 Sun. – Thur. 18:00 – 22:00
周五至周六 Fri. – Sat. 18:00 – 23:00
着装要求 Dress Code
商务休闲 Business Casual
人均消费 Per Capita Consumption
午餐 200 元 Lunch 200 RMB
晚餐 400 元 Dinner 400 RMB

开放式厨房可以让人领略到地道意大利厨房的料理动态：大厨们时而如魔术师般将食材变换成饕餮之宴，时而严谨地展示着刀功，时而如指挥官般发出口令，让用餐者们在品赏美食的间隙也大饱眼福。

There is an open kitchen to let diners watch the cooking process of authentic Italian dishes. Chefs like magicians, using their experienced technique to transform simple ingredients to amazing dishes; or like generals, commanding the whole kitchen work effectively and providing diners a wonderful cooking show.

无限卡特权

天下一品
Tianxia Yi Pin

官府菜
Official Cuisine

必应 搜索热度 Search priority 8.6

电话 /Tel
+86 10 6601 4466-162

地址 /Address
北京市西城区复兴门内大街 51 号
民族饭店 2 层
2F, Minzu Hotel, No.51, Fuxingmen Inner Street, Xicheng District, Beijing

营业时间 Opening Hours
午餐 Lunch 11:00 - 14:00
晚餐 Dinner 17:00 - 21:00
着装要求 Dress Code
优雅便服 / 商务正装
Smart Casual / Business Attire
人均消费 Per Capita Consumption
300 元 300 RMB

天下一品餐厅整体环境古朴典雅，散发着浓郁的中国味道。餐厅主打创意官府菜，在保留和继承传统烹调技艺的同时，融合了现代人的饮食风尚。
The integrated environment of the restaurant is simple and elegant with rich Chinese flavors. It features the old official cuisine inheriting traditional cooking technique and blending with modern diet customs.

万丽轩
WanLi

粤菜
Cantonese Cuisine

必应 搜索热度 Search priority 3.8

电话 /Tel
+86 10 6520 8847

地址 /Address
北京东城区王府井大街 57 号
北京金茂万丽酒店 2 层
2F, Renaissance Beijing Wangfujing Hotel, No.57, Wangfujing Street, Dongcheng District, Beijing

营业时间 Opening Hours
午餐 Lunch 11:30 - 14:00
晚餐 Dinner 18:00 - 22:00
着装要求 Dress Code
无特别着装要求 Non-specified
人均消费 Per Capita Consumption
250 元 250 RMB

万丽轩是以正宗粤菜而闻名的餐厅。其环境高雅清静，每个包间都以北京的胡同命名，非常适合朋友聚会和商务宴请，其中各种点心和烧味更是来此用餐的食客不容错过的美味。
As a restaurant known for authentic Cantonese cuisine, it has an elegant and quiet environment with each private room named after a Beijing Hutong, and is very suitable for friends gathering and business dinners. A variety of desserts and roast meats are signature dishes which diners must have a try.

万叶海鲜炉端烧
Man Yo

日本料理
Japanese Cuisine

2.8 必应搜索热度 Search priority

电话 /Tel
+86 10 6521 2511
+86 185 1517 0281

地址 /Address
北京市朝阳区建国门外大街 16 号
3 号楼底商 W-4 号
Shop W-4, Building 3, No.16, Jianguomen Outer Street, Chaoyang District, Beijing

营业时间 Opening Hours
午餐 Lunch 11:30 - 14:00
晚餐 Dinner 17:30 - 22:00
着装要求 Dress Code
无特别着装要求 Non-specified
人均消费 Per Capita Consumption
300 ~ 500 元 300 ~ 500 RMB

炉端烧是一种风靡日本的烧烤形式，京城的万叶不仅保留了日本烧烤的传统精神同时还打造出简约雅致的新派居酒屋。除了炭烤什锦小海鲜、金吉鱼一夜干、鹅鳗鱼饭等菜品，还有各种日本清酒。

Robatayaki is a kind of barbecue sweeping Japan. This restaurant not o retains the traditional spirit of Japanese barbecue, but also builds a n simple and elegant izakaya. The menu includes a variety of delicious cuisi such as Charcoal-grilled Mixed Seafood, Dried Ginger Fish, Foir Gras Rice, as well as various Japanese sakes.

文华扒房 & 酒吧
Mandarin Grill & Bar

西餐
Western Cuisine

2.8 必应搜索热度 Search priority

电话 /Tel
+86 10 8509 8810

地址 /Address
北京市王府井大街 269 号
No.269, Wangfujing Street, Beijing

营业时间 Opening Hours
午餐 Lunch 11:30 - 14:30
晚餐 Dinner 18:00 - 22:00
周一休息 Monday Rest
着装要求 Dress Code
休闲舒适 Leisure Comfort
人均消费 Per Capita Consumption
800 元 800RMB

顶级有机食材和当季美味餐点是文华扒房的菜单精髓，再配合厨师精妙的手法和创意，让食客感到惊喜不断。另外，餐厅的环境极富低调奢华气质，整体空间典雅高贵，令每一位来此用餐的客人都能满意而归。

The essences of menu here are the top organic ingredients and seasonal delicacies which will surprise diners constantly together with chef's exquisite culinary arts. In addition, it has a luxury and elegant environment to satisfy each diner who dining here.

屋里厢
WuLixiang Shanghai Cuisine

上海菜
Shanghai Cuisine

必应 搜索热度 Search priority 3.6

电话 /Tel
+86 10 6539 8660

地址 /Address
北京市朝阳区工人体育场北路甲 2 号
盈科中心临街底商 1 层
1F, Pacific Century Place, No.2A, Gongti North Road, Chaoyang District, Beijing

营业时间 Opening Hours
午餐 Lunch 11:00 - 14:00
晚餐 Dinner 17:00 - 21:00
着装要求 Dress Code
商务休闲 Business Casual
人均消费 Per Capita Consumption
200 元 200 RMB

屋里厢，源于地道上海话“家”的发音，餐厅遵循传统，环境充满老上海风情，并用匠心精神，志在打造正宗本帮菜餐厅，将上海老弄堂里的好味道带到北京，让你于味蕾间感受到家里吃饭的融洽与归属之感。

Its name is originated from the pronunciation of "home" in Shanghai dialect. This restaurant follows traditions and builds the environment full of old Shanghai style. With a spirit of ingenuity, it aims to provide an authentic local cuisine, bringing the good tastes of old Shanghai alley to Beijing, and gives diners a sense of harmony and belonging through tastes.

沃夫冈牛排馆
Wolfgang's Steak House

西餐
Western Cuisine

必应 搜索热度 Search priority 3.9

电话 /Tel
+86 10 6592 4946

地址 /Address
北京市朝阳区工体北路甲 2 号
盈科中心 B 座 1 层
1F, Building B, Pacific Century Place, No.2A, Gongti North Road, Chaoyang District, Beijing

营业时间 Opening Hours
11:30 - 22:00
着装要求 Dress Code
优雅便服 Smart Casual
人均消费 Per Capita Consumption
1000 元 1000 RMB

来自纽约的沃夫冈牛排馆迎来了在北京的第一家分店，在过去 12 年的时光里，沃夫冈坚持用干式熟成的方式让每一块牛排保有其本来的滋味。来到这里的顾客除了能够品尝到最纯正的美国牛排，还可以感受到这里轻松愉悦的用餐氛围，享受美式闲适生活。

Wolfgang's Steak House from New York made its debut in Beijing finally. In the past 12 years, Wolfgang has been insisted on dry-aged method to enhance the original taste of each piece of steak. Everyone who comes here can taste the most authentic American-style steak in a nice and joyful atmosphere and enjoy the leisure life in an American way.

梧桐
Wish

中餐
Chinese Cuisine

10.0 必应搜索热度
Search priority

电话 /Tel
+86 10 6438 8883
+86 10 6438 1118

地址 /Address
北京市朝阳区芳园西路 6 号
东四环霄云桥东 700 米路北丽都花园南门
South Gate, Lido Garden, 700m East of Xiaoyunqiao, East 4th Circle, No.6, Fangyuan West Road, Chaoyang District,Beijing

营业时间 Opening Hours
11:00 – 22:00
着装要求 Dress Code
商务休闲 Business Casual
人均消费 Per Capita Consumption
360 元 360 RMB

梧桐是一家以精品新派京城菜为代表的创意餐厅。菜品不仅完整继承了传统宫廷菜独特的味觉记忆，同时还结合了西式料理的精致与优雅。餐厅的招牌菜有：梧桐四味烤鸭、芒果粒三文鱼、梧桐沙拉等。

It is an innovative and exquisite restaurant characterized by new Beijing cuisine. Its dishes not only fully inherit the unique tastes of traditional palace dishes, but also combine them with the delicate and elegant western cuisine. Its signature dishes are: Wutong Four-flavor Roast Duck, Mango Salmon, Wutong Salad and so on.

梧桐 Plus
Wish Plus

中餐
Chinese Cuisine

4.0 必应搜索热度
Search priority

电话 /Tel
+86 10 5352 1539

地址 /Address
北京市工人体育场东门辅路向南 150 米
150m South, Auxiliary Road, East Entrance Workers' Stadium, Beijing

营业时间 Opening Hours
午餐 Lunch 11:00 – 14:30
晚餐 Dinner 17:00 – 22:00
着装要求 Dress Code
商务休闲 Business Casual
人均消费 Per Capita Consumption
550 元 550 RMB

梧桐 Plus 位于北京最繁华的三里屯，餐厅在布置方面讲究体现自然气息，采用大量的实木材料及皮质摆设，再配上餐厅主打的冲击味蕾的创意北京菜，为在梧桐餐厅用餐的食客带来无尽的视觉与味觉的愉悦情绪。

Located at Sanlitun, the most prosperous area in Beijing, it is decorated with a large number of solid wood furniture and leather articles which convey natural atmosphere, together with creative signature,Beijing cuisine, bringing diners into infinite pleasure mood through seeing and tasting.

羲和三里
XIHE Sanli

中餐
Chinese Cuisine

必应 搜索热度 Search priority 3.1

电话 /Tel
+86 10 6417 6082

地址 /Address
北京市朝阳区三里屯路 19 号院
9 号楼 3 层 S9-33 单元
Unit S9-33, 3F, Building 9, No.19, Sanlitun Road, Chaoyang District, Beijing

营业时间 Opening Hours
午餐 Lunch 11:00 - 14:00
晚餐 Dinner 17:00 - 21:00
着装要求 Dress Code
优雅便服 Smart Casual
人均消费 Per Capita Consumption
165 元 165 RMB

客人可在这里一边望着路上的潮流男女，一边品尝着传统的中式美味，能够拥有不一样的美妙体验。椒汁肥牛、海胆豆腐、宫保虾球、羲和烤鸭、羲和自制酸奶等几乎是客人必点的菜品。

Watching the trendy ladies and gentlemen passing by while tasting traditional Chinese cuisine must be an interesting dining experience. Pepper Juice Fat Cattle, Sea Urchin Tofu, Gongbao Shrimp Ball, Soup and Roast Duck, Soup and Self-Made Yoghurt are almost necessary dishes for guests.

羲和小馆（金融街店）
XIHE Bistro(Financial Street)

中餐
Chinese Cuisine

必应 搜索热度 Search priority 2.7

电话 /Tel
+86 10 6621 6061

地址 /Address
北京市西城区金城坊街 3-1 号及 3-2 号
Shop 3-1 and Shop 3-2, Jinchengfang Street, Xicheng District, Beijing

营业时间 Opening Hours
11:00 - 21:30
着装要求 Dress Code
优雅便服 Smart Casual
人均消费 Per Capita Consumption
150 元 150 RMB

羲和小馆（金融街店）在周边的餐厅中人气颇高，不仅仅是因为其古色古香的装潢和匠心独具的餐厅布局，更重要的是其菜品在北京菜的基础上又融合了诸多创意。

XIHE Bistro (Financial Street) is rather popular in nearby block, not only because of its classical decoration and thoughtful layout, but its creative dishes as well.

羲和雅苑（国贸店）
XIHE Ya Court(China World)

中餐
Chinese Cuisine

2.7 必应搜索热度 Search priority

电话 /Tel
+86 10 65056587
+86 10 65056927

地址 /Address
北京市朝阳区建国门外大街国贸商城 B1 层 SB127 和 SB128
SB127&SB128, B1, China World, Jianguomen Outer Street, Chaoyang District, Beijing

营业时间 Opening Hours
11:00 – 21:30
着装要求 Dress Code
优雅便服 Smart Casual
人均消费 Per Capita Consumption
190 元 190 RMB

羲和雅苑（国贸店）位于北京最为繁华的 CBD（中央商务区）地段，为食客提供极具传统特色且添加创意元素的中式菜品。诸如宫保虾球、张氏狮子头、酸汤肥牛等特色菜，都非常值得一试。

XIHE Ya Court (Guomao) stands in the most bustling area of the CBD, serving each diner with the most traditional but also creative Chinese cuisine. Special dishes such as Gongbao shrimp balls, Zhang's Lion's Head, Sour Soup and Fat Fattle are also worth trying.

羲和雅苑（平安店）
XIHE Ya Court(Ping'an)

中餐
Chinese Cuisine

2.7 必应搜索热度 Search priority

电话 /Tel
+86 10 59761355
+86 10 59761366

地址 /Address
北京市朝阳区新源南路 1 号都汇天地 3 层 302
Room 302, 3F, City Mall, No.1, Xinyuan South Road, Chaoyang District, Beijing

营业时间 Opening Hours
午餐 Lunch 11:00 – 14:00
晚餐 Dinner 17:00 – 22:00
着装要求 Dress Code
优雅便服 Smart Casual
人均消费 Per Capita Consumption
225 元 225 RMB

店内主厨师出杭帮菜，结合自己的创新，融合创造出诸如干煸口蘑、井冈山豆皮、椒汁肥牛等特色中式美食。如果您想品味传统中餐的独到韵味，羲和雅苑会是您的不二之选。

In-store chefs produce Hangzhou dishes and combine their own innovations to create Chinese cuisines with characteristics such as Dried Mushrooms, Jinggangshan Bean Skins, and Fat Cattle with Pepper juice. If you want to enjoy traditional flavor in a busy center, XIHE Ya Court must be a perfect choice.

夏宫
Summer Palace

粤菜 淮扬菜
Cantonese Cuisine and Huaiyang Cuisine

Private Rooms

必应 搜索热度 Search priority 7.6

电话 /Tel
+86 10 6505 2266-34

地址 /Address
北京市朝阳区建国门外大街 1 号
中国大饭店大堂
Lobby, China World Hotel, No.1, Jianguomen Outer Street, Chaoyang District, Beijing

营业时间 Opening Hours
午餐 Lunch 11:30 - 14:30
晚餐 Dinner 17:30 - 22:00
着装要求 Dress Code
优雅便服 Smart Casual
人均消费 Per Capita Consumption
300 ~ 400 元 300 ~ 400 RMB

夏宫餐厅可为客人提供经典传统粤菜、创新淮扬美食、具有深厚文化底蕴的中国茶，以及高级侍酒师推荐的法国波尔多葡萄酒。另外，餐厅每日中午还供应品种多样的美味点心。

Summer Palace serves classic traditional Cantonese cuisine, creative Huaiyang cuisine, and Chinese tea with profound culture as well as fine wine with its sommelier's exclusive selection of French Bordeaux vintages. Summer Palace also serves a popular dim sum lunch daily.

乡味小厨
Country Kitchen

中餐
Chinese Cuisine

Private Rooms　Terrace Dining

必应 搜索热度 Search priority 7.6

电话 /Tel
+86 10 6536 0066

地址 /Address
北京市朝阳区呼家楼京广中心北京瑰丽酒店 3 层
3F, Beijing Rosewood Hotel, Jing Guang Center, Hujialou, Chaoyang District, Beijing

营业时间 Opening Hours
午餐 Lunch 11:30 - 14:30
晚餐 Dinner 17:30 - 22:30
着装要求 Dress Code
优雅便服 Smart Casual
人均消费 Per Capita Consumption
300 ~ 400 元 300 ~ 400 RMB

餐厅主打中国北方风味家乡美食，内设开放式厨房和燃木烤炉，厨师们精心烹制着地道的北京烤鸭、中式面条和各式饺子等。

It mainly provides Northern Chinese specialties. With an open kitchen and a wood roasting oven, chefs demonstrate their culinary arts, such as Hand-pulled Chinese Noodles, Beijing Roast Duck and a variety of dumplings.

香守
Samesoul

港式火锅
Hong Kong Hotpot

2.7 必应搜索热度 Search priority

电话 /Tel
+86 10 5969 6666

地址 /Address
北京市华贸广场路华贸 JW 万豪酒店 2 层
2F, JW Marriott, Huamao Guangchang Road, Beijing

营业时间 Opening Hours
11:30 - 22:00
着装要求 Dress Code
无特别着装要求 Non-specified
人均消费 Per Capita Consumption
400 元 400 RMB

再简单的食物都有自己的魂魄，再复杂的食材也不过人间五味。香守遵奉港式火锅的追求并还原食材的鲜美，守住香守的味道，将人间烟火气化在一口恰到好处的锅里，将食材原本的鲜香体现得淋漓尽致。

The simplest food has its own soul, and the most complex ingredients just can give five tastes to human beings. This restaurant pursues to restore the freshness of ingredients, and puts the life of human beings in a proper pot while retaining the original flavors, and gives the original freshness and fragrance of ingredients incisively and vividly.

湘爱（凤凰汇店）
Inlove(Fenghuanghui)

中餐
Chinese Cuisine

2.7 必应搜索热度 Search priority

电话 /Tel
+86 10 5866 8358
+86 10 5866 8339

地址 /Address
北京市朝阳区曙光西里甲 5 号院
No.5A, Shuguangxili, Chaoyang District, Beijing

营业时间 Opening Hours
11:00 - 22:00
着装要求 Dress Code
无特别着装要求 Non-specified
人均消费 Per Capita Consumption
280 元 280 RMB

湘爱餐厅环境安静优雅、服务恰到好处，以严格的原料把控、精细的刀工、令人称叹的厨艺和匠心独运的装盘艺术，打造出不同于传统印象的新式湖南菜，重新组合了湖南“辣”的味觉拼图。

It has a quiet and elegant environment with considerate services. Based on the strictly selected raw materials, refined cutting techniques, remarkable culinary skills and inventive plate presentation, it builds a new Hunan cuisine different from the traditional dishes, and sets up new combinations of Hunan spicy tastes.

湘爱（三里屯店）
Inlove(Sanlitun)

中餐
Chinese Cuisine

梧桐餐饮集团旗下的湘爱三里屯店，环境时尚动感，菜品传承湘西、湘江和洞庭湘菜支系的各家所长，辅以复合的辣感，将醇厚且富有个性的辣感从舌尖传递，并令此种愉悦蔓延至全身。此外，桥底辣炒宁海蟹是餐厅的招牌菜。

As a member of Wutong Catering Group, it has a fashionable and dynamic environment. The dishes inherit various advantages of Hunan cuisine, Xiangjiang River cuisine and Dongting cuisine with compound spicy tastes, which conveys the rich and specific spicy feeling from tongue tip and spreads this pleasure to the whole body. In addition, the Under Bridge Spicy Crab is the restaurant's signature dish.

必应 搜索热度 Search priority 2.7

电话 /Tel
+86 10 5352 0033
+86 10 5352 1533

地址 /Address
北京市工人体育场东门辅路向南 150 米
150m South, Auxiliary Road, East Entrance Workers' Stadium, Beijing

营业时间 Opening Hours
午餐 Lunch 11:00 – 14:30
晚餐 Dinner 17:00 – 22:00
着装要求 Dress Code
无特别着装要求 Non-specified
人均消费 Per Capita Consumption
400 元 400 RMB

湘爱（祥云店）
Inlove(Xiangyun)

中餐
Chinese Cuisine

湘爱秉持着令食客在用餐时能够分享精致美好生活方式和美食的理念，打造舒适清新的环境，并采用体现原汁原味的烹饪手法，表达湖南菜纯粹的色、香、味。餐厅主打菜为：石锅牛蛙、馋嘴鸭头、非常臭鳜鱼等。

It upholds the concept of making diners sharing exquisite and beautiful life style and delicious food during eating, provides a comfortable and fresh environment, and expresses the color, fragrance and taste of Hunan cuisine through authentic cooking techniques. Its signature dishes are: Stone Pot Bullfrog, Glutton Duck Head, Smelly Mandarin Fish and so on.

必应 搜索热度 Search priority 2.7

电话 /Tel
+86 10 6860 6066

地址 /Address
北京市安泰大街祥云小镇南区 6 号院 9 号楼 105 号
No.105, Building 9, No.6, Xiangyun County South, Antai Street, Beijing

营业时间 Opening Hours
午餐 Lunch 11:00 – 14:30
晚餐 Dinner 17:00 – 21:30
着装要求 Dress Code
无特别着装要求 Non-specified
人均消费 Per Capita Consumption
260 元 260 RMB

小大董（侨福店）

Taste of Dadong(Parkview Green)

创意菜
Creative Cuisine

3.6 必应搜索热度 Search priority

电话 /Tel
+86 10 5208 6061

地址 /Address
北京市朝阳区东大桥路 9 号
侨福芳草地 LG2-11A
LG2-11A, Parkview Green, No.9, Dongdaqiao Road, Chaoyang District, Beijing

营业时间 Opening Hours
11:00 - 22:00
着装要求 Dress Code
优雅便服 Smart Casual
人均消费 Per Capita Consumption
200 元 200 RMB

作为大董旗下的时尚餐饮品牌，小大董的空间设计在中式风格中透露着轻松愉悦的就餐氛围。来到这里，食客无须花费太多就能品尝到与大董一脉相承的精致创意菜肴。

Subordinated to the fashionable restaurant brand Da Dong , Taste of Dadong gives a touch of leisure and joy in its Chinese-style space design. The creative dishes are as good as Da Dong's at an affordable price.

小红门港式海鲜火锅（永安里店）

Red Door(Yonganli)

火锅
Hotpot

7.7 必应搜索热度 Search priority

电话 /Tel
+86 10 6568 1861

地址 /Address
北京市永安东里甲 3 号
No.3A, Yongandongli, Beijing

营业时间 Opening Hours
11:00 - 22:30
着装要求 Dress Code
无特别着装要求 Non-specified
人均消费 Per Capita Consumption
300 ~ 500 元 300 ~ 500 RMB

美食能激发人的美好情感和对生活的热情，小红门火锅以精益求精的认真态度，在快节奏的繁华都市保持中华传统，用匠心制作美食。餐厅食材鲜美，环境格调温馨。

Delicacy can inspire human's good feelings and enthusiasm for life. This restaurant holds on a serious attitude of perfecting, inherits Chinese traditions in the fast-paced bustling city, and cooks food with ingenuity. It provides a warm environment and fresh ingredients for diners.

小红袍香港私房火锅料理（王府井店）
Xiaohongpao(Wangfujing)

火锅
Hotpot

必应 搜索热度 Search priority 2.6

电话 /Tel
+86 10 6526 9560
+86 130 1102 7156

地址 /Address
北京市王府井大街王府中环西座 408 室
Room 408, Building West, Wangfu Central, Wangfujing Street, Beijing

营业时间 Opening Hours
11:30 – 22:30
着装要求 Dress Code
无特别着装要求 Non-specified
人均消费 Per Capita Consumption
350 元 350 RMB

小红袍私房火锅是北京打边炉中口味比较纯正的一家，整个餐厅的用餐氛围轻松又愉悦，餐厅的服务人员还会过来帮你涮肉、煮菜，服务热情又周到。餐厅有许多招牌菜品，如：鬼马虾饺、长崎蟹柳、安格斯肥牛等。

As an authentic hotpot in Beijing, it provides a relaxing and pleasant dining atmosphere. Its staff will help diners rinse the meat and vegetables with enthusiastic and considerate services. It has many signature dishes, such as: Ghost Shrimp Dumplings, Nagasaki Crab Sticks, and Angus Beef.

小红门港式海鲜火锅（丽都店）
Red Door(Lidu)

火锅
Hotpot

必应 搜索热度 Search priority 7.7

电话 /Tel
+86 10 6568 1862

地址 /Address
北京市芳园西路 2 号 2 楼和乔丽晶西门对面
Opposite of Chateau Regency West Entrance, 2F, No.2, Fangyuan West Road, Beijing

营业时间 Opening Hours
11:30 – 24:00
着装要求 Dress Code
无特别着装要求 Non-specified
人均消费 Per Capita Consumption
320 元 320 RMB

小红门港式海鲜火锅作为众多海鲜火锅餐厅中的佼佼者之一，自开业以来，一直坚持使用最新鲜营养的食材，以最纯熟的烹饪手法服务于新老食客。餐厅环境时尚，现代感十足，并以一道海味浓鸡汤征服了诸多食客的心。

As one of excellent seafood hotpot restaurants, it has always insisted in using the freshest and most nutritious ingredients and serving diners with the most skillful culinary arts since its opening. It has a fashionable and modern environment, and has won the hearts of numerous diners with its seafood chicken soup.

新加坡海鲜（国贸店）
Singapore Seafood(China World)

东南亚菜
Southeast Asian Cuisine

2.7 必应搜索热度 Search priority

电话 /Tel
+86 10 8595 0291

地址 /Address
北京市朝阳区建国门外大街 1 号
国贸商城北区 4 层 NL4010
NL4010, 4F, China World North, No.1, Jianguomen Outer Street, Chaoyang District, Beijing

营业时间 Opening Hours
11:00 – 22:00
着装要求 Dress Code
优雅便服 Smart Casual
人均消费 Per Capita Consumption
292 元 292 RMB

新加坡海鲜致力于以高质量、高标准甄选食材，用心料理，为每一位顾客提供最上等的海鲜，再加上店内优雅的环境，满足每一位挑剔的食客。星洲辣椒螃蟹、黑胡椒螃蟹、黄金炸鱼皮等招牌菜是这里的必点菜品。

It devotes to selecting ingredients based on the high quality and standards, and provides the best seafood with carefully cooking techniques for each diner. The elegant environment can satisfy all picky diners. Its signature dishes include must-try specialties, such as Singapore Chili Crab, Black Pepper Crab, and Golden Fried Fish Skin.

西村
Nishimura

无限卡特权

日本料理
Japanese Cuisine

5.9 必应搜索热度 Search priority

电话 /Tel
+86 10 6841 2211-6719

地址 /Address
北京市海淀区紫竹院路 29 号
北京香格里拉饭店景阁 2 层
2F, Garden Pavilion of Shangri-La Hotel, No.29, Zizhuyuan Road, Haidian District, Beijing

营业时间 Opening Hours
午餐 Lunch 11:30 – 14:30
晚餐 Dinner 17:30 – 22:00
着装要求 Dress Code
优雅便服 Smart Casual
人均消费 Per Capita Consumption
300 元 300 RMB

餐厅内设现场制作美食的独立寿司吧和铁板烧台，以及私密包间和日式榻榻米包间供私人聚会之用。这里提供纯正精致的日本料理，刺身、铁板虾球沙拉、西村寿司精选和天妇罗精选等都大受好评。

There is a free-standing sushi bar and teppanyaki table for onsite cooking, and private rooms and Tatami VIP rooms for friend gatherings. Nishimura stays true to Japanese flavors and brings in sophisticated Japanese cuisine, such as sashimi, Teppanyaki-fried Shrimp Salad, Nishimura Sushi Combination and Tempura, which are highly praised by diners.

行运打边炉
Xing Yun

粤菜
Guangdong Cuisine

必应 搜索热度 Search priority 3.0

电话 /Tel
+86 10 6552 9801

地址 /Address
北京市工体北路 15 号 VICS 旁
VICS, No.15, Gongti North Road, Beijing

营业时间 Opening Hours
周一至周五 Mon. – Fri.
11:30–14:00 17:00 – 02:00
周六、周日 Sat. – Sun. 11:00 – 02:00
着装要求 Dress Code
无特别着装要求 Non–specified
人均消费 Per Capita Consumption
290 元 290 RMB

边炉是一道色香味俱全的粤菜名肴。行运打边炉餐厅以其新鲜营养的菜品和充香港风格的环境受到京城食客的青睐。餐厅招牌菜为：金牌花胶鸡煲、招牌黄泡饭、芝士龙虾虾饺等。其中金牌花胶鸡煲汤底浓厚，最受食客的喜爱。

is a famous Cantonese cuisine with perfect combination of color aroma iste and appearance. With its fresh and nutritious dishes and Hong Kong–tyle environment, it is popular among Beijing diners. The restaurant's gnature dishes include: Golden Fish Maw Chicken Pot, Signature Golden orridge, Cheese Lobster Dumplings, etc. The Golden Fish Maw Chicken ot is the most popular among diners with thick soup base.

席 Feast
Feas

素食
Vegetarian Cuisine

必应 搜索热度 Search priority 7.5

电话 /Tel
+86 10 8620 0250

地址 /Address
北京市朝阳区建国路 93 号院
17 号楼 102 号商铺
Shop 102, Building 17, No.93, Jianguo Road, Chaoyang District, Beijing

营业时间 Opening Hours
11:00 – 22:00
着装要求 Dress Code
无特别着装要求 Non–specified
人均消费 Per Capita Consumption
520 元 520 RMB

餐厅用创意、精细、正本清源的态度对待素菜的种种演化，不以素食荤吃迎合现代人的口味，还原素菜食材原本的清甜与雅致。餐厅还十分注重营造用餐环境，以雅致的环境衬托食物的无限美味。

It proposes to treat the development of vegetarian dishes with creativity, delicacy and purity, and does not mix meat and vegetables which caters to the taste of modern people, so as to retain the original sweetness and elegance of vegetarian dishes. It still pays attention to building a dinning environment to provide the infinite delicacy of food against elegant environment.

岩极
A Stone Grill House

烤肉
Barbecue

2.6 必应搜索热度 Search priority

电话 /Tel
+86 10 8590 0332

地址 /Address
北京市工体北路
三里屯 SOHO 办公 A 座 5 层
5F, Building A, Sanlitun SOHO, Gongti North Road, Beijing

营业时间 Opening Hours
10:00 – 23:30
着装要求 Dress Code
无特别着装要求 Non-specified
人均消费 Per Capita Consumption
150 元 150 RMB

岩极主打东北风味烤肉，店内提供二十多种酱料，不同的肉、不同部位，都有对应的最佳酱料，每天需要以不同的手法提前腌制好，才能上桌给客人烤制。餐厅老板还专门从东北定制了石板烤盘，就为了还原自己家乡的味道。

It mainly provides Northeast barbecue with more than 20 kinds of sauces corresponding to different parts of meats. The meats are pickled well in advance every day using different approaches, and serve to the table for diners to bake. The owner of this restaurant specially customized stone baking pan from Northeast China to restore flavors of his hometown.

亚洲风尚
Asian Bistro

无限卡特权

自助餐
Buffet

4.4 必应搜索热度 Search priority

电话 /Tel
+86 10 5908 8511

地址 /Address
北京市朝阳区建国路 83 号 JW 万豪酒店 1 层
1F, JW Marriott Hotel Beijing, No.83, Jianguo Road, Chaoyang District, Beijing

营业时间 Opening Hours
早餐 Breakfast 06:30 – 10:30
午餐 Lunch 11:30 – 14:30
晚餐 Dinner 18:00 – 22:00
着装要求 Dress Code
无特别着装要求 Non-specified
人均消费 Per Capita Consumption
300 元 300 RMB

空灵的顶部设计与炫美灯光相融合，亚洲风尚为客人提供充满活力的用餐环境，四个开放式厨房分别供应来自泰国、印度、日本与中国的优质亚洲风味。

Combining the ethereal top design with dazzling lights, the Asian Bistro provides guests with an energetic dining environment. Four open kitchens provide high-quality Asian taste from Thailand, India, Japan and China respectively.

叶奈日式料理
Hana by Hatsune

日本料理
Japanese Cuisine

必应 搜索热度 Search priority 3.7

电话 /Tel
+86 10 8599 6131

地址 /Address
北京市朝阳区国贸商城北区 6 层 NL6006
NL6006, 6F, China World North, Chaoyang District, Beijing

营业时间 Opening Hours
午餐 Lunch 11:30–14:00
晚餐 Dinne 17:30–22:00
着装要求 Dress Code
无特别着装要求 Non-specified
人均消费 Per Capita Consumption
350 元 350 RMB

奈，日语为“花”的意思，店内以温馨、优美的“竹林雅居”环境设计惊艳业界。奈主张甄选顶级食材，沿用加州日料的创新做法激活食材的天然美味，搭配焕一新。点一道缤纷寿司，其口感上佳。

atsune means "followers" in Japanese; therefore its environmental esign of "refined house around by bamboo forest" amazes the restaurant dustry, leaving a warm and elegant feeling. It devotes to selecting top gredients, and inspiring natural delicacies of ingredients through the novative approach of California-Japanese cuisine. Ordering a piece of olorful sushi with new arrangement, diners will enjoy a delicious taste.

叶叶菩提（大望路店）
L.Bodhi Restaurant(Dawanglu)

素食
Vegetarian Cuisine

必应 搜索热度 Search priority 2.6

电话 /Tel
+86 135 5268 6209

地址 /Address
北京市光华路 2 号楼阳光 100F 座底商
1F, Building F, Sunshine 100, No.2, Guanghua Road, Beijing

营业时间 Opening Hours
09:30 – 21:30
着装要求 Dress Code
无特别着装要求 Non-specified
人均消费 Per Capita Consumption
600 元 600 RMB

作为新素食餐厅中的佼佼者，精致、细腻、含蓄、素雅的美学是叶叶菩提的品质定位。叶叶菩提旨在宣传饮食有节、饮食有度、饮食有择的养生法则，精心组配极品素食健康佳肴。此外，餐厅的用餐环境也是令人心旷神怡。

As an outstanding restaurant among new vegetarian restaurants, it pursues a dining quality of exquisite, delicate, implicit, simple and elegant aesthetics. It aims to promote healthy eating habits of controlled and selected diet, and carefully combines the best and healthy vegetarian dishes. In addition, the dining environment is also pleasant and refreshing.

叶书
Hagaki

中餐
Chinese Cuisine

7.4 必应搜索热度 Search priority

电话 /Tel
+86 10 8414 9815

地址 /Address
北京市朝阳区酒仙桥路 22 号北京东隅 2 层
2F, EAST Beijing, No.22, Jiuxianqiao Road, Chaoyang District, Beijing

营业时间 Opening Hours
午餐 Lunch 11:30 – 14:30
晚餐 Dinner 17:30 – 22:00
着装要求 Dress Code
优雅便服 Smart Casual
人均消费 Per Capita Consumption
150 元 150 RMB

叶书是一家颇具格调的现代日本餐厅，风格独树一帜。除供应一些特色卷寿司、吉列猪扒、天妇罗、乌冬面等经典日本料理外，叶书还专门烹制加州风味的日式美食，并在餐厅内设置了动感寿司吧。

It is a modern Japanese restaurant with unique style. It not only serves traditional Japanese dishes such as some specialty Maki Sushi, Gillet Pork Chop, Tempura and Udon Noodles, but also specializes in "California flavors" Japanese cuisine and has a dynamic Sushi Bar inside restaurant.

一品淮扬中餐厅
Yipin Chinese Restaurant

无限卡特权

淮扬菜
Huaiyang Cuisine

2.8 必应搜索热度 Search priority

电话 /Tel
86 10-8599 6666-6508

地址 /Address
北京市万达索菲特大饭店 6 层
6F, Sofitel Wanda Hotel, Beijing

营业时间 Opening Hours
午餐 Lunch 11:30 – 14:00
晚餐 Dinner 17:30 – 22:00
着装要求 Dress Code
得体 Decent
人均消费 Per Capita Consumption
500 元 500 RMB

一品淮扬中餐厅由蒋应荣师傅主理，他的刀功、烹饪方式精细而不做作，餐厅招牌菜品包括响油鳝糊、清蒸狮子头、雨花石汤圆等。

Yipin Chinese Restaurant recruits Chef Jiang Yingrong who is a master of slicing technique and culinary skills, with signatures such as Ring Oil Eel Paste, Steamed Meat Ball, and Pebble-like Tang-yuan, etc.

意秀
Italian Trattoria

意大利菜
Italian Cuisine

必应 搜索热度 3.8
Search priority

电话 /Tel
+86 10 8437 1188

地址 /Address
北京市朝阳区北辰西路 8 号北辰洲际酒店 2 层
2F, InterContinental Beijing Beichen Hotel, No.8, Beichen West Road, Chaoyang District, Beijing

营业时间 Opening Hours
晚餐 Dinner 17:30 – 22:00
着装要求 Dress Code
优雅便服 Smart Casual
人均消费 Per Capita Consumptions
260 ~ 320 元 260 ~ 320 RMB

意秀为名流和老饕们量身定制精致的意大利美食。厨师团队精选当季新鲜食材，并运用独特的烹饪方法，如食烹香草煮海鲜汤，虾、扇贝、贻贝等海鲜加上香草的独特香味，层次丰富。

It mainly provides exquisite Italian cuisine for celebrities and gourmets. Chef team selects the seasonal fresh ingredients and adopts unique cooking methods. For example, its seafood soup with champignon, shrimps, scallops, mussels and other seafood mixing with vanilla has unique flavors and rich tastes.

意库（新源里店）
Bottega(Xinyuanli)

西餐
Western Cuisine

必应 搜索热度 3.6
Search priority

电话 /Tel
+86 10 6410 9800

地址 /Address
北京市朝阳区新源里西 20 号金尚 1 层
1F, Jinshang, No.20, Xinyuanlixi, Chaoyang District, Beijing

营业时间 Opening Hours
早餐 Breakfast 11:00
午餐 Lunch 12:00 – 15:00
晚餐 Dinner 16:00 – 24:00
着装要求 Dress Code
无特别着装要求 Non-specified
人均消费 Per Capita Consumption
172 元 172 RMB

拥有意大利风情的披萨名店意库为北京城增添一丝热情，主厨团队一直致力于不断为食客带来惊喜，无论是日式现烤菠菜烘蛋、意大利茴香猪肉香肠，还是美味的配菜热烤土豆，都会给食客带来无比的愉悦和满足的体验。

As a famous pizza restaurant with Italian style, it makes Beijing more enthusiastic. The chef team has been committed to constantly bringing surprises to diners. Whether the Japanese-style Freshly Baked Frittata, Italian Fennel Pork Sausage, or delicious side dishes such as Hot Roasted Potatoes, the diners will have an extremely pleasant and satisfied experience.

意库（三里屯店）
Bottega(Sanlitun)

西餐
Western Cuisine

4.4 必应搜索热度 Search priority

电话 /Tel
+86 10 6416 1752

地址 /Address
北京市三里屯北路 81 号那里花园 2 层
2F, Nali Patio, No.81, Sanlitun North Road,Beijing

营业时间 Opening Hours
早餐 Breakfast 11:00
午餐 Lunch 12:00 – 15:00
晚餐 Dinner 16:00 – 24:00
着装要求 Dress Code
无特别着装要求 Non-specified
人均消费 Per Capita Consumption
172 元 172 RMB

作为充满格调与异域风情的餐厅，意库（三里屯店）结合了高品质的食材与意大利大厨的精湛厨艺，推出的菜品一向兼具高水准与性价比。除了必点的披萨，其丰富的午间套餐也刷新了北京午餐的新高度。

It is a restaurant with attractive and exotic style. Based on the high-quality ingredients and exquisite culinary arts of Italian chef, its dishes are not only high level but also cost-effective. In addition to the must-try pizza, its luxuriant lunch packages also lift the level of Beijing lunch.

壹炖饭
One Meal

中餐
Chinese Cuisine

4.1 必应搜索热度 Search priority

电话 /Tel
+86 10 8517 2808

地址 /Address
北京市朝阳区建国门外大街 2 号
银泰中心 in01 地下 1 层
B1, Yintai Centre, No.2, Jianguomen Outer Street, Chaoyang District, Beijing

营业时间 Opening Hours
午餐 Lunch 11:00 – 14:00
晚餐 Dinner 17:00 – 21:30
着装要求 Dress Code
商务休闲 Business Casual
人均消费 Per Capita Consumption
150 元 150 RMB

壹炖饭作为中餐连锁品牌，主要经营炖菜及烤鸭，其中以炖鱼头为主。壹炖饭采用明档厨房，它能使客人看到菜品制作的全过程或部分过程，使客人不仅在用餐上更放心，同时还能欣赏带有艺术特色的烹调文化。

As a chain brand of Chinese cuisine, it is focused on stewed dishes and roast duck. For stewed dishes, the stewed fish head is first recommended. Through its open kitchen, it provides diners with a whole or partial cooking show with artistic characteristics, in order to make them appreciate the cooking culture while have more confidence in the dishes.

隐泉日式料理（8 号公馆店）
Hatsune(No. 8 Residence)

无限卡特权

日本料理
Japanese Cuisine

必应 搜索热度 Search priority 2.7

电话 /Tel
+86 10 6508 2889

地址 /Address
北京市朝阳区朝阳公园西门 8 号公馆院内
No. 8 Residence, West Gate of Chaoyang Park, Chaoyang District, Beijing

营业时间 Opening Hours
午餐 Lunch 11:30 – 14:00
晚餐 Dinner 17:30 – 22:00
着装要求 Dress Code
优雅便服 Smart Casual
人均消费 Per Capita Consumption
350 元 350 RMB

隐泉是源自加州的日式料理，菜单上颇受欢迎的火警虾及蝴蝶卷等，正是隐泉力图呈现加州创意日料的代表作。

Originated from California, Hatsune is a Japanese cuisine restaurant. The long-term popular dishes like Fire Shrimp and Butterfly Roll are exactly the representative Japanese dishes in California concept.

隐泉日式料理（三里屯店）
Hatsune(Sanlitun)

无限卡特权

日本料理
Japanese Cuisine

必应 搜索热度 Search priority 2.7

电话 /Tel
+86 10 6415 3939

地址 /Address
北京市朝阳区三里屯 19 号院南区 3 层 S8-30
S8-30, 3F, South Area, No.19, Sanlitun, Chaoyang District, Beijing

营业时间 Opening Hours
午餐 Lunch 11:30 – 14:00
下午茶 Afternoon Tea 14:00 – 17:30
晚餐 Dinner 17:30 – 22:00
着装要求 Dress Code
优雅便服 Smart Casual
人均消费 Per Capita Consumption
230 元 230 RMB

隐泉是中国首家源自加州的日式料理，提供高品质、新鲜的海鲜食材，从原产地直飞而来的各类刺身用生鱼，吸引了各路食家光临。

Hatsune is the first Japanese cuisine restaurant originating from California in China,offering high-quality and fresh seafood, including various fishes for sashimi from source areas, which attracts numerous guests.

隐厨
Hidden Kitchen

中餐
Chinese Cuisine

2.7 必应搜索热度
Search priority

电话 /Tel
+86 10 5621 5783

地址 /Address
北京市三里屯南路通盈中心 4 层 4-1 号
Room 4-1, 4F, InterContinental Sanlitun Beijing, Sanlitun South Road, Beijing

营业时间 Opening Hours
11:30 – 22:00
着装要求 Dress Code
无特别着装要求 Non-specified
人均消费 Per Capita Consumption
150 元 150RMB

隐厨是一家主打中国民间菜的餐厅，餐厅自开业以来，就将“抛弃繁杂工艺，拒绝一切重料，只留原始本味”作为烹饪的坚持。餐厅环境极具中国特色，将古典与现代完美结合。蜂蜜地瓜、小米油渣土豆丝、高压芋头牛腩是餐厅的特色菜。

It mainly provides Chinese folk cuisine, and abandons complicated techniques and various seasonings to retain original flavors of materials since its opening. It has a classical and modern environment with Chinese characteristics. The signature dishes include Honey Sweet Potato, Shredded Potato with Millet Oil Residue, and High Pressure Taro Sirloin.

玉
Yu

粤菜
Cantonese Cuisine

9.7 必应搜索热度
Search priority

电话 /Tel
+86 10 5908 8111

地址 /Address
北京市朝阳区华贸中心建国路甲 83 号
No.83A, Jianguo Road, China Central Place, Chaoyang District, Beijing

营业时间 Opening Hours
午餐 Lunch 11:30 – 14:00
晚餐 Dinner 18:00 – 22:00
着装要求 Dress Code
优雅便服 Smart Casual
人均消费 Per Capita Consumption
500 ~ 1000 元 500 ~ 1000 RMB

这里的各种精品粤菜用料讲究，口味地道，同时加入了厨师团队的独创风格。特色美食如吊炉脆皮鸡，经典甜品如杨枝甘露，都获得了广大食客乃至名人明星的称赞。

A variety of refined and authentic Cantonese cuisine with creative style of chef team is provided here. Its specialties and classic desserts, like Crisp Grilled Chicken and Chilled Mango Sago Cream with Pomelo, are highly praised by many diners, even some celebrities and stars.

粤秀轩
DI Restaurant

中餐
Chinese Cuisine

必应 搜索热度 Search priority 3.6

电话 /Tel
+86 10 8437 1188

地址 /Address
北京市朝阳区北辰西路 8 号北辰洲际酒店 1 层
1F, InterContinental Beijing Beichen Hotel, No.8, Beichen West Road, Chaoyang District, Beijing

营业时间 Opening Hours
午餐 Lunch 11:30 – 14:00
晚餐 Dinner 17:30 – 22:00
着装要求 Dress Code
优雅便服 Smart Casual
人均消费 Per Capita Consumption
300 元 300 RMB

餐厅呈现的是极富代表性的粤菜和其他地方风味菜肴，如梅子鹅肝、葱烧辽参、特色芝麻鸡、石锅银鳕鱼等，能够让食客的味蕾得到极大满足。

DI Restaurant offers a fine selection of typical Cantonese cuisine and other local flavor features such as Plum Foie Gras, Braised Sea Cucumber with Scallion, Sesame Chicken, and Stone Bowl Codfish, which can greatly satisfy various diners.

盈中餐
Ying Chinese

粤菜
Cantonese Cuisine

必应 搜索热度 Search priority 3.6

电话 /Tel
+86 10 8516 0066

地址 /Address
北京三里屯通盈中心洲际酒店 3 层
3F, InterContinental Sanlitun Beijing, Beijing

营业时间 Opening Hours
早餐 Breakfast 6:30 – 10:00
午餐 Lunch 11:30 – 14:30
晚餐 Dinner 17:30 – 21:30
着装要求 Dress Code
无特别着装要求 Non-specified
人均消费 Per Capita Consumption
300 元 300 RMB

盈中餐以粤菜闻名，主厨将对传统烹饪的推崇融入到富有新意的中餐创作中，并将甄选自各地的新鲜时令食材幻化成全新滋味的招牌菜式。餐厅空间是一个载体，承载着美食与人文的故事。

Known for its Cantonese cuisine, its chefs integrate the worship of traditional cooking into the creation of new Chinese cuisine, and cook the fresh seasonal ingredients selected from different places into signature dishes with new flavors. It just likes a carrier, carrying the story of food and humanity.

悦尚
N'Joy

自助餐
Buffet

8.4 必应搜索热度 Search priority

电话 /Tel
+86 10 5926 8281

地址 /Address
北京市朝阳区将台路甲 2 号北京诺金酒店 1 层
1F, NUO Hotel Beijing, No. 2A, Jiangtai Road, Chaoyang District, Beijing

营业时间 Opening Hours
午餐 Lunch
周一至周五 Mon. - Fri. 11:30 - 14:00
周六、周日 Sat. - Sun. 11:30 - 14:30
晚餐 Dinner 17:30 - 21:30
着装要求 Dress Code
优雅便服 Smart Casual
人均消费 Per Capita Consumption
300 元 300 RMB

位于北京诺金酒店 1 层的悦尚全日制餐厅，拥有北京星级酒店中面积最大的自助餐台及开放式厨房。整个空间设计感十足，将中国元素与国际化色彩相结合。
N'Joy is an all-day dining restaurant located at 1F of NUO Hotel Beijing, with the largest buffet counter and open kitchen in Beijing's 5-star hotels. The whole space presents a sense of design mixing Chinese elements and global tunes.

者火 · 善造
Zenzo

日本料理
Japanese Cuisine

5.7 必应搜索热度 Search priority

电话 /Tel
+86 10 8556 0566

地址 /Address
北京市青年路朝阳大悦城 7 层拾间主题区内
Shijian Theme Zone, 7F, Joy City, Qingnian Road, Beijing

营业时间 Opening Hours
周一至周五 Mon. - Fri.
11:30 - 14:30 17:30 - 21:30
周六、周日 Sat. - Sun. 11:30 - 21:30
着装要求 Dress Code
无特别着装要求 Non-specified
人均消费 Per Capita Consumption
250 元 250 RMB

者火 · 善造是京城难得主打寿喜锅的日式餐厅，餐厅装修充满和风气息，令人感到温暖。还有层次丰富、肉质出众的安格斯牛小排和肩颈肉，蘸上生鸡蛋液，口感鲜嫩清甜，让食客体会到来自美食的幸福感和满足感。
It is a Japanese restaurant focused on Sukiyaki Pot, which is rare in Beijing. It is decorated in a warm Japanese style. The multiple and superior Angus Short Ribs and Boneless Boston Shoulder dipping with raw egg liquid will give diners a fresh and sweet taste and bring them experience a sense of happiness and satisfaction from delicious food.

紫膳
Cafe Zi

亚洲菜
Asian Cuisine

必应 搜索热度 Search priority 2.6

电话 /Tel
+86 10 8509 8820

地址 /Address
北京市王府井大街 269 号
北京王府井文华东方酒店 5 层
5F, Mandarin Oriental Wangfujing, No.269, Wangfujing Street, Beijing

营业时间 Opening Hours
早餐 Breakfast 06:30 – 10:30
午餐 Lunch 11:30 – 14:30
晚餐 Dinner 17:30 – 22:00
着装要求 Dress Code
优雅便服 Smart Casual
人均消费 Per Capita Consumption
300 元 300 RMB

紫膳餐厅作为种类齐全的自助餐厅，菜品包含了中西菜式和各类精致美味的甜品。餐厅提供海鲜、烤肉和各类寿司，只为全力满足食客的需求。餐厅环境高端典雅，融合了现代与古典的风格，成功俘获了诸多食客的心。

As a buffet restaurant, it provides all kinds of dishes, including Chinese and western food and various delicious desserts. This restaurant serves seafood, barbecue and various types of sushi, in order to meet the demands of diners. It has a high-end and elegant environment with combination style of modern and classics, which has successfully captured the hearts of many diners.

中 8 楼
Zhong 8 Lou

云南菜
Yunnan Cuisine

必应 搜索热度 Search priority 2.6

电话 /Tel
+86 10 6415 8858
+86 10 6415 9889

地址 /Address
北京市三里屯太古里南区 4 层
4F, Taikoo Li Sanlitun South, Beijing

营业时间 Opening Hours
11:30 – 22:00
着装要求 Dress Code
无特别着装要求 Non-specified
人均消费 Per Capita Consumption
130 元 130 RMB

中 8 楼缘起于创始人对彩云之南的顾念，餐厅把对云南的爱和对美食的执着，转化为美味的菜肴。餐厅的环境也是充满了云南风情，四大云南菜品系列：云缘、素念、蘑界和辣道，让食客体味原始纯真的云南美味。

It is originated from the memories of South of the Clouds and converts the love for Yunnan and the persistence to food into delicious dishes. This restaurant has a Yunnan style environment and four major Yunnan dishes series: Yunyuan, Sunian, Mushroom and Spicy, bringing diners the original and authentic Yunnan delicacies.

上海
SHANGHAI

无限卡特权

58° 扒房
Fifty 8° Grill

西餐
Western Cuisine

必应 搜索热度 Search priority 3.6

电话 /Tel
+86 21 2082 9938

地址 /Address
上海市浦东新区浦东南路 111 号上海浦东文华东方酒店公寓 1 层
1F, Mandarin Oriental Pudong Shanghai, No. 111, Pudong South Road, Pudong New District, Shanghai

上等新鲜食材配以出色的烹制技艺，58° 扒房为食客奉上现代派法国美食。餐厅位于上海浦东文华东方酒店 1 层，与室外贯通，并有露天花园餐桌，洋溢着 20 世纪 20 至 30 年代上海滩装饰艺术的氛围。

With top fresh ingredients and prominent culinary arts, Fifty 8° Grill mainly provides modern French cuisine. Located at the 1F of Mandarin Oriental Pudong Shanghai and connecting with outdoor area, this restaurant has garden tables with rich artful flavors of the Bund in 1920s and 1930s.

营业时间 Opening Hours
午餐 Lunch 11:30 – 14:30
晚餐 Dinner 17:30 – 22:30
着装要求 Dress Code
优雅便服 Smart Casual
人均消费 Per Capita Consumption
500 元 500 RMB

无限卡特权

8 ½ Otto e Mezzo BOMBANA（上海）
8 ½ Otto e Mezzo BOMBANA(Shanghai)

意大利菜
Italian Cuisine

必应 搜索热度 Search priority 3.2

电话 /Tel
+86 21 6087 2890

地址 /Address
上海市黄浦区圆明园路 169 号 协进大楼 6 层
6F, Associate Mission Building, No. 169, Yuanmingyuan Road, Huangpu District, Shanghai

上海 8 ½ Otto e Mezzo BOMBANA 是世界名厨 Umberto Bombana 在中国大陆地区开设的首家餐厅。主厨 Bombana 和行政主厨精选来自世界各地的食材，为食客带来顶级意大利美食。

The 8 ½ Otto e Mezzo BOMBANA is the first restaurant opened by world famous chef Umberto Bombana in Mainland China. Chef Bombana and Executive Chef search and select products across the world, bring customers to experience the Italian fragrant and tasty dishes.

营业时间 Opening Hours
午餐 Lunch 11:30 – 14:30
（仅周日开放 Sunday Only）
晚餐 Dinner 18:00 – 23:00
着装要求 Dress Code
优雅便服 Smart Casual
人均消费 Per Capita Consumption
2000 元 2000 RMB

艾利爵士
Sir Elly's Restaurant & Terrace

无限卡特权

西餐
Western Cuisine

2.9 必应搜索热度 Search priority

电话 /Tel
+86 21 5308 1188

地址 /Address
上海市中山东一路 32 号半岛酒店 13 层
13F, Peninsula Hotel, No.32, First Zhongshan East Road, Shanghai

营业时间 Opening Hours
周一至周四 Mon. - Thur.
12:00 - 14:30 18:00 - 22:30
周日 Sun. 11:30 - 14:30 18:00 - 22:30
着装要求 Dress Code
优雅便服 Smart Casual
人均消费 Per Capita Consumption
1300 元 1300 RMB

艾利爵士顶层餐厅位于半岛酒店顶楼，环境幽雅，装饰大气。顶部的露天酒吧能够一览江景，食客可一边欣赏江景一边品尝美食。其中餐厅菜单的银鳕鱼肉质鲜美，给食客留下深刻的印象。

Located in the top floor of Peninsula Hotel, it has an elegant environment and splendid decoration. The outdoor bar at the top provides a panoramic view of river, and diners can enjoy the delicious food while appreciating the beautiful view. Among the restaurant menu, Cod Meat leaves a deep impression to diners with its tasty meat.

宝丽轩中餐厅
Bvlgari

中餐
Chinese Cuisine

8.7 必应搜索热度 Search priority

电话 /Tel
+86 21 3606 7788

地址 /Address
上海市河南北路 33 号
No.33, Henan North Road, Shanghai

营业时间 Opening Hours
午餐 Lunch 11:30 - 14:00
晚餐 Dinner 17:30 - 22:00
着装要求 Dress Code
优雅便服 Smart Casual
人均消费 Per Capita Consumption
910 元 910 RMB

餐厅建筑是由上海总商会的旧址改造而成的，整体环境极具历史气息，内部装修色调以黑白为主，并用红色加以点缀，使得餐厅的用餐氛围既庄重优雅，又有一轻松活泼的气息。餐厅招牌菜为：玫瑰豉油鸡、鲍鱼酥和牛芦笋等。

Its building is renovated from the former site of Shanghai General Chamb of Commerce, which has an overall environment full of historical flavors a interior decoration mainly in black and white color tones adorned with r color, making the dining environment both solemn and elegant with a relaxi and lively atmosphere. Its signature dishes: Rose Wine & Soy Poach Chicken, Baked Abalone Pastry, Beef Asparagus, etc.

标帜餐厅
The Kitchen Table

西餐
Western Cuisine

必应 搜索热度
Search priority 5.8

电话 /Tel
+86 21 2286 9960
+86 21 2286 9999

地址 /Address
上海市旅顺路 66 号上海外滩 W 酒店 W 层
W, W Hotel, Shanghai Bund, No.66, Lvshun Road, Shanghai

营业时间 Opening Hours
06:30 – 22:30
着装要求 Dress Code
优雅便服 Smart Casual
人均消费 Per Capita Consumption
460 元 460 RMB

标帜餐厅位于上海外滩附近，食客可欣赏到繁华的上海城市景观。餐厅极具纽约市小酒馆的现代风格，室内设计由餐厅团队精心打造，致力于展现出传统与现代的碰撞。餐厅招牌菜为：黑松露土豆泥、巧克力熔岩蛋糕、西冷和牛等。

Located near the Bund of Shanghai, it provides diners the beautiful bustling Shanghai cityscape. It has a modern style of New York bistro with an interior decoration carefully designed by the restaurant team, which is dedicated to displaying a mixture of tradition and modernity. The restaurant's signature dishes: Baked Potatoes with Bacon and Truffle, Chocolate Lava Cake, Sirloin Wagyu Beef, etc.

无限卡特权

长泰华府
Chamtime Chinese Restaurant

宫廷菜
Imperial Cuisine

必应 搜索热度
Search priority 4.0

电话 /Tel
+86 21 5080 3912

地址 /Address
上海市浦东新区金科路 2889 弄长泰广场 7 座 2 层
2F, Building 7, Chamtime Square, Lane 2889, Jinke Road, Pudong New District, Shanghai

营业时间 Opening Hours
午餐 Lunch 11:00 – 14:30
晚餐 Dinner 17:00 – 21:30
着装要求 Dress Code
正装 Formal
人均消费 Per Capita Consumption
2 层 400 元 Second Floor 400 RMB
3 层 200 元 Third Floor 200 RMB

秉承宫廷菜的传统，长泰华府在原料上很是讲究。除了原料产地、质地、大小、部位都有严格要求外，还注重菜品的足斤足两。对食材精心挑选，对烹饪精益求精。

Following the imperial cuisine traditions, Chamtime Chinese Restaurant has strict principles on ingredient selection, from the origin, texture, size to parts, as well as the quantity of each dish. It pays attention to the high standard of ingredients and remarkable culinary arts.

Da Ivo 意大利魔镜餐厅
Da Ivo

无限卡特权

西餐
Western Cuisine

4.4 必应搜索热度
Search priority

电话 /Tel
+86 21 5717 1757
+86 21 6303 0021

地址 /Address
上海市金陵东路 1 号
No.1, Jinling East Road, Shanghai

营业时间 Opening Hours
11:30 – 22:30
着装要求 Dress Code
优雅便服 Smart Casual
人均消费 Per Capita Consumption
900 元 900 RMB

作为有着餐饮界传奇之称的意大利魔镜餐厅，凭借其一流的美食和优雅的环境，成了如今上海外滩最出名的餐厅之一。餐厅致力于创新意大利美食，其中威尼斯魔镜甜品、西冷牛排和白芦笋套餐都是最负盛名的菜品。

Known as a legend of food industry, it has become one of the most famous restaurants in the Bund of Shanghai with its first-class delicacies and elegant environment. This restaurant devotes to innovating Italian cuisine, among which Venice Magic Mirror Dessert, Sirloin Steak and White Asparagus Package are the most famous dishes.

大蔬无界 · 外滩和美馆
WUJIE The Bund

无限卡特权

素菜
Vegetarian Cuisine

3.6 必应搜索热度
Search priority

电话 /Tel
400 920 1517
+86 21 6375 2818

地址 /Address
上海市黄浦区中山东二路外滩 22 号 4 层
4F, Bund 22, Second Zhongshan East Road, Huangpu District, Shanghai

营业时间 Opening Hours
午餐 Lunch 11:00 – 14:00
晚餐 Dinner 17:00 – 22:00
着装要求 Dress Code
优雅便服 Smart Casual
人均消费 Per Capita Consumption
300 ~ 500 元 300 ~ 500 RMB

在这里，风景不仅仅是指窗外独特的城市景观，餐厅精心选用的来自不同地方的食材，通过厨师们的精彩演绎，带着人与土地的故事，亦成为盘子里的风景。

At WUJIE, the beautiful dining environment designed with nature in mind, serves to complement the scene on the diner's plate. WUJIE is inspired by ingredients from all over the world and the diligence of our farmers and the land. It's their duty and pleasure to weave these components together.

大董（越洋广场店）
Da Dong(Park Place)

北京菜
Beijing cuisine

必应 搜索热度 Search priority 2.8

电话 /Tel
+86 21 3253 2299

地址 /Address
上海市南京西路 1601 号越洋广场 5 楼
5F, Park Place, No.1601, Nanjing West Road, Shanghai

营业时间 Opening Hours
11:00 – 22:00
着装要求 Dress Code
优雅便服 Smart Casual
人均消费 Per Capita Consumption
420 元 420RMB

大董作为一家深得食客喜爱的餐厅，主营创意特色菜与北京烤鸭。北京烤鸭酥香鲜嫩，由刀工精湛的厨师当场切片，集美味与观赏于一体。值得一提的是，菜品的摆盘极为讲究，中式的做法搭配上西式的摆盘，令人赏心悦目。

As a popular restaurant, it specializes in creative cuisine and Peking Duck. Its Peking Duck is crispy and tender, and sliced by skilled chef on the spot, which is not only delicious but also spectacle. It is worth mentioning that the dishes presentation is extremely exquisite and delightful with Chinese culinary arts and Western presentation.

大董（环贸店）
Da Dong(iapm mall)

北京菜
Beijing cuisine

必应 搜索热度 Search priority 2.8

电话 /Tel
+86 21 5466 5758

地址 /Address
上海市淮海中路 999 号环贸 iapm 商场 L6 室
Room L6, iapm mall, No.999, Huaihai Central Road, Shanghai

营业时间 Opening Hours
11:00 – 22:00
着装要求 Dress Code
优雅便服 Smart Casual
人均消费 Per Capita Consumption
380 元 380 RMB

大董无论是菜品还是环境，都讲究“意境”二字。这里运用中国古典文学、陶瓷器皿、写意绘画、书法等艺术手段综合表达菜品的意境，顾客品尝到的不仅仅是菜品在唇齿之间留下的美妙和雅味，更是将顾客对艺术的感知提升到精神层面。

It pays attention to "artistic conception" in both dishes and environment and presents the artistic conception of dishes through Chinese classical literature, ceramic vessels, freehand paintings, calligraphies and other art media. This restaurant not only provides diners with beautiful and elegant dishes left between the lip and teeth, but also improves the artistic perception of diners to the spiritual level.

东来居港式米其林火锅
King's Garden

无限卡特权

港式火锅
Hong Kong Style Hotpot

4.1 必应搜索热度 Search priority

电话 /Tel
+86 21 5270 0277

地址 /Address
上海市长宁区虹桥路 1482 号
No.1482, Hongqiao Road, Changning District, Shanghai

营业时间 Opening Hours
午餐 Lunch 11:30 – 14:00
晚餐 Dinner 17:30 – 21:30
着装要求 Dress Code
优雅便服 Smart Casual
人均消费 Per Capita Consumption
400 元 400 RMB

这家新派港式火锅餐厅获得过不少餐饮界的殊荣。其香港分店名声在外，不少明星都是该店常客，招牌美食包括火爆一时的“120 元的餐蛋饭”。

This is an award-winning new-style Hong Kong hotpot restaurant. Its Hong Kong branch has won tremendous fame and even attracts many stars to be their regulars. Its signatures include 120-Yuan Fried Rice with Egg.

贰千金
Lady Bund

无限卡特权

创意菜
Creative Cuisine

3.7 必应搜索热度 Search priority

电话 /Tel
+86 21 6333 1798

地址 /Address
上海市黄浦区中山东二路 22 号 4 层
4F, No. 22, Second Zhongshan East Road, Huangpu District, Shanghai

营业时间 Opening Hours
午餐 Lunch 11:30 – 14:00
下午茶 Afternoon Tea 14:30 – 17:00
晚餐 Dinner 17:30 – 22:00
着装要求 Dress Code
优雅便服 Smart Casual
人均消费 Per Capita Consumption
400 元 双人午餐
Lunch Course for Two 400 RMB
晚餐 550 元 Dinner 550 RMB

贰千金由法国知名设计师托马斯 · 达里埃尔打造，充满了文身元素的软装，加上外滩少有的全景落地玻璃窗，处处隐含华丽的细节。与中西合璧的装修氛围相映衬的，是其融合了风格的美食，既有精致欧陆料理，又有摩登中餐菜单。

Designed by the good-fame French designer Thomas Dariel, Lady Bund is full of tattoo elements with 3 full-height windows and implying the gorgeous details everywhere. Echoing its ambiance, the food here is also a good combination between east and west.

无限卡特权

二二二餐酒馆
OPPOSITE by Jenson & Hu

西餐
Western Cuisine

必应 搜索热度 Search priority 3.6

电话 /Tel
+86 21 6427 0127

地址 /Address
上海市徐汇区建国西路 222 号 1-2 层
1-2F, No.222, Jianguo West Road, Xuhui District, Shanghai

营业时间 Opening Hours
周末早午餐 Brunch at Weekends
12:00 – 15:00
（最后点单 Last Order 14:30）
晚餐 Dinner 18:00 – 23:00
（最后点单 Last Order 22:30）
着装要求 Dress Code
优雅便服 Smart Casual
人均消费 Per Capita Consumption
600 ~ 800 元 600 ~ 800 RMB

2 楼餐厅，由行政主厨领衔的厨师团队主打新派欧式菜系，主厨擅长混搭，有些菜肴巧妙地融入了亚洲食材。1 楼酒吧，帅气的首席调酒师艾伦制作的各种特调鸡尾酒营造出整体氛围。
In 2F, the Executive Chef leads his team to create new Continental cuisine. He knows the magic of fusion and mixes the Asian ingredients skillfully in his dishes. After a feast, it's a good choice to enjoy a drink in 1F bar where Allen, a handsome bartender, lights up the whole area by his awesome cocktails.

Frasca
Frasca

西餐
Western Cuisine

必应 搜索热度 Search priority 3.0

电话 /Tel
+86 21 3216 8168

地址 /Address
上海市石门一路 366 号镛舍 1 层
1F, The Middle House, No.366, First Shimen Road, Shanghai

营业时间 Opening Hours
周一至周五 Mon. – Fri.
11:30 – 14:30 18:00 – 22:00
周六、周日 Sat. – Sun.
11:30 – 15:00 18:00 – 22:00
着装要求 Dress Code
优雅便服 Smart Casual
人均消费 Per Capita Consumption
375 元 375 RMB

Frasca 提供惬意并富有魅力的意大利餐厅氛围，玻璃屋和露台会令你感受到意大利最原始的情怀，无论是手工意大利面，还是意式经典提拉米苏，都将令你全方位地感受到意大利风情及美味餐食。
It creates a cozy and charming Italian restaurant atmosphere. Dinners will feel the most original Italian flavors from the glass house and terrace, and enjoy Italian style and delicious meals in an all-round manner, such as Handmade Pasta and Italian Classic Tiramisu.

翡翠 36 餐厅
Jade on 36 Restaurant

法餐
French Cuisine

3.1 必应搜索热度
Search priority

电话 /Tel
+86 21 2828 6888

地址 /Address
上海市浦东新区富城路 33 号
浦东香格里拉大酒店紫金楼 36 层
36F, Grand Tower, Pudong Shangri-La,
East Shanghai No.33 Fucheng Road,
Pudong New District, Shanghai

营业时间 Opening Hours
11:30 – 14:00 18:00 – 22:00
着装要求 Dress Code
优雅便服 Smart Casual
人均消费 Per Capita Consumption
530 元 530 RMB

翡翠 36 餐厅将新鲜、时令、本地的选材融入亚洲元素，持续奉上经典美食，使客在舒适放松的环境下，尽享愉悦轻松的用餐体验。复古摩登的餐厅设计，为宾提供独特的用餐体验，宾客也可同时欣赏到曼妙的浦西天际线。

It blends the fresh, seasonal and local ingredients with Asian flavors a serves authentic delicacies, bringing diners a pleasant and relaxing dini experience under such comfortable and cozy environment. Diners will en a unique dining experience and appreciate the graceful skyline of Shang Puxi area in such a retro and modern environment at the same time.

福和慧
Fu He Hui

无限卡特权

素菜
Vegetarian Cuisine

5.6 必应搜索热度
Search priority

电话 /Tel
+86 21 3980 9188

地址 /Address
上海市长宁区愚园路 1037 号
No.1037, Yuyuan Road, Changning
District, Shanghai

营业时间 Opening Hours
午餐 Lunch 11:15 – 14:00
晚餐 Dinner 17:15 – 22:00
着装要求 Dress Code
优雅便服 Smart Casual
人均消费 Per Capita Consumption
400 ~ 1000 元 400 ~ 1000 RMB

素食餐厅福和慧是喧嚣城市中的一片净土，由荣获多个国际设计大奖的青年设计师吕永中与餐厅老板共同构思打造，以石头、木头、布头为主要元素，清雅脱俗的细节让人凝神静心、体验美好。

This veggie restaurant, co-designed by the award-winning young designer Lv Yongzhong and its owner, creates a peaceful space in the busy city by stone, wood and fabric. Elegant and refined design details make customers feel peaceful and fragrant.

无限卡特权

斐霓丝
PHENIX Eatery & Bar

西餐
Western Cuisine

必应 搜索热度 Search priority 3.6

电话 /Tel
+86 21 2216 6988

地址 /Address
上海市常德路 1 号璞丽酒店 2 层
2F, Puli Hotel, No.1, Changde Road, Shanghai

营业时间 Opening Hours
周一至周六 Mon. - Sat. 06:30 - 10:30
12:00 - 17:30 18:00 - 22:00
周日 Sun. 06:30 - 10:30 11:30 - 21:00
着装要求 Dress Code
优雅便服 Smart Casual
人均消费 Per Capita Consumption
600 元 600 RMB

斐霓丝无论是细小的陈列还是整体的布置风格，都透露着自然与古典相融合的气质。以优质的天然食材为灵感源泉，本色呈现法式料理精髓，回归食材本源，展现生活本味。

It reveals an atmosphere of nature and classics in small furnishings and overall decorations. Taking high-quality natural ingredients as sources of inspiration, it presents the essences of French cuisine in original flavors to reflect the original tastes of life.

桂花楼
Gui Hua Lou

中餐
Chinese Cuisine

必应 搜索热度 Search priority 5.6

电话 /Tel
+86 21 2828 6888

地址 /Address
上海市浦东新区富城路 33 号
浦东香格里拉大酒店浦江楼 1 层
1F, River Wing, Pudong Shangri-La, East Shanghai, No.33 Fucheng Road, Pudong New District, Shanghai

营业时间 Opening Hours
周一至周五 Mon. - Fri.
11:30 - 15:00 17:30 - 22:00
周六、周日 Sat. - Sun.
11:00 - 15:00 17:30 - 22:00
着装要求 Dress Code
优雅便服 Smart Casual
人均消费 Per Capita Consumption
400 元 400 RMB

桂花楼中餐厅主营淮扬菜，辅以川菜和本帮菜，开业以来屡获殊荣，已成为沪上著名中餐厅之一。高晓生率领其精英厨师团队不断创新，为食客们奉上匠心独具的菜品。其中，红汤蒸鲥鱼、迷你葫芦八宝鸭等头牌菜深受食客喜爱。

As an award-winning and one of famous Chinese restaurants since its opening, it mainly provides Huaiyang cuisine, some Sichuan cuisine and Shanghai cuisine. Chef Gao Xiaosheng leads elite chefs to constantly innovate and provide unique dishes with great ingenuity for diners. Among dishes, Red Soup Steamed Shad, Mini Calabash Eight Treasure Duck and other signature dishes are favored by diners.

华懋阁
Cathay Room

西餐
Western Cuisine

3.6 必应搜索热度 Search priority

电话 /Tel
+86 21 6138 6881

地址 /Address
上海市南京东路 20 号和平饭店 9 层
9F, Peace Hotel, No.20, Nanjing East Road, Shanghai

营业时间 Opening Hours
午餐 Lunch
周一至周五 Mon. – Fri. 12:00 – 14:30
周日 Sun. 11:30 – 14:30
晚餐 Dinner 18:00 – 22:30
露台 Terrace Dining
12:00 – 22:30（应季 In season）
着装要求 Dress Code
优雅便服 Smart Casual
人均消费 Per Capita Consumption
700 元 700 RMB

华懋阁西餐厅在外滩享有盛名，荟萃欧式顶级美食，食客可一边俯瞰外滩的优美景致，一边品尝雅致、时尚相融的欧陆式佳肴，尊享无与伦比的用餐体验。华懋阁的开放式露台是餐前酒后的最佳去处，提供特色鸡尾酒及欧式小食。

It has a good reputation in the Bund for providing top European cuisine. While overlooking the beautiful scenery of the Bund, diners can enjoy the elegant and fashionable Continental cuisine and leave an unparalleled dining experience. Its open terrace is the best place before dining and after drinking and provides featured cocktails and European snacks.

Il Ristorante – Niko Romito
Il Ristorante – Niko Romito

西餐
Western Cuisine

4.0 必应搜索热度 Search priority

电话 /Tel
+86 21 3606 7788

地址 /Address
上海市河南北路 33 号上海宝格丽酒店 47 层
47F, Bvlgari Hotel Shanghai, No.33, Henan North Road, Shanghai

营业时间 Opening Hours
12:00 – 14:30 18:00 – 22:00
着装要求 Dress Code
优雅便服 Smart Casual
人均消费 Per Capita Consumption
1200 元 1200 RMB

意大利餐厅内部装饰豪华大气，有包房，有卡座，靠窗的位置还可以尽情欣赏外面的美景。招牌脆皮小乳猪，搭配特制酱料，又香又脆，还有餐前面包和开胃汤，均可见厨师的别具用心。

It is an Italian restaurant with luxurious interior decoration. There are private rooms, booths and window seats for diners to enjoy the beautiful scenery outside window. The ingenuity of chefs is shown everywhere, such as the fragrant Signature Crispy Porchette matching with special sauce, as well as the bread and appetizer soups.

无限卡特权

Jean Georges
Jean Georges

西餐
Western Cuisine

必应 搜索热度 Search priority 6.6

电话 /Tel
+86 21 6321 7733

地址 /Address
上海市中山东路一路 3 号外滩 3 号 4 层
4F, Bund 3, No.3, First Zhongshan East Road, Shanghai

营业时间 Opening Hours
周一至周五 Mon. – Fri. 18:00 – 22:30
周六、周日 Sat. – Sun.
11:30 – 15:00 18:00 – 22:30
着装要求 Dress Code
优雅便服 Smart Casual
人均消费 Per Capita Consumption
1000 元 1000 RMB

上海的 Jean Georges 法国餐厅室内环境活力洋溢，装饰高端时尚。餐厅以创新的菜式、丰富的藏酒以及无微不至的服务成为上海当代高端餐饮的典范，接待无数饕餮食客。

The Jean Georges is a French restaurant with a vibrant interior environment and stylish high-end decoration. It has become a model of contemporary high-end restaurants in Shanghai by its innovative dishes, rich wine collection and considerate services, and has served numerous diners.

嘉府壹号
Mansion on One

中餐
Chinese Cuisine

必应 搜索热度 Search priority 2.6

电话 /Tel
+86 21 3680 6766

地址 /Address
上海市北苏州路 188 号
上海苏宁宝丽嘉酒店大堂
Lobby, Bellagio Shanghai, No.188, Beisuzhou Road, Shanghai

营业时间 Opening Hours
午餐 Lunch 11:30 – 14:30
晚餐 Dinner 17:30 – 22:30
着装要求 Dress Code
优雅便服 Smart Casual
人均消费 Per Capita Consumption
560 元 560RMB

嘉府壹号致力于为食客献上纯正的上海菜与经典粤菜。手工砌造而成的北京烤鸭挂炉呈现出传统地道的果木烤鸭。复古的老上海风情弥漫在华贵典雅的包房内，每一间包房都拥有自己的主题与色调，是商务宴请、家庭聚餐的不二之选。

This restaurant is dedicated to providing authentic Shanghai cuisine and classic Cantonese cuisine. The hand-built Beijing roast duck fireplace presents the traditional and authentic fruit wood roast ducks. Each luxurious and elegant private room gives a retro old Shanghai style with its own theme and color, which is the best choice for business banquets and family gatherings.

吉品轩
Ji Pin

粤菜
Cantonese Cuisine

3.5 必应搜索热度
Search priority

电话 /Tel
+86 21 6469 9969
+86 21 6428 9799

地址 /Address
上海市乌鲁木齐南路 55 号
No.55, Wulumuqi South Road, Shanghai

营业时间 Opening Hours
11:30 – 22:00
着装要求 Dress Code
优雅便服 Smart Casual
人均消费 Per Capita Consumption
800 元 800 RMB

吉品轩格调雅致摩登，尽显海派文化包容之气。餐厅以温润灵动的木质地板和饰面贯穿空间。餐厅主打矜贵海鲜、地道烧味、精致点心等，选用上乘当季食材，在传统技法中融入新派元素，为食客们呈现品相精美的粤式佳肴。

With elegant and modern style, it shows an inclusiveness of Shanghai regional culture. The dining room is covered with warm and flexible wooden floors and finishes. Its main signature dishes include exquisite seafood, authentic roast meat and refined desserts. It selects excellent seasonal food materials and integrates new elements with traditional techniques to present diners with luxurious Cantonese cuisine.

锦厨西餐厅
Kwee Zeen

自助餐
Buffet

2.7 必应搜索热度
Search priority

电话 /Tel
+86 21 3669 6666

地址 /Address
上海市泰虹路 666 号虹桥索菲特酒店 B1 层
B1, Sofitel Shanghai Hongqiao, No.666, Taihong Road, Shanghai

营业时间 Opening Hours
6:00–24:00
着装要求 Dress Code
优雅便服 Smart Casual
人均消费 Per Capita Consumption
300 元 300 RMB

锦厨作为下沉式自助餐厅，可同时容纳 198 人。高挑的落地窗及下沉式的空间设计让人尽享城市美景，由法国籍大厨主持的 8 个开放式厨房提供丰盛的环球美味，更会推出不同主题的特色自助餐饮，为宾客们提供常来常新的体验。

As a Parisian lifestyle restaurant offering diners a unique interactive kitchen concept with eight live ateliers, Kwee Zeen could offer dinning experience for 198 people at the same time. Immerse yourself in a city oasis as you take in the breathtaking views over our cascading waterfall and different themes of buffet all around the year.

金轩中餐厅
Jin Xuan

中餐
Chinese Cuisine

必应 搜索热度 Search priority 4.0

电话 /Tel
+86 21 2020 1717
+86 21 2020 1768

地址 /Address
上海市世纪大道 8 号上海国金中心
上海浦东丽思卡尔顿酒店 53 楼
53F, Ritz-Carlton Shanghai Pudong,
Shanghai IFC, No.8, Shiji Road, Shanghai

坐在餐厅窗边望着浦江对岸的万国建筑群，优雅的环境、旷远的景致、精巧的摆盘、细致的搭配，令人心旷神怡。美景配美食，牛肉和腰果碰撞出新的火花，酱汁锁在嫩嫩的牛肉中，腰果恰到好处地升华了牛肉的香味。

Sitting by the window and looking at the group of buildings on the other side of Huangpu River, diners will feel pleasant with exquisite presentation and collocation under such elegant environment. Beautiful scenery goes with delicacies. The beef and cashew give new tastes with sauce locked in tender beef, and the cashew properly improves the fragrance of beef.

营业时间 Opening Hours
周一至周五 Mon. - Fri.
11:30 - 14:00 17:30 - 22:00
周六、周日 Sat. - Sun.
12:00 - 14:30 17:30 - 22:00
着装要求 Dress Code
优雅便服 Smart Casual
人均消费 Per Capita Consumption
1200 元 1200 RMB

无限卡特权

菁禧荟
Amazing Chinese Cuisine

粤菜
Cantonese Cuisine

必应 搜索热度 Search priority 3.6

电话 /Tel
+86 21 6262 5677

地址 /Address
上海市虹桥路 1665 号 B5 幢别墅
B5 Villa, No.1665, Hongqiao Road, Shanghai

餐厅坚守着享受美味、专注菜品的理念。餐厅仅五间包房，无散台，但长期供货商超过二十家，餐厅寻遍各地，做出的菜式也不仅局限于“潮汕”美味。后厨人潮州人，卤水汁是一大亮点，特制不同的调味汁用来卤不同的菜品。

eres to the concept of enjoying delicious food and focuses on the excellent . This restaurant only has five private rooms with no extra seats. However, are more than 20 food suppliers providing long-term ingredients. It has ned food materials all over the country and produces dishes beyond shan" cuisine. The chefs are all from Chaozhou. The Chinese marinades lly made for different dishes are its important seasonings.

营业时间 Opening Hours
11:00 - 14:00 17:00 - 22:00
着装要求 Dress Code
优雅便服 Smart Casual
人均消费 Per Capita Consumption
1250 元 1250 RMB

晶采轩（恒隆广场店）
Jing Cai Xuan(Hang Lung Plaza)

粤菜
Cantonese Cuisine

2.8 必应搜索热度
Search priority

电话 /Tel
+86 21 6241 2779
+86 21 6245 7739

地址 /Address
上海市南京西路 1266 号恒隆广场 4-5 层
4-5F, Hang Lung Plaza, No.1266, Nanjing West Road, Shanghai

营业时间 Opening Hours
11:00 - 14:00 17:00 - 21:30
着装要求 Dress Code
优雅便服 Smart Casual
人均消费 Per Capita Consumption
500 元 500 RMB

晶采轩的每一道菜都是对美好事物的追求。以粤菜为基础，辅以江南特色烹饪工艺，引入日本传统怀石料理，呈现出别具一格的佳肴美馔。拥有贯通商场四、五层的内部旋转楼梯，环境静谧幽雅，是宴请重要宾客的绝佳之地。

All its dishes pursue the beautiful things. Based on Cantonese cuisine with South River special cooking techniques, it introduces traditional Japanese Kaiseki cuisine to present unique and distinctive delicacies. With an inner spiral staircase connecting the fourth and fifth floors of the shopping mall and a quiet and elegant environment, it is a perfect place to entertain important guests.

LAGO by Julian Serrano 意大利餐厅
LAGO by Julian Serrano

无限卡特权

西餐
Western Cuisine

4.5 必应搜索热度
Search priority

电话 /Tel
+86 21 3680 6777

地址 /Address
上海市北苏州路 188 号
上海苏宁宝丽嘉酒店 6 层
6F, Bellagio Shanghai, No.188, Beisuzhou Road, Shanghai

营业时间 Opening Hours
周一至周五 Mon. - Fri.
午餐 Lunch 11:30 - 15:00
晚餐 Dinner 18:00 - 22:30
着装要求 Dress Code
优雅便服 Smart Casual
人均消费 Per Capita Consumption
590 元 590 RMB

屡获殊荣的名厨 Julian Serrano 被业界公认为天赋异禀的烹饪奇才。他将自己意大利餐厅以及全新的用餐理念引入上海。设计现代的餐厅拥有超大室外露台和间私密别致的钟楼式包房。宾客们可以边享用美食，边欣赏上海的迷人景致。

Award-winning chef Julian Serrano is widely regarded as a culinary tale He opened his Italian restaurant with a new dining concept in Shangh His restaurant designed in modern decoration has a large outdoor terra and a private bell-tower-style room. Diners can enjoy delicious food wh appreciating the charming scenery of Shanghai.

无限卡特权

Le Comptoir de Pierre Gagnaire
Le Comptoir de Pierre Gagnaire

西餐
Western Cuisine

必应 搜索热度 Search priority 4.3

电话 /Tel
+86 21 5466 9928

地址 /Address
上海市建国西路 480 号
No.480, Jianguo West Road, Shanghai

营业时间 Opening Hours
周一至周五 Mon. - Fri.
07:00 - 10:00 12:00 - 14:00
14:00 - 16:30 18:00 - 22:00
着装要求 Dress Code
优雅便服 Smart Casual
人均消费 Per Capita Consumption
750 元 750 RMB

Le Comptoir de Pierre Gagnaire 是一家休闲并充满时尚气息的餐厅，轻松的氛围是举办庆祝活动的首选场所。餐厅的菜品用简单、真诚、优雅的法式菜肴，辅以创新大胆的味道直击灵魂，使食客体会到不一样的用餐体验。

It is the first choice to hold celebrations for its casual and fashionable environment and relaxing atmosphere. This restaurant provides simple, sincere, and elegant French dishes in innovative and bold tastes which will hit the bud and leave a different dining experience for diners.

莱美露滋（上海中心店）
Maison Lameloise(Shanghai Center)

西餐
Western Cuisine

必应 搜索热度 Search priority 3.8

电话 /Tel
+86 21 6881 6789

地址 /Address
上海市银座中路 501 号上海中心大厦 68 层
68F, Shanghai Center, No.501, Yinzuo Central Road, Shanghai

营业时间 Opening Hours
周一至周五 Mon. - Fri.
11:30 - 13:30 18:00 - 21:00
周六、周日 Sat. - Sun.
18:00 - 21:00
着装要求 Dress Code
优雅便服 Smart Casual
人均消费 Per Capita Consumption
2300 元 2300 RMB

备受食客赞誉的莱美露滋能俯视整个外滩的美景，优雅精致的装饰为整个餐厅增色不少。造型独特的鸭肝，精心腌制过的鳌虾，再搭配正宗的法式甜点，带来味觉和视觉的双重享受。

Highly praised by diners, this restaurant can overlook the beautiful scenery of the Bund, and the elegant and delicate decoration enriches the whole restaurant. It brings double enjoyment of taste and vision for diners with unique styling duck liver and elaborately pickled lobster, together with authentic French desserts.

兰庭厉家菜

Family Li Imperial Cuisine

宫廷菜
Imperial Cuisine

2.6 必应搜索热度
Search priority

电话 /Tel
+86 21 5308 8071

地址 /Address
上海市中山东一路 487 号黄浦公园 1 层
1F, Huangpu Park, No.487, First Zhongshan East Road, Shanghai

营业时间 Opening Hours
11:00 – 14:30 17:30 – 21:30
着装要求 Dress Code
优雅便服 Smart Casual
人均消费 Per Capita Consumption
1100 元 1100 RMB

厉家菜源自清朝的宫廷御膳，创始人为已故的厉善麟，而兰庭厉家菜现由厉善麟的儿子厉晓麟亲自主理。位于上海的兰庭厉家菜秉持着宫廷菜精致的风骨，力求将更好的菜品带给食客。餐厅招牌菜为：糖醋排骨、翡翠豆腐等。

Founded by the late Li Shanlin, the Family Li Cuisine originates from the Peking Court cuisine of Qing Dynasty, and now managed by Li Shanlin's son, Li Xiaolin. Located in Shanghai, it upholds the exquisite style of royal cuisine and strives to bring the best dishes to diners. Its signature dishes include: Sweet and Sour Spare Ribs, Emerald-Jade Bean Curd, etc.

岚亭

L'Atrium

西餐
Western Cuisine

3.6 必应搜索热度
Search priority

电话 /Tel
+86 21 5153 3300-3708

地址 /Address
上海市长宁区仙霞路 369 号
No.369, Xianxia Road, Changning District, Shanghai

营业时间 Opening Hours
早餐 Breakfast 06:30 – 10:30
午餐 Lunch 11:30 – 14:30
晚餐 Dinner 18:00 – 22:00
着装要求 Dress Code
优雅便服 Smart Casual
人均消费 Per Capita Consumption
200 元 200 RMB

岚亭餐厅是一家极富当代艺术气息的欧陆风味餐厅，其挑高的中庭，配以巨型壁画装饰，独具一格。餐厅环境优雅舒适，恬淡柔和，各式各样的佳肴美馔别具风味，配以多款口感香醇的甄选美酒，定能让食客流连忘返。

It is a Continental cuisine restaurant full of contemporary artistic air with a high and unique atrium decorated with giant murals. It has an elegant and comfortable environment and quiet and soft atmosphere, matching with numerous delicious food and special flavors, as well as various selected wines, making diners linger.

老干杯（外滩本店）
Kanpai Classic(Bund)

日式烧肉
Japanese Grill

必应 搜索热度 Search priority 3.3

电话 /Tel
+86 21 6340 0767

地址 /Address
上海市黄浦区广东路 20 号外滩 5 号 5 层
5F, Bund 5, No.20, Guangdong Road, Huangpu District, Shanghai

营业时间 Opening Hours
晚餐 Dinner 17:00 – 24:00
着装要求 Dress Code
优雅便服 Smart Casual
人均消费 Per Capita Consumption
100 ～ 800 元 100 ～ 800 RMB

全程冷藏熟成、从澳大利亚牧场直送到餐桌的高端澳洲和牛，雪花肉等级都在 8 ～ 9 级，并根据不同部位，以薄切、厚切、角切、牛排等方式料理，以达到最佳口感。

The top Australian Wagyu beef ranking M8-9 level is directly delivered from Australian farms in freezer and at dry aging condition. According to their parts, they are cut in different ways to reach their best taste.

无限卡特权

鹿园
Moose

江浙菜
Jiangzhe Cuisine

必应 搜索热度 Search priority 8.3

电话 /Tel
+86 21 6205 5058

地址 /Address
上海市长宁区新华路 119 弄 1 号
No.1, Lane 119, Xinhua Road, Changning District, Shanghai

营业时间 Opening Hours
午餐 Lunch 11:00 – 15:00
晚餐 Dinner 17:00 – 22:00
着装要求 Dress Code
优雅便服 Smart Casual
人均消费 Per Capita Consumption
350 元 350 RMB

鹿园创始人艾瑞斯 · 林将餐厅置入洋房，把花园别墅恢复为旧式风格，室内布置高贵典雅，每个细节都抓人眼球，俨然一幅老上海大户人家的迤逦画卷。

Iris Lin, the founder of Moose, is so fond of aged garden villa, she locates the restaurant inside villa and tries her best to restore the villa to its original architectural style. Indoor layout of the villa are noble and elegant, and all the details of the restaurant are eye-catching, just like a glamorous picture of a big family at old times of Shanghai.

Mercato
Mercato

无限卡特权

意大利菜
Italian Cuisine

9.6 必应搜索热度
Search priority

电话 /Tel
+86 21 6321 9922

地址 /Address
上海市黄浦区中山东一路 3 号外滩 3 号 6 层
6F, Bund 3, No.3, First Zhongshan East Road, Huangpu District, Shanghai

营业时间 Opening Hours
晚餐 Dinner 17:30 – 23:00
着装要求 Dress Code
优雅便服 Smart Casual
人均消费 Per Capita Consumption
400 ~ 500 元 400 ~ 500 RMB

简・乔治西餐厅旗下的意大利餐厅 Mercato，充满意大利家庭般的氛围，温暖又令人放松。菜肴也是摩登农场风，简单、自然，充满创意和活力。
Subordinated to the brand Jean Georges, the Italian restaurant Mercato looks just like a warm and relaxing Italian home. Its dishes feature the modern farm style that is simple, natural, creative and energetic.

Mr & Mrs Bund-Modern Eatery by Paul Pairet
Mr & Mrs Bund-Modern Eatery by Paul Pairet

法国菜
French Cuisine

3.2 必应搜索热度
Search priority

电话 /Tel
+86 21 6323 9898

地址 /Address
上海市黄浦区中山东一路 18 号外滩 18 号 6 层
6F, Bund 18, No.18, First Zhongshan East Road, Huangpu District, Shanghai

营业时间 Opening Hours
早午餐 Brunch
周六、周日 Sat. – Sun. 11:30 – 14:30
晚餐 Dinner 17:30 – 22:30
夜宵 Midnight Snack
周四至周六 Thur. – Sat. 23:30 – 02:00
着装要求 Dress Code
优雅便服 Smart Casual
人均消费 Per Capita Consumption
600 ~ 1000 元 600 ~ 1000 RMB

餐厅主题是简单与流行，将法餐的文化精髓通过富有新意的方式呈现，在烹饪方式和配菜的选择上随性发挥。在这里还能体验到主厨极具创意的分子料理，造型与口感都令人惊艳不已。
The theme of restaurant is the simple and fashion, and the restaurant dedicates to presenting the essence of French cuisine through a creative way by flexibly selecting culinary methods and ingredients. And the Chef's molecular gastronomy is astonishing both in palate and taste.

莫尔顿海鲜牛排坊
Morton's Steak & Seafood Grill

无限卡特权

西餐
Western Cuisine

必应 搜索热度 Search priority 2.6

电话 /Tel
+86 21 6067 7888

地址 /Address
上海市徐汇区淮海中路 999 号
环贸 iapm 商场 4 层
4F, iapm mall, No.999, Huaihai Central Road, Xuhui District, Shanghai

营业时间 Opening Hours
周日至周四 Sun. – Thur. 11:30 – 22:00
周五至周六 Fri. – Sat. 11:30 – 23:00
着装要求 Dress Code
优雅便服 Smart Casual
人均消费 Per Capita Consumption
600 元 600 RMB

餐厅的招牌美食除了上乘的进口熟成谷饲牛排，还包括从美国、法国、澳大利亚和新西兰运抵的 9 种新鲜生蚝，生蚝以冰镇的方式供客人享用。菜单上的海鲜品种丰富，极具亚洲特色，分量充足。

It provides signature dishes, such as superior imported grain-fed steaks, and 9 kinds of fresh oysters delivered from United States, France, Australia and New Zealand, which are served on ice for diners. The restaurant also provides a variety of Asian-style seafood in sufficient quantity.

莫尔顿牛排坊（上海）
Morton's of Chicago,The Steakhouse(Shanghai)

无限卡特权

西餐 牛排
Western Cuisine and Steak House

必应 搜索热度 Search priority 3.0

电话 /Tel
+86 21 6075 8888

地址 /Address
上海市浦东新区世纪大道 8 号
国金中心 4 层 15-16 商铺
Shop 15-16, 4F, IFC, No.8, Shiji Road, Pudong New District, Shanghai

营业时间 Opening Hours
周日至周四 Sun. – Thur. 11:30 – 22:00
周五至周六 Fri. – Sat. 11:30 – 23:00
着装要求 Dress Code
优雅便服 Smart Casual
人均消费 Per Capita Consumption
800 元 800 RMB

上海莫尔顿牛排坊为莫尔顿旗舰店，以顶级谷物喂养的牛及新鲜鱼类、波士顿大龙虾、羊排、鸡肉等美食而著称，也以备受好评的酒单闻名遐迩。餐厅设有 9 间包房，阳台则可举办露天晚宴和酒会。

Shanghai Morton is the flagship store of the Mortons, famous for its superior grain-fed beef, fresh fishes, Boston lobster, lamb, chicken and its highly-praised wine list. There are 9 VIP Rooms, and the terrace is suitable for outdoor banquet and cocktail party.

明阁
Ming Court

中餐
Chinese Cuisine

5.5 必应搜索热度
Search priority

电话 /Tel
+86 21 5263 9618

地址 /Address
上海市申虹路 333 号
上海虹桥康得思酒店 B1 层
B1, Cordis Shanghai Hongqiao, No.333, Shenhong Road, Shanghai

营业时间 Opening Hours
午餐 Lunch
周一至周五 Mon. - Fri. 11:30 - 14:30
周六、周日 Sat. - Sun. 11:30 - 15:00
晚餐 Dinner 17:30 - 22:00
着装要求 Dress Code
优雅便服 Smart Casual
人均消费 Per Capita Consumption
681 元 681 RMB

明阁中餐厅的内部装饰灵感来自 20 世纪 30 年代“十里洋场”的老上海，餐厅的资深中餐行政总厨苏巍青带领他的厨师团队，只选用上乘新鲜的食材，以精湛的烹调技术，将地道的“上海口味”融于明阁，让食客们品味到创新粤菜的精髓。

The interior decoration of this restaurant is inspired from the old Shangha of "metropolis infested with foreign adventurers" in the 1930s. The senio Chinese executive chef Su Weiqing leads his chef team and selects high quality and fresh ingredients with exquisite culinary arts to make authentic "Shanghai tastes" and provide diners with the essence of innovative Cantonese cuisine.

迷 · 上海
Shang-High Cuisine

江浙菜
Jiangzhe Cuisine

3.6 必应搜索热度
Search priority

电话 /Tel
+86 21 3858 0768
+86 21 3858 0760

地址 /Address
上海市梅花路 1108 号
卓美亚喜玛拉雅酒店 6 层
6F, Jumeirah Himalayas Hotel Shanghai, No.1108, Meihua Road, Shanghai

营业时间 Opening Hours
11:30 - 14:30 17:30 - 22:30
着装要求 Dress Code
优雅便服 Smart Casual
人均消费 Per Capita Consumption
642 元 642RMB

在酒店充满艺术气息的六层建筑中，有大气的前厅和幽静的入口，冷色调的中式复古风，让整个餐厅变得更加厚重有深度。冷菜熏鱼，甜而不腻，入口松脆。三黄鸡肉质鲜嫩，也俘获了大批食客的心。

Located at a 6-floor artistic hotel building, it has a fabulous lobby and quiet entrance; the cool Chinese retro style decoration makes the whole restaurant more glorious and serious. Cold dishes including smoked fish are sweet and crisp without greasy. The Sanhuang Chicken has also captured the favor of numerous diners with its fresh and tender meat.

PHO 东田越南粉
PHO

越南菜
Vietnamese Cuisine

必应 搜索热度 7.4
Search priority

电话 /Tel
+86 21 6330 7758

地址 /Address
上海市湖滨路 168 号无限极荟购物广场 B1 层
B1, PwC Shanghai Innovation Center, No.168, Hubin Road, Shanghai

营业时间 Opening Hours
11:00 – 22:00
着装要求 Dress Code
无特别着装要求 Non-specified
人均消费 Per Capita Consumption
90 元 90RMB

一碗河粉，看似简单，但想要完全重现越南的当地风味却绝非易事。PHO 东田越南粉餐厅为了给食客带来最正宗的一碗火车头牛肉河粉，坚持选用最新鲜的食材，加上厨师团队的精心烹饪，最后才能成就一碗地道美味的越南河粉。

A bowl of PHO seems simple, but it's difficult to reproduce the local flavors in Vietnam. In order to bring the most authentic locomotive beef PHO to diners, this restaurant insists on using the freshest ingredients with culinary arts of chef team to produce the authentic and delicious PHO.

POP 美式餐厅与酒吧
POP American Brasserie

西餐
Western Cuisine

必应 搜索热度 9.3
Search priority

电话 /Tel
+86 21 6321 0909

地址 /Address
上海市黄浦区中山东一路 3 号外滩 3 号 7 层
7F, Bund 3, No.3, First Zhongshan East Road, Huangpu District, Shanghai

营业时间 Opening Hours
11:00 – 23:00
着装要求 Dress Code
优雅便服 Smart Casual
人均消费 Per Capita Consumption
300 ~ 500 元 300 ~ 500 RMB

位于上海外滩 3 号顶层的 POP，弥漫着奢华与闲适兼备的气息。典雅空间中点缀着复古的美国波普文化和装饰主义细节，宽阔露台可一览外滩全景。菜品兼具美式精神与法式风格，包括美式经典美食、烧烤肉类与海鲜盛宴。

Located at the top floor of No.3 of the Bund, POP has a good balance between luxury and leisure. The elegant space is decorated by American Pop Art and Art Deco elements; the grand terrace overlooks the Bund. Its dishes blend with American spirit and French styles, including classic American dishes, grills and seafood feast.

浦之舟
The Voyage of Pu Jiang

海鲜
Seafood

2.6 必应搜索热度 Search priority

电话 /Tel
+86 21 5840 0318
+86 21 5840 0090

地址 /Address
上海市滨江大道 3688 号
No.3688, Binjiang Road, Shanghai

营业时间 Opening Hours
11:30 – 13:30
14:00 – 16:00
17:00 – 22:00
着装要求 Dress Code
优雅便服 Smart Casual
人均消费 Per Capita Consumption
750 元 750 RMB

浦之舟的装修风格偏现代化设计理念中的花园式。餐厅以“融合菜”为方向，以“招牌口碑菜和传统菜”为灵魂，创新又不失本味。窗外黄浦江的旖旎美景，将老上海的怀旧与当下的繁华灵动地贯穿在一起。

It is decorated based on the modern garden design philosophy. This restaurant provides "fusion cuisine" and "signature dishes and traditional dishes" with innovative natural techniques. The beautiful scenery of Huangpu River outside the window brings a nostalgia style of old Shanghai and present prosperity together.

鮨直辉
Sushi Naoki

无限卡特权

日本料理
Japanese Cuisine

3.1 必应搜索热度 Search priority

电话 /Tel
+86 21 5473 0595

地址 /Address
上海市闵行区古北路 1838 号
No.1838, Gubei Road, Minhang District, Shanghai

营业时间 Opening Hours
晚餐 Dinner 18:00 – 23:00
着装要求 Dress Code
优雅便服 Smart Casual
人均消费 Per Capita Consumption
1800 元 1800 RMB

日本料理中的“割烹”主要是指料理师傅在餐台前当面操刀，为不同客人量身定做美食。走精致路线的鮨直辉，主打各类高级进口鱼生和日本江户前握寿司，以无菜单料理方式呈现。

Kappou means a Japanese chef customizes dishes for each diner on site. Sushi Naoki features top imported sashimi and nigiri-sushi and serves by Omakase non-menu way.

柒厢食事雅谈
Qi Xiang

粤菜
Cantonese Cuisine

必应 搜索热度 Search priority 3.1

电话 /Tel
+86 158 2114 7917

地址 /Address
上海市广中西路 737 号
No.737, Guangzhong West Road, Shanghai

营业时间 Opening Hours
11:00 – 22:00
着装要求 Dress Code
优雅便服 Smart Casual
人均消费 Per Capita Consumption
800 元 800 RMB

正如其店名一样，柒厢的“柒”代表了一年四季一日三餐，颇具意义。餐厅装修风格低调奢华，别具一格，客人坐在房间里会十分悠闲自得。无论是菜品的摆盘、厨师用心的烹饪，还是优雅舒适的环境，无不体现出一个“雅”字。

As its name means, the meaningful "Qi" represents three meals a day and four seasons a year. This restaurant has a low-key luxury and unique decoration, making diners feel comfortable and cosy when sitting here. No matter the dishes presentation, the chef's culinary art, or the elegant and comfortable environment, all reflect its "elegance".

无限卡特权

乔尔 · 卢布松美食坊（上海）
L'Atelier de Joël Robuchon(Shanghai)

法国菜
French Cuisine

必应 搜索热度 Search priority 2.6

电话 /Tel
+86 21 6071 8888

地址 /Address
上海市黄浦区中山东一路 18 号 3 层
3F, No.18, First Zhongshan East Road, Huangpu District, Shanghai

营业时间 Opening Hours
午餐 Lunch
周六、周日 Sat. – Sun. 11:30 – 14:00
晚餐 Dinner
周日 – 周三 Sun. – Wed. 17:30 – 22:30
周四 – 周六 Thur. – Sat. 17:30 – 23:00
着装要求 Dress Code
优雅便服 Smart Casual
人均消费 Per Capita Consumption
1500 元 1500 RMB

法国美食界的传奇人物乔尔 · 卢布松在中国大陆的首家餐厅——乔尔 · 卢布松美食坊（上海），呈现极富法国韵味的风格美食。餐厅位于上海外滩的中心地段，在这里可以俯瞰黄浦江两岸美景。

The legendary French chef Joël Robuchon made his debut in China in L'Atelier de Joël Robuchon (Shanghai), presenting upmost French-style cuisines. The restaurant just locates at the heart of the Bund. It has magnificent view of overlooking the beautiful Huangpu River.

荣新馆（金汇广场 4 号店）
Japanese Restaurant Sakae Shinkan(Jinhui Square)

日本料理
Japanese Cuisine

2.9 必应搜索热度 Search priority

电话 /Tel
+86 21 3471 1198
+86 21 5429 0118

地址 /Address
上海市红松路 148 号金汇广场 4 层
4F, Jinhui Square, No.148, Hongsong Road, Shanghai

营业时间 Opening Hours
17:30 – 23:00
着装要求 Dress Code
优雅便服 Smart Casual
人均消费 Per Capita Consumption
370 元 370 RMB

餐厅整体格调大气十足，其中包间是典型的日式榻榻米，让你不经意间仿佛置身于日本的餐厅。餐厅主打日料主题，食材的新鲜是菜品的基础，精湛的刀工和精美的摆盘，让这间餐厅成为众多食客的用餐地。

It has a glorious environment with typical Japanese tatami private rooms which make diners inadvertently as if they are in a Japanese restaurant. This restaurant mainly serves Japanese cuisine with fresh food materials, masterful cutting techniques and exquisite plate presentation, becoming a dining location for numerous diners.

Scarpetta
Scarpetta

无限卡特权

意大利菜
Italian Cuisine

7.4 必应搜索热度 Search priority

电话 /Tel
+86 21 3376 8223

地址 /Address
上海市黄浦区蒙自路 33 号
No. 33, Mengzi Road, Huangpu District, Shanghai

营业时间 Opening Hours
晚餐 Dinner 17:30 – 22:00
（最后点单 Last Order 21:30）
着装要求 Dress Code
优雅便服 Smart Casual
人均消费 Per Capita Consumption
250 元 250 RMB

餐厅名字 Scarpetta 的有趣含义是：在家里吃完意大利面后，因为太美味了而用面包将盘里的酱汁也抹了个干净。Scarpetta 不照搬任何意大利传统风味，用新鲜和高品质的食材，带来简单而富有独创性的意大利风味美食。

Scarpetta is an Italian word describing the action that you take bread after enjoying spaghetti to wipe your plate clean of all remaining sauce at home. Scarpetta has not copied any Italian traditional flavor, brings simple and original Italian food to the table by insisting on fresh and high quality ingredients.

Shanghai Tavern 西餐厅
Shanghai Tavern

西餐
Western Cuisine

必应 搜索热度 Search priority 4.3

电话 /Tel
+86 21 5368 9511

地址 /Address
上海市南京东路 199 号上海艾迪逊酒店 1 层
1F, Shanghai Edition, No.199, Nanjing East Road, Shanghai

营业时间 Opening Hours
06:00 – 23:00
着装要求 Dress Code
优雅便服 Smart Casual
人均消费 Per Capita Consumption
400 元 400 RMB

餐厅的环境设计借鉴并展示了华东电力大厦的悠久历史底蕴，餐厅中心有着极富线条设计感的展示厨房，米其林星级厨师 Jason Atherton 将在这里随着季节变化为食客呈现摩登英式佳肴。其中，牛肉鞑靼最受食客的欢迎。
The environment design of this restaurant displays the long history of East China Electric Power Building. There is a show kitchen with rich line designs in the center of this restaurant, where the Michelin-starred chef Jason Atherton will present modern British cuisine to diners in accordance with seasonal changes. Among the dishes, Steak Tartare is the most popular among diners.

Stone Brewing Tap Room
Stone Brewing Tap Room

西餐
Western Cuisine

必应 搜索热度 Search priority 3.7

电话 /Tel
+86 21 6226 2510

地址 /Address
上海市愚园路 1107 号 1 号楼 1 层
1F, Building 1, No.1107, Yuyuan Road, Shanghai

营业时间 Opening Hours
周一至周三，周日 Mon. – Wed. Sun.
11:30 – 24:00
周四至周六 Thur. – Sat. 11:30 – 02:00
着装要求 Dress Code
优雅便服 Smart Casual
人均消费 Per Capita Consumption
180 元 180 RMB

Stone Brewing 原是来自美国加利福尼亚的一家独立精酿酒厂，餐厅沿袭了酿酒厂工业风的装饰以及“原生，天然，手工精致”的理念，并用对啤酒同样的执着呈现特色美食。餐厅招牌菜有“发泄”鸡翅、巨石 BBQ 汉堡和战斧牛排等。
Grew out of an independent brewery in California, this restaurant follows the decorations of brewery's loft style, upholds the concept of "raw, natural and delicate craft", and devotes such efforts to its cuisine. Its signature dishes include "Vent" Chicken Wings, Rock BBQ Burger and Tomahawk.

上海滩餐厅（新天地店）
Shanghai Tang Café(Xintiandi)

无限卡特权

上海菜
Shanghai Cuisine

3.6 必应搜索热度
Search priority

电话 /Tel
+86 21 6377 3333

地址 /Address
上海市黄浦区黄陂南路 373 号
No.373, Huangbei South Road, Huangpu District, Shanghai

营业时间 Opening Hours
午餐 Lunch 11:00 – 14:00
晚餐 Dinner 17:30 – 22:30
着装要求 Dress Code
正装 / 优雅便服 Formal / Smart Casual
人均消费 Per Capita Consumption
300 ~ 500 元 300 ~ 500 RMB

本店呈现的是由江南名厨俞斌执掌的创意上海料理，在尊重中国传统烹饪工艺的同时，注重风格形式上的突破与超越。如牛油果西红柿、十年陈花雕醉虾等，特色鲜明的口感令食客流连忘返。
Shanghai Tang Café recruits the famous Jiangnan chef Yu Bin as its executive chef who respects the traditional cuisine but also tries his best to make breakthroughs in style and form. The distinctive flavors of his works like Avocado and Tomato, Wine-steeped Shrimp in 10-year-old Hua Diao Wine are all fascinating and attractive.

上海青年酒厂餐厅（歌斐中心店）
Shanghai Beer Factory(Gefei Center)

无限卡特权

西餐
Western Cuisine

2.7 必应搜索热度
Search priority

电话 /Tel
+86 21 6160 0116

地址 /Address
上海市黄浦区蒙自路 757 号
歌斐中心 2 层 206 室
Room 206, 2F, Gefei Center, No. 757, Mengzi Road, Huangpu District, Shanghai

营业时间 Opening Hours
午餐 Lunch 11:30 – 14:00
晚餐 Dinner 17:30 – 21:30
着装要求 Dress Code
优雅便服 Smart Casual
人均消费 Per Capita Consumption
150 元 150 RMB

上海青年酒厂餐厅，是上海少有的一家啤酒全程冷链保存在 2~6℃环境下的啤酒主题餐厅。和啤酒相配的美食，从欧式烤鸡到美式汉堡，甚至东南亚风味的各路海鲜，一应俱全。
Shanghai Beer Factory is a beer-themed restaurant with all beers kept in 2~6 ℃ during the whole freezing chain, which is rare in Shanghai. It offers the tasty food covering European-style grilled chicken, American hamburger and Southeast Asian flavor seafood to match with beer.

无限卡特权

苏浙总会
Jade Mansion

淮扬菜 粤菜
Huaiyang Cuisine and Cantonese Cuisine

必应 搜索热度 Search priority 3.6

电话 /Tel
+86 21 5012 7728

地址 /Address
上海市浦东新区世纪大道 8 号
国金中心商场 4 层
4F, IFC, No.8, Shiji Road, Pudong New District, Shanghai

苏浙总会的首家餐厅位于上海国金中心商场，环境融合古典宫廷元素与现代美学，有 10 余间私密雅致的包厢，在服务上则注重客人的个性化需求。
As the first restaurant of Jade Mansion located in IFC, it mixes the classical palace elements with modern aesthetics in its interior design. And there are over 10 elegant and private VIP rooms to satisfy the diner's individual demands.

营业时间 Opening Hours
午餐 Lunch 11:00 – 14:00
晚餐 Dinner 17:00 – 22:00
着装要求 Dress Code
优雅便服 Smart Casual
人均消费 Per Capita Consumption
480 元 480 RMB

无限卡特权

三号黄浦会
Canton Table

粤菜
Cantonese Cuisine

必应 搜索热度 Search priority 4.0

电话 /Tel
+86 21 6321 3737

地址 /Address
上海市中山东一路 3 号外滩 3 号 5 层
5F, Bund 3, No. 3, First Zhongshan East Road, Shanghai

粤式餐厅三号黄浦会位于知名的时尚生活地标外滩 3 号，以雍容雅致的上海滩海派为主角缀以现代简约风格。餐厅追溯经典粤菜本源，从家喻户晓的家常菜到名贵山珍海味，都坚持甄选优质新鲜食材，用料广博、百里挑一。
Located at the Bund 3, as the most famous landmark in Shanghai, it serves Shanghai cuisine in modern simple styles. This restaurant traces back to the origin of traditional Cantonese food, and selects quality and fresh ingredients to produce well-known home dishes and superior delicacies; all adhere to the best and extensive selections of high quality fresh ingredients.

营业时间 Opening Hours
周一至周五 Mon. – Fri.
11:30 – 14:30 17:30 – 23:00
周六、周日 Sat. – Sun.
11:30 – 15:00 17:30 – 23:00
着装要求 Dress Code
正装 Formal
人均消费 Per Capita Consumption
530 元 530 RMB

Terra Shanghai
Terra Shanghai

西餐
Western Cuisine

2.6 必应搜索热度
Search priority

电话 /Tel
+86 21 3253 5722

地址 /Address
上海市南京西路 1601 号芮欧百货 5 层
5F, Reel Shanghai, No.1601, Nanjing West Road, Shanghai

营业时间 Opening Hours
17:30 – 22:00
着装要求 Dress Code
优雅便服 Smart Casual
人均消费 Per Capita Consumption
1200 元 1200 RMB

Terra Shanghai 只设有 20 个坐席，每天仅晚餐营业，在静谧的夜晚为客人提供全方位的用餐体验。延续 Terra 的美食理念，所有菜肴都源于自然元素和纯有机食材。主厨 Heinrich Schneider 为 Terra Shanghai 研发新菜单，由主厨 Sandro Zheng 来演绎。

It only has 20 seats and provides dinner every day, serving all-around dining experiences to diners under quiet nights. Based on the Terra' culinary philosophy, all dishes here are made of natural and pure organi food materials. Chef Heinrich Schneider has created a new menu for Terr Shanghai which is made by Chef Sandro Zheng from Terra Shanghai.

The MEAT · 扒餐厅
The MEAT

无限卡特权

西餐 牛排
Western Cuisine and Steak House

4.4 必应搜索热度
Search priority

电话 /Tel
+86 21 6169 8886

地址 /Address
上海市浦东新区花木路 1388 号
上海浦东嘉里大酒店 2 层
2F, Kerry Hotel Pudong Shanghai, No.1388, Huamu Road, Pudong New District, Shanghai

营业时间 Opening Hours
午餐 Lunch 11:30 – 15:00
晚餐 Dinner 17:30 – 22:00
着装要求 Dress Code
优雅便服 Smart Casual
人均消费 Per Capita Consumption
700 元 700 RMB

The MEAT · 扒餐厅是一家兼具现代感与时尚休闲感的牛排烧烤餐厅，肉制品玻璃储藏室镶嵌在皮革拼凑成墙的餐厅入口，非常抢眼。食客还能在可视醒肉房中挑选自己中意的部位交由厨师炮制。

The MEAT is a modern and leisure steak house and grill restaurant. A glass meat pre-treatment room is built in at the entrance where there is a wall patched with leathers. Diners can pick up the meat they like there and hand to chef for cooking.

无限卡特权

天庭
Patoi

茶廊
Tea Lounge

必应 搜索热度 Search priority 7.5

电话 /Tel
+86 21 5047 8838

地址 /Address
上海市浦东新区世纪大道 88 号金茂大厦
金茂君悦大酒店 56 层
56F, Grand Hyatt Shanghai, Jin Mao Tower, No. 88, Shiji Road, Pudong New District, Shanghai

有 33 层楼高的天庭，华丽至极，是上海金茂君悦大酒店最具特色的休闲餐饮之地。天庭提供各色甜品、小食和咖啡茶饮，下午茶更是精致有加，值得推荐。
With a 33-storey atrium, Patio is the most special tea lounge in Grand Hyatt Shanghai. It offers various desserts, snacks, coffee and tea; especially the exquisite afternoon tea is highly recommended.

营业时间 Opening Hours
下午茶 Afternoon Tea 14:00 – 17:00
着装要求 Dress Code
优雅便服 Smart Casual
人均消费 Per Capita Consumption
368 元 +15% 服务费
368 RMB+15% Service Fee

唐阁
T'ang Court

粤菜
Cantonese Cuisine

Private Rooms

必应 搜索热度 Search priority 5.3

电话 /Tel
+86 21 2330 2430

地址 /Address
上海市黄浦区马当路 99 号
上海新天地朗廷酒店 5 层
5F, Langham Xintiandi Shanghai, No.99, Madang Road, Huangpu District, Shanghai

以中国历史上繁盛的唐朝命名的唐阁，同样盛名远扬。餐厅整体氛围充满中国风情，拥有 9 间豪华包房和雅致用餐区域，格调典雅。
Named after Tang, the most prosperous dynasty in Chinese history, T'ang Court restaurant is also very famous. The restaurant features in Chinese cultural traditions and has nine luxury private dining rooms and elegant dining areas.

营业时间 Opening Hours
午餐 Lunch 11:30 – 14:00
晚餐 Dinner 17:30 – 22:00
着装要求 Dress Code
优雅便服 Smart Casual
人均消费 Per Capita Consumption
800 元 800 RMB

泰安门
Taian Table

西餐
Western Cuisine

5.4 必应搜索热度
Search priority

电话 /Tel
+86 173 0160 5350

地址 /Address
上海市镇宁路 465 弄 161 号
愚园里 1 号楼 101 室
Room 101, Building 1, No.161, Yuyuanli, Lane 465, Zhenning Road, Shanghai

营业时间 Opening Hours
18:00 – 23:00
着装要求 Dress Code
优雅便服 Smart Casual
人均消费 Per Capita Consumption
1600 元 1600 RMB

餐厅开放式的厨房设计让人领略到地道的西餐文化，每一道菜品的食材原料和创作搭配，仿佛都在厨师们的指尖舞蹈。厨师变魔术一般将食材在食客眼前变换成饕餮盛宴，让食客们在享受美味的同时也过足了眼瘾。

Its open kitchen design brings diners to appreciate the authentic Western food culture. The combination of ingredients and creative collocation of each dish seem like a dancing in chefs' fingertips. Chefs transform the general ingredients into a feast in front of eyes just like a magic, so that diners can enjoy the delicacies while watching an interesting show.

Ultraviolet by Paul Pairet
Ultraviolet by Paul Pairet

西餐
Western Cuisine

5.8 必应搜索热度
Search priority

地址 /Address
上海某处 仅接受官网订位
Shanghai Website Reservation Only
http://www.uvbypp.cc//

营业时间 Opening Hours
晚餐 Dinner
周二至周六 Tue. – Sat. 18:30 – 23:00
着装要求 Dress Code
优雅便服 Smart Casual
人均消费 Per Capita Consumption
6000 元 6000 RMB

Ultraviolet by Paul Pairet 是一家自成一格、无法被归类的餐厅。餐厅只有一张长桌、10 个座位、20 种菜式左右的套餐，但加入了多重感知科技的支持，带来 5 种感官的全面体验。

This is the first restaurant beyond classification with its own style. It has only one communal table of 10 seats and a set-course of about 20 dishes, but it blends with multi-sensible technology and supports 5-sense experience.

VANILLA(外滩店)
VANILLA(Bund)

东南亚菜
Southeast Asian Cuisine

必应 搜索热度 Search priority 6.7

电话 /Tel
+86 21 6339 1579

地址 /Address
上海市北京东路 130 号中实大楼 B1101 号
Room 1101, Building B, Zhongshi Building, No.130, Beijing East Road, Shanghai

营业时间 Opening Hours
11:00 – 22:00
着装要求 Dress Code
优雅便服 Smart Casual
人均消费 Per Capita Consumption
300 元 300 RMB

餐厅以灰色为主色调的装修布置简约又不失大气，玻璃窗外是车水马龙的城市，窗内却是一片宁静的氛围。泰国地处热带又临近海洋，水果和海鲜的产量极其丰富，所以泰式料理最经典的菜品就是一碗酸酸辣辣的海鲜汤，让食客回味无穷。

It has a simple and elegant decoration in its primary color of gray, with bustling city outside window and halcyon atmosphere inside window. Thailand is located in the tropical region and close to the ocean, therefore it has abundant production of fruits and seafood, so the most classic Thai cuisine is a bowl of sour and spicy seafood soup, leaving diners endless flavors aftertaste.

王品牛排
Wang Steak

西餐
Western Cuisine

必应 搜索热度 Search priority 6.6

电话 /Tel
+86 21 620 84292

地址 /Address
上海市长宁区仙霞路 80 号
No.80, Xianxia Road, Changning District, Shanghai

营业时间 Opening Hours
午餐 Lunch 11:30 – 16:00
晚餐 Dinner 17:30 – 21:00
着装要求 Dress Code
优雅便服 Smart Casual
人均消费 Per Capita Consumption
396 元 +10% 服务费
396 RMB+10% Service Fee

王品上海店服务亲切，对美味牛排有着自己的严格定义：选取一头牛第六至第八对肋骨作为原料。这六块牛排，再历经数十种中西香料的 10 小时腌浸、高温烘烤后，才能呈现在客人面前。

Wang Steak provides kindly service and has its own definition to tasty steak. That is, only the six pieces of steak from the 6th to 8th rib of cattle are suitable, and then cure them over 10 hours by the spices from east and west before baking.

绚景楼
Aurora

无限卡特权

西餐
Western Cuisine

9.2 必应搜索热度
Search priority

电话 /Tel
+86 400 1800 000

地址 /Address
上海市申迪西路上海迪士尼乐园酒店 8 层
8F, Disneyland Hotel Shanghai, Shendi West Road, Shanghai

营业时间 Opening Hours
17:30 – 22:00
着装要求 Dress Code
优雅便服 Smart Casual
人均消费 Per Capita Consumption
800 元 800 RMB

绚景楼位于上海迪士尼度假区，由绚景楼眺望，童话城堡的梦幻全景尽收眼底。餐厅提供的“水牛芝士番茄沙拉”及“菲力牛柳与香煎橙味萝卜与黑椒汁”等菜品，相信会为您开启一段奇妙的美食之旅。

It is located in Shanghai Disney resort. Looking from here, diners will have a panoramic view of fairy tale castles. This restaurant offers "Buffalo Cheese Tomato Salad","Filet Mignon and Fried Orange Radish and Black Pepper Juice" and other dishes which will bring diners to start an amazing delicacies tour.

蟹家大院（外滩店）
Cejerdary(Bund)

海鲜
Seafood

3.0 必应搜索热度
Search priority

电话 /Tel
+86 21 6969 7777

地址 /Address
上海市广东路 59 号
No.59, Guangdong Road, Shanghai

营业时间 Opening Hours
11:00 – 21:30
着装要求 Dress Code
优雅便服 Smart Casual
人均消费 Per Capita Consumption
320 元 320 RMB

餐厅没有过多的装饰，桌椅都是原木色，大厅中央有景观隔断、微观植物、假山小僧，禅意十足，初心就是为了回归自然。餐厅只有三种菜品，蟹黄金、蟹肉、蟹太极，但每一道菜都力求尽善尽美。

It has a simple decoration with natural color tables and chairs. There is a landscape partition, with micro plants, rockery and a little monk in Buddhis mood in the hall center, presenting its original heart of returning to nature There are only three dishes in this restaurant: Golden Crab Roe, Crab Meat and Crab Tai Chi, but each dish reaches the acme of perfection.

无限卡特权

香港百合居（南丰城店）
House of Lily(The Place)

粤菜
Cantonese Cuisine

必应 搜索热度 Search priority 3.0

电话 /Tel
+86 21 6273 0533
+86 21 6273 0535

地址 /Address
上海市长宁区遵义路 150 号虹桥南丰城北区 6 层
6F, Northern Zone of The Place, No. 150, Zunyi Road, Changning District, Shanghai

营业时间 Opening Hours
午餐 Lunch
周一到周五 Mon. – Fri. 11:00 – 14:00
周六、周日 Sat. – Sun. 11:00 – 15:00
晚餐 Dinner 17:00 – 22:00
着装要求 Dress Code
优雅便服 Smart Casual
人均消费 Per Capita Consumption
150 元 150 RMB

餐厅的装修沿袭了“古法香港，摩登清新”的新粤风，加上明亮宽敞的落地玻璃窗，清雅而疏朗。热气腾腾的开放式厨房里烹制着品种丰富的粤式菜品、点心与靓汤。
The interior of House of Lily is in New Cantonese style which inherits the old Hong Kong style with a touch of modern and freshness; the massive French window makes it more elegant, spacious and bright. The steaming hot open kitchen makes a diversity of Cantonese dishes, dim sums and soup under preparation.

喜粤 8 号
Canton 8

粤菜
Cantonese Cuisine

必应 搜索热度 Search priority 5.8

电话 /Tel
+86 21 6330 8217

地址 /Address
上海市南京东路 139 号美伦大楼 5 层 501
Room 501, 5F, Meilun Building, No.139, Nanjing East Road, Shanghai

营业时间 Opening Hours
11:00 – 14:00 17:00 – 21:00
着装要求 Dress Code
优雅便服 Smart Casual
人均消费 Per Capita Consumption
210 元 210 RMB

喜粤 8 号是一家深藏于外滩的餐厅，环境温馨，令人有归属感，这不仅仅是因为其典雅的装修，更重要的是餐厅对每一道菜品的用心。蚝黄叉烧酥，外皮酥脆，散发奶香，搭配肉的咸腻，恰到好处地实现了升华。
Hidden in the Bund, it has a warm and cozy environment giving a sense of belonging and elegant decoration. This restaurant devotes to presenting each dish with ingenuity. The Oyster BBQ Pork Pastry with crispy skin and milk fragrance matches with salty meat, perfectly lifting the flavors.

新荣记（外滩店）
Xin Rong Ji(Bund)

江浙菜
Jiangzhe Cuisine

3.8 必应搜索热度 Search priority

电话 /Tel
+86 21 6303 7977

地址 /Address
上海市中山东二路 558 号 N3 幢 3 层
3F, Building N3, No.558, Second Zhongshan East Road, Shanghai

营业时间 Opening Hours
11:30 – 14:30 17:30 – 21:30
着装要求 Dress Code
优雅便服 Smart Casual
人均消费 Per Capita Consumption
590 元 590 RMB

地处黄埔江边的新荣记，餐厅窗外夜景“秀色可餐”。店内装修雅致，低调奢华的风格很有质感。餐厅菜名颇具寓意，比如醉生梦死、风生水起、醉龙闻香、年年有余等，其中醉龙闻香的口感会有多个层次的变化，带来全新体验。

Located by the Huangpu River, it has a beautiful night view outside the window. The interior decoration is elegant, modest luxury and distinctive. Its dishes' names are very meaningful such as "A Befuddled Life", "Spring Up", and "Drunk Dragon Smell". The "Drunk Dragon Smell" will have several levels of taste changes, which is innovative and refreshing.

新肴珍宝海鲜（国金店）
Jumbo Seafood(IFC)

无限卡特权

新加坡菜
Singapore Cuisine

3.5 必应搜索热度 Search priority

电话 /Tel
+86 21 6895 3977

地址 /Address
上海市浦东新区世纪大道 8 号
国金中心商场 L3-10
L3-10, IFC, No.8, Shiji Road, Pudong New District, Shanghai

营业时间 Opening Hours
午餐 Lunch 11:30 – 15:00
（最后点单 Last Order 14:15）
晚餐 Dinner 17:30 – 22:00
（最后点单 Last Order 21:00）
着装要求 Dress Code
优雅便服 Smart Casual
人均消费 Per Capita Consumption
450 元 450 RMB

餐厅的招牌菜无疑是螃蟹，东南亚特有的香辛料调和出风味独具的酱料，不仅成就了海鲜所特有的甘甜鲜美，更带来了多层次的丰富口感。

The crabs doubtlessly become Jumbo's signature, which keeps the tasty of seafood and takes rich flavors by the special Southeast Asian spices and the impressive sauces.

言盐西餐厅
Stone Sal

西餐
Western Cuisine

必应 搜索热度 Search priority 3.5

电话 /Tel
+86 21 5465 1765

地址 /Address
上海市东湖路 9 号上海地产大厦裙房 1M 号
No. 1M, Podium, Shanghai Real Estate Building, No.9, Donghu Road, Shanghai

营业时间 Opening Hours
11:00 – 01:00
着装要求 Dress Code
优雅便服 Smart Casual
人均消费 Per Capita Consumption
600 元 600 RMB

Stone Sal，即 stone salt，意指喜马拉雅山脉 600 米深矿开采出来的矿物盐。店内装修以金属和岩石为主，盐岩相互映衬，加上宽敞明亮的开放式厨房，整体感觉赏心悦目。餐厅招牌菜包括：战斧牛排、法国生蚝和松露意大利面等。
Stone Sal, or stone salt, refers to mineral salts from the mine 600 meters deep in the Himalayas. It is decorated with reflecting and shining metals and rocks, together with a spacious and bright open kitchen, giving an overall pleasant feeling pleasing to diners. Signature dishes include Tomahawk, French Oysters and Truffle Pasta.

宴遇
YANYU

无限卡特权

创意菜
Creative Cuisine

必应 搜索热度 Search priority 4.4

电话 /Tel
+86 21 6685 5556

地址 /Address
上海市静安区愚园路 68 号晶品中心 4 层
4F, Crystal Galleria, No.68, Yuyuan Road, Jing'an District, Shanghai

营业时间 Opening Hours
午餐 Lunch 11:15 – 14:15
晚餐 Dinner 17:00 – 21:15
着装要求 Dress Code
优雅便服 Smart Casual
人均消费 Per Capita Consumption
150 元 150 RMB

宴遇以创意中国菜闻名，在各方面都营造出十分新颖的用餐氛围。仅空间设计就足够摩登，让人眼前一亮。更重要的是菜品的设计，搭配、烹调、摆盘也不落俗套。
YANYU is famous for its creative Chinese cuisine and succeeds to create an innovative dining experience in every aspect. The dining hall is modern enough to impress the diners at the very beginning. And the most important feature is its idea for dish design, combination, cooking, and plate presentation.

洋房火锅（新天地店）
Hot Pot Sun(Xintiandi)

火锅
Hotpot

2.8 必应搜索热度
Search priority

电话 /Tel
+86 21 6333 8778

地址 /Address
上海市黄坡南路 376 号新天地南里
Xintiandi of Shanghai, No.376, Huangpo South Road, Shanghai

营业时间 Opening Hours
11:00 － 04:00
着装要求 Dress Code
优雅便服 Smart Casual
人均消费 Per Capita Consumption
960 元 960 RMB

餐厅古典优雅的老洋房环境以及精致的设计，每一处细节都体现了老上海的气派。洋房火锅主要经营高档海鲜火锅，食材精挑细选，用的是金华黑毛猪秘制汤底，香浓的汤底夹着淡淡的胡椒味和蔬菜的清香，有着不一般的温暖。
It has a classic and elegant old-house environment with exquisite design, reflecting a style of old Shanghai in details. It mainly provides high-level seafood hotpot with carefully selected ingredients and Jinhua black pig secret soup base. The fragrant soup base with a touch of pepper taste and vegetable fragrance will give diners a unique feeling of warmth.

怡咖啡
Yi Café

无限卡特权

自助餐
Buffet

2.9 必应搜索热度
Search priority

电话 /Tel
+86 21 2828 6888

地址 /Address
上海市浦东新区富城路 33 号
浦东香格里拉大酒店紫金楼 2 层
2F, Grand Tower, Shangri-La Hotel, No.33, Fucheng Road, Pudong New District, Shanghai

营业时间 Opening Hours
早午餐 Brunch 12:00 – 15:00
午餐 Lunch 11:30 – 14:30
晚餐 Dinner 17:30 – 22:00
着装要求 Dress Code
优雅便服 Smart Casual
人均消费 Per Capita Consumption
250 元 250 RMB

推陈出新的怡咖啡，汇集 11 个档口、170 种美食单品，由 30 位厨师现场烹饪，每个档口都有不容错过的美食。面现做，披萨现烤，生鱼片现切，印度烤鸡现做，香气袅袅飘荡在整个空间中。
With sustaining innovation, Yi Café has 11 counters, 170 delicacies and 30 chefs cooking on site. On the counters, some chefs are making noodles, some baking pizza, some cutting sashimi and others baking Indian-style chicken. And flavors surround the entire space.

逸龙阁
Yi Long Court

粤菜
Cantonese Cuisine

必应 搜索热度 Search priority 4.1

电话 /Tel
+86 21 2327 2888

地址 /Address
上海市中山东一路 32 号半岛酒店 2 层
2F, Peninsula Hotel, No.32, First Zhongshan East Road, Shanghai

营业时间 Opening Hours
午餐 Lunch 11:30 – 14:30
晚餐 Dinner 18:00 – 22:30
着装要求 Dress Code
优雅便服 Smart Casual
人均消费 Per Capita Consumption
664 元 664 RMB

餐厅拥有古色古香的中式屏风和深沉的棕红色木椅桌子，仿佛让人穿越回了旧上海，和外面繁华的大都市形成了鲜明的对比。厨房玻璃墙让每道菜品从制作到出炉均全程可观。推荐菜品有叉烧、燕窝和东星斑。

It is decorated with antique Chinese-style screens and deep brownish red wooden chairs and tables, leading diners returning to the old Shanghai, and forming a bright contrast with outside flourishing metropolis. The glass wall of kitchen makes every dish from making to presentation transparent. Recommended dishes include Roast Port, Bird's Nest and East Star Spot.

意膳坊
Thought for Food

无限卡特权

西餐
Western Cuisine

必应 搜索热度 Search priority 4.9

电话 /Tel
+86 21 33384666

地址 /Address
上海市徐汇区建国西路 357 号
No. 357, Jianguo West Road, Xuhui District, Shanghai

营业时间 Opening Hours
早餐 Breakfast 07:00 – 10:00
午餐 Lunch12:00 – 14:30
晚餐 Dinner 18:00 – 22:00
着装要求 Dress Code
优雅便服 Smart Casual
人均消费 Per Capita Consumption
280 元 280 RMB

意膳坊专注于经营由精心搭配的天然有机食材烹饪而成的美馔。时令菜单由享誉全球的行政总厨亚历山大 · 比特林及西医认证营养师陈珊珊倾力打造。

Thought for Food focuses on organic delicacy with elaborate mixes. Seasonal menus are created by the global-fame Chef Alexander Bitterling and the certificated dietitian Chen Shanshan.

雍福会
The Yong Foo Elite

上海菜
Shanghai Cuisine

4.4 必应搜索热度
Search priority

电话 /Tel
+86 21 5466 2727

地址 /Address
上海市徐汇区永福路 200 号
No.200, Yongfu Road, Xuhui District, Shanghai

营业时间 Opening Hours
午餐 Lunch 11:30 – 14:00
（最后点单 Last Order 13:45）
晚餐 Dinner 17:30 – 22:00
（最后点单 Last Order 21:30）
着装要求 Dress Code
商务休闲 Business Casual
人均消费 Per Capita Consumption
800 ~ 1500 元 800 ~ 1500 RMB

会所内外环境雅致、花木茂盛，还陈列了近千件艺术精品及古董。雍福会以经典上海菜闻名，菜式融入古法烹调，使用自制酱料，注重刀工和火候，口味精致清淡。

The Yong Foo Elite soaks in elegance with plants surrounding and nearly 1000 pieces of artworks and antiques in display. Famous for Shanghai cuisines, this restaurant insists on the traditional culinary methods and adopts its self-made sauces; its chef's magical cutting skills and accurate sense of time are rather impressive.

雍颐庭
Yong Yi Ting

江浙菜
Jiangzhe Cuisine

3.8 必应搜索热度
Search priority

电话 /Tel
+86 21 2082 9978

地址 /Address
上海市浦东南路 111 号文华东方酒店 LG 层
LG, Mandarin Oriental Hotel, No.111, Pudong South Road, Shanghai

营业时间 Opening Hours
11:30 – 14:30 17:30 – 22:30
着装要求 Dress Code
优雅便服 Smart Casual
人均消费 Per Capita Consumption
680 元 680 RMB

雍颐庭在食客中口碑极佳，不仅仅是因为其拥有深具文化底蕴的中国风设计和规整布局，更重要的是其美味的菜品。餐厅的招牌菜熏鲳鱼、山核桃小牛肉、宋嫂鱼羹和太湖河虾仁等，均广受好评。

This restaurant has a good reputation among diners, not only because of its profound cultural heritage of Chinese-style design and the overall layout structure, but also its delicious dishes which are more importantly. Its signature dishes have been well received, such as Smoked Pomfret, Pecan Veal, Sister Song's Fish Broth and Taihu River Shrimp.

甬府

Yong Fu

江浙菜
Jiangzhe Cuisine

必应 搜索热度 Search priority 4.0

电话 /Tel
+86 21 3356 6777

地址 /Address
上海市茂名南路 59 号锦江饭店锦北楼 12 楼
12F, Jinbei Building, Jinjiang Hotel, No.59, Maoming South Road, Shanghai

营业时间 Opening Hours
11:00 – 13:30 17:00 – 21:00

着装要求 Dress Code
优雅便服 Smart Casual

人均消费 Per Capita Consumption
840 元 840 RMB

不境洋溢着浓浓的老宅风情，古色古香，地方不大但足够温馨，装修优雅，怀旧风卡极具艺术感，包房宽敞舒适，餐具摆放考究。餐厅名菜宁氏十八斩，将红膏白蟹舌切成大小均匀的十八块，片片有膏，入口生津。

environment of this restaurant gives a strong feeling of old house. It is but gives diners an antique, warm and nostalgia atmosphere with elegant rations. The private rooms are spacious and comfortable, matching with site tableware. Its famous dish "Ningshi Eighteen Cuts" is produced through g the red cream white crab after sudden freezing into 18 uniform pieces with pieces stained with crab cream, which is delicious and attractive.

御宝轩

Imperial Treasure Fine Chinese Cuisine

粤菜
Cantonese Cuisine

必应 搜索热度 Search priority 4.9

电话 /Tel
+86 21 5308 1188

地址 /Address
上海市北京东路 99 号益丰外滩源 4 层
4F, Bund Origin, Yifeng Building, No.99, Beijing East Road, Shanghai

营业时间 Opening Hours
周一至周五 Mon. – Fri.
11:00 – 14:30 17:00 – 22:00
周六、周日 Sat. – Sun.
11:00 – 15:00 17:00 – 22:00

着装要求 Dress Code
优雅便服 Smart Casual

人均消费 Per Capita Consumption
370 元 370 RMB

御宝轩所处的大楼前身是益丰洋行，一幢五层砖木结构的上海早期建筑。如今餐厅结合了现代化的装饰，使古典与现代相得益彰。餐厅粤式早茶最为经典，晶莹剔透的虾饺和流光溢彩的流沙包都是必尝的美味。

Located in a building formerly known as Abraham E Building, it is an early Shanghai style brick-wood building with five stories. Now, this restaurant combines with the modern interior decoration to make the classical and modern styles complement with each other. Its Cantonese morning tea is the most popular, crystal shrimp dumplings and colorful cream custard bun are must-try delicious.

御京都
Meiji Kyoto

无限卡特权

日本料理
Japanese Cuisine

2.6 必应搜索热度
Search priority

电话 /Tel
+86 21 5403 4528
+86 21 5403 2976

地址 /Address
上海市静安区巨鹿路 913 号
No. 913, Julu Road, Jing'an District, Shanghai

营业时间 Opening Hours
午餐 Lunch 11:30 – 14:00
晚餐 Dinner 17:30 – 23:00
着装要求 Dress Code
优雅便服 Smart Casual
人均消费 Per Capita Consumption
500 元 500 RMB

位于上海旧法租界巨鹿路的御京都餐厅，其所在建筑已有近百年历史，庭院充满幽雅之气。餐厅主打的是日本关西风格料理，即京都、大阪等地具有代表性的菜肴，擅长以蒸煮法进行烹饪。

Standing in the previous French Concession, Julu Road, Meiji Kyoto embeds in a hundred-year-old architecture with a peaceful garden. It features the dishes that are the signatures in Kyoto and Osaka regions made by steaming and stewing.

源咖啡 · 全日餐厅
Commune

自助餐
Buffet

7.5 必应搜索热度
Search priority

电话 /Tel
+86 21 6766 1888

地址 /Address
上海市辰花路 5888 号上海佘山世茂洲际酒店
Inter Continental Shanghai Wonderland, No.5888, Chenhua Road, Shanghai

营业时间 Opening Hours
6:30 – 22:30
着装要求 Dress Code
优雅便服 Smart Casual
人均消费 Per Capita Consumption
410 元 410RMB

源咖啡·全日餐厅拥有多个互动式开放厨房，汇聚亚洲美食及丰盛的西式自助餐，为食客呈现诱人的特色佳肴。特别设计的儿童游乐园区，能让孩子们在源咖啡度过愉快的用餐时光。

It has several interactive open kitchens which provide Asian cuisine and sumptuous Western buffet, bringing attractive specials to diners. The specially designed adventure playground for children allows children to have a pleasant meal here.

欣舍
Shinpaku

日本料理
Japanese Cuisine

必应 搜索热度 Search priority 2.6

电话 /Tel
+86 21 6323 0093

地址 /Address
上海市中山东一路 3 号外滩 3 号 2 层
2F, Bund 3, No. 3, First Zhongshan East Road, Shanghai

营业时间 Opening Hours
17:30 – 1:00

着装要求 Dress Code
优雅便服 Smart Casual

人均消费 Per Capita Consumption
500 元 500 RMB

舍餐厅的灵感来源于日本社交文化的精髓，即崇尚分享与相聚。欣舍餐厅厨师团甄选上乘食材，无论是传统的日式炭烧、寿司或刺身，抑或是以现代烹饪技巧所现的创新菜式，在重视季节感的同时，又最大限度利用食材的色泽、香味与口感。

spired by the essence of Japanese social culture, that is sharing and thering, it selects the best ingredients to bring seasonal flavors and ovide beautiful color, aroma and taste of food ultimately, no matter ditional Japanese skewers, premium fresh seafood, or innovative dishes h modern cooking techniques.

广州

GUANGZHOU

7 号主场
NO.7 Host

西餐
Western Cuisine

必应 搜索热度 Search priority 2.9

电话 /Tel
+86 20 8765 8961

地址 /Address
广州市达道路保安前街 3-5 号
No.3-5, Baoanqian Street, Dadao Road, Guangzhou

营业时间 Opening Hours
11:00 – 22:30

着装要求 Dress Code
无特别着装要求 Non-specified

人均消费 Per Capita Consumption
300 元 300 RMB

7 号主场由两座有着上百年历史的洋房互通而成，曾在英国生活的老板将自己感受到的独特文化融入餐厅的环境中，这里有许多摆设物件都是老板的珍藏。餐厅出品的菜式皆有精美雕饰，食客可品尝到纯正美味。

Built by connecting two foreign houses with a history of over one hundred years, it has a unique environment reflecting the special culture which the owner felt during living in the UK. There are many cherished furnishings displayed in this restaurant. It provides beautifully garnished and authentic dishes to diners.

Alan's Kitchen
Alan's Kitchen

西餐
Western Cuisine

必应 搜索热度 Search priority 3.7

电话 /Tel
+86 20 8758 8563

地址 /Address
广州市珠江东路 6 号 K11 购物艺术中心 B131-132 铺
Shop B131-132, K11 Art Mall, No. 6, Zhujiang East Road, Guangzhou

营业时间 Opening Hours
11:00 – 22:00

着装要求 Dress Code
无特别着装要求 Non-specified

人均消费 Per Capita Consumption
250 元 250 RMB

Alan's Kitchen 是一家环境时尚、空间宽敞的西餐厅。餐厅的装修简洁大气又不失精致，开放式厨房窗明几净，干净整齐，令客人放心。餐厅以惠灵顿牛扒最为出名，牛扒口感鲜嫩，是食客来店必点的一道菜。

It is a western restaurant with fashionable style and spacious environment. It has a simple and elegant decoration and a clean open kitchen which seems comforting. The restaurant is best known for its fresh and tender Beef Wellington, which is a must-try dish.

Allegria 意大利餐厅
Allegria

意大利菜
Italian Cuisine

4.9 必应搜索热度 Search priority

电话 /Tel
+86 757 2927 0801

地址 /Address
广东省佛山市顺德区乐从河滨南路 3 号
佛山罗浮宫索菲特酒店 59 层
59F Sofitel Foshan 3 Hebin Road South, Lecong, Shunde District, Foshan, Guangdong Province

营业时间 Opening Hours
周一至周日 Mon. - Sun.
晚餐 Dinner 17:30 - 22:00
周六、周日 Sat. - Sun.
午餐 Lunch 11:30 - 14:30
着装要求 Dress Code
无特别着装要求 Non-specified
人均消费 Per Capita Consumption
500 元 500 RMB

Allegria 餐厅以地中海生活风尚为设计灵感，装饰布置洋溢着意大利托斯卡纳风情，开放式厨房及壁炉是餐厅亮丽的风景。在这里，食客可以享用地道的意大利美食，品尝正宗家庭风味的佳肴，享受来自优质牛排和自制风干肉类的惊喜美味。
Its design is inspired from the Mediterranean life style with decorations full of Italian Tuscan flavors. The open kitchen and fireplace constitutes beautiful scenery of the restaurant. Here, diners can enjoy authentic Italian cuisine and homemade delicacies while receiving surprises from premium steaks and homemade air-dried meats.

八月翠园（天环广场店）
Jassmine Jade(Parc Central)

中餐
Chinese Cuisine

2.6 必应搜索热度 Search priority

电话 /Tel
+86 20 8521 9202

地址 /Address
广州市天河路 212、214、216、218、220 号
天环广场 B236
B236, Parc Central, No. 212, No. 214, No. 216, No. 218 and No. 220, Tianhe Road, Guangzhou

营业时间 Opening Hours
周一至周五 Mon. - Fri. 11:00 - 22:00
周六、周日 Sat. - Sun. 10:00 - 22:00
着装要求 Dress Code
无特别着装要求 Non-specified
人均消费 Per Capita Consumption
250 元 250 RMB

八月翠园是广州最出名的餐厅之一，同样也是来广州必去的一家餐厅。餐厅环境优雅精致，来客可以一边欣赏餐厅的精巧布置，一边品尝美食。餐厅主营各种广式佳肴，招牌菜包括澳洲龙虾、拿破仑、片皮鸭等。
As one of the most famous and must-try restaurants in Guangzhou, it has an elegant and exquisite environment where diners can enjoy delicacies while appreciating its beautiful decorations. It specializes in a variety of Cantonese cuisine, including signature dishes: Australian Lobster, Napoleon, Duck Slice and so on.

无限卡特权

佰鲜汇
Catch

海鲜
Seafood

必应 搜索热度 Search priority 9.1

电话 /Tel
+86 20 8883 3300

地址 /Address
广州市珠江西路 5 号
国际金融中心四季酒店 100 层
100F, Four Seasons Hotel, International Financial Center, No. 5, Zhujiang West Road, Guangzhou

营业时间 Opening Hours
午餐 Lunch 11:30 – 14:30
晚餐 Dinner 18:00 – 23:00
（最迟点餐时间为 22:00）
着装要求 Dress Code
高雅休闲 Business Casual
人均消费 Per Capita Consumption
800 ~ 1000 元 800 ~ 1000 RMB

佰鲜汇是一家极具特色的亚洲风味海鲜餐厅，其举目繁星的用膳空间是由国际著名室内设计师梁志天打造的，诠释了花城商务社交的聚所。餐厅菜单荟萃了来自世界各地的新鲜海鲜产品，为宾客带来崭新的奢华美食体验。

As a seafood restaurant with special Asian styles, it has a starry dining space designed by the internationally famous interior designer Steve Leung, and is suitable for gatherings and business banquets. Its menu gathers the fresh seafood around the world together to bring a new luxury dining experience to diners.

无限卡特权

弁庆日本料理铁板烧
Benkay

日本料理
Japanese Cuisine

必应 搜索热度 Search priority 3.6

电话 /Tel
+86 20 6631 5070

地址 /Address
广州市华观路 1961 号广州日航酒店 1 层
1F, Hotel Nikko Guangzhou, No. 1961, Huaguan Road, Guangzhou

营业时间 Opening Hours
午餐 Lunch 11:30 – 14:30
晚餐 Dinner 18:00 – 22:00
着装要求 Dress Code
时尚休闲 Fashion Leisure
人均消费 Per Capita Consumption
200 ~ 500 元 200 ~ 500 RMB

弁庆日本料理餐厅每周从日本空运海鲜到店，当日海鲜由日本早晨直运，晚餐即可送至餐桌。餐厅氛围日式与西式相结合，既有传统榻榻米个室，又有多间西式包房，满足各种宴请需求。

As a Japanese cuisine restaurant, its seafood is transported from Japan by air every week. The seafood is shipped from Japan in the morning and can be delivered to the table for dinner. The restaurant is decorated in a combination of Japanese and Western, with both traditional tatami rooms and various Western rooms, which can meet the needs of different banquets.

炳胜公馆

Bing Sheng

粤菜
Cantonese Cuisine

4.4 必应搜索热度
Search priority

电话 /Tel
+86 20 3803 5000
+86 20 3803 5111

地址 /Address
广州市珠江新城冼村路 2 号首府大厦 5 层
5F, Capital Mansion, No. 2, Xiancun Road, Zhujiang New Town, Guangzhou

营业时间 Opening Hours
周一至周五 Mon. – Fri.
10:00 – 15:00 17:00 – 22:00
周六、周日 Sat. – Sun.
09:00 – 15:00 17:00 – 22:00
着装要求 Dress Code
时尚休闲 Fashion Leisure
人均消费 Per Capita Consumption
300 元 300 RMB

炳胜公馆团队亲赴实地挑选各地新鲜特有的食材，在烹饪方式上追求匠人及传承精神，力求每一道菜品精益求精，并将粤菜的原汁原味发挥得淋漓尽致，用心研制出一道道精致的粤式美味。

The chef team of this restaurant goes to different places to select fresh local food materials, pursues to the spirit of craftsman and heritage in the cooking methods in order to perfect every dish and present the original flavors of Cantonese cuisine incisively and vividly, and prepares delicious Cantonese food with heart.

炳胜私厨

Bing Sheng Private Kitchen

粤菜
Cantonese Cuisine

3.8 必应搜索热度
Search priority

电话 /Tel
+86 20 8757 5699

地址 /Address
广州市天河东路 178 号
No.178 Tianhe East Road, Guangzhou

营业时间 Opening Hours
午餐 Lunch 11:00 – 14:30
晚餐 Dinner 17:00 – 02:00
着装要求 Dress Code
无特别着装要求 Non-specified
人均消费 Per Capita Consumption
500 ~ 600 元 500 ~ 600 RMB

炳胜私厨主营健康、原味的私房菜。所有菜品均选用绿色食材、优质山泉水和精制食用油烹调。餐厅应季节和气候变化悉心准备佳肴，再配合清新静谧的环境，使食客在用餐过程中身心舒畅，从而引导食客健康饮食。

It provides healthy and original private home cuisine. All dishes here are made with green ingredients, quality spring water and refined cooking oil. With delicious dishes prepared according to seasons and climate changes, diners will feel comfortable and cozy during dining under such a fresh and quiet environment, and aware of healthy diet.

无限卡特权

大哥茶餐厅
Big Brother Restaurant

粤港菜
Cantonese Cuisine and Hong Kong Cuisine

必应 搜索热度 Search priority 3.6

电话 /Tel
+86 20 8460 7002

地址 /Address
广州市番禺区市桥街西丽南路 90 号
No. 90, Xili South Road, Shiqiao Street, Panyu District, Guangzhou

营业时间 Opening Hours
07:30 – 24:00

着装要求 Dress Code
便服 Casual

人均消费 Per Capita Consumption
100 元 100 RMB

大哥茶餐厅开业十多年来一直是广州港式茶餐厅的代表之一。虽然餐厅本身比较低调，但独具特色的地道美味和坚持如一的品质原则，令其人气爆棚。

Since the opening over 10 years ago, Big Brother Restaurant has been one of the leading Hong Kong-style tea restaurant in Guangzhou. Without many promotions, it is still rather popular for its special regional delicacies and consistent food quality.

无限卡特权

东南小馆
Southeastern Pub

东南亚菜
Southeast Asian Cuisine

必应 搜索热度 Search priority 2.7

电话 /Tel
+86 20 8917 6498

地址 /Address
广州市海珠区会展东路 1 号
广州香格里拉大酒店 2 层
2F, Shangri-La Hotel Guangzhou, No.1, Huizhan East Road, Haizhu District, Guangzhou

营业时间 Opening Hours
晚餐 Dinner
周二至周日 Tue. – Sun. 18:00 – 23:00

着装要求 Dress Code
优雅便服 Smart Casual

人均消费 Per Capita Consumption
190 元 190 RMB

东南小馆不仅食物可口，还推出了独具东南亚热带风情的鸡尾酒饮品系列，酒店专业侍酒师精通各式调酒，特别推荐东南小馆特制的冬阴功风味鸡尾酒。

Besides the delicious food, Southeastern Pub offers a series of Southeast Asian flavor cocktail. The bartenders are good at various kinds of wine mixing, and its specialty tom yum goong flavor cocktail are awesome.

恩惠咖啡
Grace Coffee Roaster

西餐
Western Cuisine

2.6 必应搜索热度
Search priority

电话 /Tel
+86 20 2865 0805

地址 /Address
广州市西环大街西秀园北排 59 号商铺
Shop 59, Xixiuyuan North Line, Xihuan Street, Guangzhou

营业时间 Opening Hours
11:30 – 19:30
着装要求 Dress Code
无特别着装要求 Non-specified
人均消费 Per Capita Consumption
90 元 90 RMB

恩惠咖啡在番禺之南，小巷深处，是一家以小野善造的咖啡豆为常规单品的咖啡馆，也是广州为数不多的主打深烘豆的小店。餐厅招牌菜为：华夫饼、姜汁拿铁、班尼蛋等。

Located at a deep alley in the south of Panyu, it is a coffee shop that specializes in Hawana coffee beans. It also provides deep baked coffee beans which is rare in Guangzhou. Its signature dishes include Waffles, Ginger Lattes, Egg Benedict, etc.

FUEL 露台江景法餐
FUEL

西餐
Western Cuisine

8.2 必应搜索热度
Search priority

电话 /Tel
+86 20 8092 2169

地址 /Address
广州市阅江西路 118 号珠江琶醍 B 区 4、5 层
4&5F, Zone B, Pearl River, No.118, Yuejiang West Road, Guangzhou

营业时间 Opening Hours
17:30–24:00
着装要求 Dress Code
无特别着装要求 Non-specified
人均消费 Per Capita Consumption
500 元 500 RMB

FUEL 是广州法餐爱好者的打卡胜地，坐拥无敌露台江景，食客可一边欣赏美景一边品尝精致美食。FUEL 的行政主厨 Steven Chen 和主厨 Gregory Louraichi 都有着多年星级餐厅的工作经验，专注于为食客提供更好的美食体验。

It is a favorable place for French food lovers in Guangzhou. With invincible terrace river view, diners can enjoy the beautiful scenery while tasting delicacies. The Executive Chef Steven Chen and Top Chef Gregory Louraichi have years of experience in Michelin-starred restaurants, devoting to providing the best delicacies experience for diners.

无限卡特权

豪厨
The Open Kitchen

中西美食
Chinese and Western Cuisine

必应 搜索热度 Search priority 3.9

电话 /Tel
+86 20 8916 3528

地址 /Address
广州市新港东路 638 号广州南丰朗豪酒店 4 楼
4F, Langham Place Hotels Nanfeng Guangzhou, No. 638, Xingang East Road, Guangzhou

营业时间 Opening Hours
06:30 - 24:00

着装要求 Dress Code
整齐休闲服 Neat Casual Wear

人均消费 Per Capita Consumption
226 元 226 RMB

豪厨餐厅全天供应琳琅满目的自助餐和精彩纷呈的环球美馔，为食客呈献一场味蕾与感官的盛宴。食客可以在各个互动美食台与厨师交流，欣赏厨师即席烹调出一道道佳肴，并遍尝数不胜数的环球美味。

It provides various buffet and delicious global delicacies throughout the day, bringing diners a feast of taste buds and senses. Diners can communicate with chefs at various interactive food stations and enjoy a variety of dishes prepared by the chef on the spot, as well as taste numerous global delicacies.

霍公子瓷馆艺术餐厅
Huo Gongzi

西餐
Western Cuisine

必应 搜索热度 Search priority 2.6

电话 /Tel
+86 133 0228 6859

地址 /Address
广州市环市东路 367 号丽柏广场 2、3 层
2F and 3F, La Perle Plaza, No. 367, Huanshi East Road, Guangzhou

营业时间 Opening Hours
11:00 - 01:00

着装要求 Dress Code
时尚休闲 Fashion Leisure

人均消费 Per Capita Consumption
368 元 368 RMB

霍公子瓷馆作为一家艺术主题餐厅，其标识瓷、痴、吃的谐音，揭示了瓷馆最核心的内涵。在艺术的氛围中，餐厅对各国菜式进行创新融合并加以艺术化呈现，食材的精心搭配、器皿的相得益彰，勾勒出一幅美食的境画。

As an art-themed restaurant, its name is a homonym tone of porcelain, infatuated and eating in Chinese, which reveals the core connotation of this restaurant. Under the artistic environment, it innovatively integrates the dishes of different countries to present them in an artistic way. The careful collocation of food materials complemented with utensils outlines a picture of delicacies.

红棉中餐厅
Hong Mian

中餐
Chinese Cuisine

2.9 必应搜索热度 Search priority

电话 /Tel
+86 20 2826 6966

地址 /Address
广州市天河区林和中路 6 号 4 层
4F, No. 6, Linhe Central Street, Tianhe District, Guangzhou

营业时间 Opening Hours
周一至周五 Mon. - Fri.
11:30 - 14:30 17:30 - 21:30
周六、周日 Sat. - Sun.
09:00 - 14:30 17:30 - 21:30
着装要求 Dress Code
优雅便服 Smart Casual
人均消费 Per Capita Consumption
250 元（包房人均 500 元）
250 RMB (500 RMB in VIP Room)

红棉中餐厅网罗正宗时尚粤菜及中国各地名菜，令到此宾客的身心都能得到愉悦满足。装潢耀眼夺目的餐厅设有 8 个私人宴会厅，宾客可乐享私宴。

Hong Mian collects a wide range of authentic trendy Cantonese and other Chinese cuisines to bring a physical and mental feast for every diner. The dazzling restaurant has 8 VIP rooms for diners to enjoy private dining.

江 - 由辉师傅主理
Jiang By Chef Fei

粤菜
Cantonese Cuisine

3.7 必应搜索热度 Search priority

电话 /Tel
+86 20 3808 8885

地址 /Address
广州市天河区天河路 389 号
广州文华东方酒店 3 层
3F, Mandarin Oriental Guangzhou, No. 389, Tianhe Road, Tianhe District, Guangzhou

营业时间 Opening Hours
早茶 Yum Cha 10:30 - 14:30
午餐 Lunch 11:30 - 14:30
晚餐 Dinner 17:30 - 22:30
着装要求 Dress Code
优雅便服 Smart Casual
人均消费 Per Capita Consumption
午餐 450 元 Lunch 450 RMB
晚餐 800 ~ 1000 元
Dinner 800 ~ 1000 RMB

厨师善于利用独具创意的菜式设计，用简单食材烹制出令人赞叹的美味。餐厅菜单以全新的方式展现粤菜的精致与完美，同时还原传统家庭式的用餐氛围。

The Chef is good at creative dish design to bring in remarkable delicacies by those simple ingredients. The menu expresses the sophistication and perfection of Cantonese cuisine in an innovative way, and the dining ambience might be felt like a traditional home.

金井日本料理
Kanaz Zatanese Restaurant

日本料理
Japanese Cuisine

必应 搜索热度 Search priority 2.6

电话 /Tel
+86 20 8333 1000

地址 /Address
广州市环市东路 367 号
丽柏广场 5 层 505-506
Room 505-506, 5F, La Perle Plaza, No. 367, Huanshi East Road, Guangzhou

营业时间 Opening Hours
午餐 Lunch 11:00 – 14:00
晚餐 Dinner 17:00 – 22:00
着装要求 Dress Code
时尚休闲 Fashion Leisure
人均消费 Per Capita Consumption
350 元 350RMB

金井日本料理由资深日料团队管理运营，主打铁板烧、刺身及和食等高级日式美食。大部分食材、调料及炊具均按高标准选自世界各地，餐厅风格也由专业团队倾心设计，力求将上等美味呈现给有品位的食客。

It is a Japanese cuisine restaurant managed by a senior Japanese team, featuring with Teppanyaki, Sashimi, Washoku and other advanced Japanese food. Its ingredients, seasonings and cooking utensils are selected from all over the world according to the high standard. The restaurant style is also designed by a professional team, so as to present delicacies to the tasteful diners.

无限卡特权

聚味轩
Ju Wei Xuan

粤菜
Cantonese Cuisine

必应 搜索热度 Search priority 2.6

电话 /Tel
+86 20 3211 0705

地址 /Address
广州市天河区东圃汇彩路菁映路 1 号
广州东圃合景福朋喜来登酒店 2 层
2F, Four Points by Sheraton Guangzhou Dongpu, No. 1, Jingying Road, Dongpuhuicai Road, Tianhe District, Guangzhou

营业时间 Opening Hours
午餐 Lunch
周一至周五 Mon. – Fri. 11:30 – 14:30
周六、周日 Sat. – Sun. 08:00 – 14:30
晚餐 Dinner 17:30 – 22:00
着装要求 Dress Code
优雅便服 Smart Casual
人均消费 Per Capita Consumption
200 元 200 RMB

在广州，怎能不尝一尝广式点心？聚味轩为广大食客供应精品粤菜和区域特色菜，这里的粤式点心具有传统的经典口味，同时在传统点心菜式的基础上又创作出不一样的新式点心。

When you come to Guangzhou, you must try the Cantonese dim sums. Ju Wei Xuan is a perfect place where the gourmets can find the refined Cantonese cuisines and some local specialties. It features classic taste while brings in some new-styled dim sums based on the traditional flavors.

佬佬餐厅
The Buddy's Kitchen

无限卡特权

粤菜
Cantonese Cuisine

2.6 必应搜索热度 Search priority

电话 /Tel
+86 20 3903 7789

地址 /Address
广州市西里路 91 号西丽广场 4 层
4F, Xili Plaza, No.91, Xili Road, Guangzhou

营业时间 Opening Hours
午餐 Lunch 11:00 – 14:00
晚餐 Dinner 17:30 – 22:00
着装要求 Dress Code
无特别着装要求 Non-specified
人均消费 Per Capita Consumption
70 元 70 RMB

佬佬餐厅是大佬和弟弟的意思，继承了大哥餐厅的炒炉出品，让人仿佛置身于 20 世纪 50 年代的湾仔唐楼里，品尝着霸气的大排档小炒。餐厅招牌菜为：炒滑蛋咖喱牛肉饭、特色干炒牛河、菠萝生炒骨等。

Its name means big brother and younger brother. This restaurant inherits the dishes of Big Brother Restaurant and makes diners as if enjoy the arrogant large stall stir-fry in Wan Chai building in the 1950s. Its signature dishes include: Fried Egg Curry Beef Rice, Featured Stir-Fried Rice Noodles with Beef, Sweet & Soup Pork with Sliced Pineapple, etc.

岚山
Lan Shan

日本料理
Japanese Cuisine

5.7 必应搜索热度 Search priority

电话 /Tel
+86 20 3727 6663

地址 /Address
广州市星汇云锦东面首层 A07-A09 铺
Shop A07-A09, 1F, Xinghui Yunjin East, Guangzhou

营业时间 Opening Hours
周一至周五 Mon.- Fri.
午餐 Lunch 11:30 – 14:30
晚餐 Dinner 17:30 – 22:30
着装要求 Dress Code
无特别着装要求 Non-specified
人均消费 Per Capita Consumption
400 元 400 RMB

作为广州珠江新城周边著名的日本料理餐厅，岚山对食材的选择极为重视，餐厅提供的鱼鲜、刺身和各种寿司都是现场制作。此外岚山的午餐定食最受食客欢迎，食客可在闲暇的午间，在充满经典和式风格的氛围中享受美食。

As a famous Japanese cuisine restaurant in Guangzhou Zhujiang New Town, it pays great attention to the selection of food materials. The seafood, sashimi and various sushi provided by this restaurant are all made on site. In addition, its lunch set menu is the most popular among diners who can enjoy the delicious food under traditional Japanese environment in their leisure time.

利苑（越秀店）
Lai Heen(Yuexiu)

粤菜
Cantonese Cuisine

必应 搜索热度 Search priority 3.7

电话 /Tel
+86 20 8363 3268

地址 /Address
广州市建设六马路 33 号宜安广场 4 层
4F, Yi'an Plaza, No.33, Jiansheliuma Road, Guangzhou

营业时间 Opening Hours
周一至周五 Mon.- Fri.
11:30 – 15:00 17:30 – 22:00
周六、周日 Sat. -Sun.
11:00 – 15:00 17:30 – 22:00
着装要求 Dress Code
无特别着装要求 Non-specified
人均消费 Per Capita Consumption
280 元 280 RMB

利苑酒家作为高端粤菜酒楼，不仅餐厅环境一流，而且出品的皆是精致独特、色香味俱全的菜肴，尤其是点心小食，做工讲究，口感适度，味道相当出众。另外，利苑的服务也是热情周到，无微不至。

As a high-end Cantonese cuisine restaurant, it not only has a first-class environment, but also provides exquisite and distinctive dishes which are rich in color, fragrance and tastes, especially for delicious and beautiful desserts and snacks. In addition, its service is warm and considerate as well.

荔雅图
Li Chateau

西餐
Western Cuisine

必应 搜索热度 Search priority 3.0

电话 /Tel
+86 20 2986 0818

地址 /Address
广州市天河路 228 号
正佳广场万豪酒店正门左手边负夹层
Negative Layer, Marriott Hotel Front Door Left, Grandview Plaza, No.228, Tianhe Road, Guangzhou

营业时间 Opening Hours
午餐 Lunch 11:30 – 14:30
晚餐 Dinner 17:30 – 22:00
着装要求 Dress Code
时尚休闲 Fashion Leisure
人均消费 Per Capita Consumption
350 元 350 RMB

荔雅图是正佳集团与 Landmark Bistro 合作的高端法国餐厅，餐厅设计独具匠心，低调奢华。在食物出品方面走的是精致法餐路线，用心挑选最优质、最新鲜的食材，加上独特烹饪手法，给您的味蕾带来不一样的精彩感受。

Co-operated by the Excellence International Group and Landmark Bistro, it is a high-end French restaurant with inventive and low-key luxury decoration. In terms of food production, it provides delicate French cuisine with the best and freshest ingredients carefully selected and unique cooking techniques, bringing different wonderful tastes to diners.

乐排馆
Ribs

无限卡特权

西餐
Western Cuisine

7.8 必应搜索热度
Search priority

电话 /Tel
+86 20 8917 6498

地址 /Address
广州市海珠区会展东路 1 号
广州香格里拉大酒店 2 层
2F, Shangri-La Hotel Guangzhou, No.1, Huizhan East Road, Haizhu District, Guangzhou

营业时间 Opening Hours
晚餐 Dinner
周一至周六 Mon. - Sat. 18:00 - 23:00
着装要求 Dress Code
优雅便服 Smart Casual
人均消费 Per Capita Consumption
488 ~ 588 元 488 ~ 588 RMB

这里有传统美国烧烤背小排、撒满秘制香料的蒙古羊排、由三种柑橘加上香料油炸腌制的短吻鳄肋排，还有澳大利亚塔斯马尼亚三文鱼、意式白兰地龙虾浓汤等，满足食客的不同需求。

Dishes include the Carolina-Style USA Baby Pork Back Ribs, Mongolian Lamb Ribs using secret spicy ingredients, the most exotic Gator Ribs served with a citrus trio and a spice combo, and more global selections of ribs. Guests can enjoy an international selection of Western cuisine, including Tasmanian Salmon, Lobster Bisque and more.

丽轩中餐厅
Lai Heen

无限卡特权

粤菜
Cantonese Cuisine

3.8 必应搜索热度
Search priority

电话 /Tel
+86 20 3813 6689

地址 /Address
广州市兴安路 3 号富力丽思卡尔顿酒店 3 层
3F, Ritz-Carlton Guangzhou, No.3, Xing'an Road, Guangzhou

营业时间 Opening Hours
周一至周五 Mon. - Fri.
11:30 - 14:00 17:30 - 22:00
周六、周日 Sat. - Sun.
10:30 - 14:00 17:30 - 22:00
着装要求 Dress Code
无特别着装要求 Non-specified
人均消费 Per Capita Consumption
700 元 700RMB

丽轩中餐厅是广州最奢华的粤式主题餐厅之一，格调古朴典雅，食客可以在这里品尝到精致正宗的粤菜佳肴、传统点心以及节日美食。侍酒师为食客搜集了 400 种葡萄酒和干邑，将美酒与佳肴完美搭配。

As a Cantonese-themed restaurant, it is the most luxurious one in Guangzhou. With classically elegant environment, diners will enjoy exquisite and authentic Cantonese cuisine, traditional dim sum and festive delicacies here. Its sommeliers have collected 400 wines and cognac for diners to enjoy with their food.

Mr. F180° 夜景露台餐厅
Mr. F180°

西餐
Western Cuisine

必应 搜索热度 Search priority 2.6

电话 /Tel
+86 189 2959 6044

地址 /Address
广州市中山三路 33 号
中华国际中心 B 座 54 层 413 室
Room 413, 54F, Building B, China International Center, No.33, Third Zhongshan Road, Guangzhou

如果你想欣赏广州的美丽夜景，那么就一定要来 Mr. F180° 夜景露台餐厅。这家餐厅不仅拥有能俯览城区的夜景露台，其装饰与布置也极富浪漫情调。食客可伴着凉爽的晚风，品尝店里精心准备的套餐，享受一段浪漫时光。

If you want to appreciate the beautiful night view in Guangzhou, you must come to the night view terrace of this restaurant. It not only has a night view terrace with a panoramic city view, but also possesses romantic and affective decoration and arrangement. Diners can enjoy romantic moments with elaborately delicious packages and cool evening breeze.

营业时间 Opening Hours
18:00 – 22:00
着装要求 Dress Code
无特别着装要求 Non-specified
人均消费 Per Capita Consumption
250 元 250 RMB

无限卡特权

明阁
Ming Court

粤菜
Cantonese Cuisine

必应 搜索热度 Search priority 5.5

电话 /Tel
+86 20 8916 3588

地址 /Address
广州市海珠区新港东路 638 号
广州朗豪酒店 3 层
3F, Langham Place Guangzhou, No.638, Xingang East Road, Haizhu District, Guangzhou

广州明阁以现代手法呈现新派粤菜精品。餐厅设计灵感来自广州独有的“西关大屋”建筑风格，并摆放有近代艺术品，东方韵味十足。

Ming Court specializes in presenting new Cantonese cuisine by modern cooking methods. The interior design is inspired by the regional Xiguan House with a display of modern Chinese artworks, evoking a mood of Oriental glamour.

营业时间 Opening Hours
午餐 Lunch
周一至周五 Mon. – Fri. 11:00 – 14:30
周末及节假日 Weekends and Holidays
09:00 – 14:30
晚餐 Dinner 17:30 – 22:00
着装要求 Dress Code
优雅便服 Smart Casual
人均消费 Per Capita Consumption
200 ~ 300 元 200 ~ 300 RMB

莫尔顿牛排坊（广州）
Morton's of Chicago,The Steakhouse(Guangzhou)

西餐
Western Cuisine

4.4 必应搜索热度
Search priority

电话 /Tel
+86 20 8708 5888

地址 /Address
广州市珠江新城兴民路 222 号
IGC 天汇广场 L505-L603
L505-L603, IGC, No.222, Xingmin Road,
Zhujiang New Town, Guangzhou

营业时间 Opening Hours
周五、周六 Fri. Sat. 11:30 – 23:00
周一至周四，周日 Mon. – Thur. Sun.
11:30 – 22:00
着装要求 Dress Code
时尚休闲 Fashion Leisure
人均消费 Per Capita Consumption
600 元 600 RMB

莫尔顿是全球连锁牛扒坊的佼佼者之一，其招牌牛扒以其上乘的肉质、精湛的烹饪手法和一流的口感受到许多食客的喜爱，是食客来餐厅必点的精品菜肴。餐厅环境优雅，可俯视珠江景色，适合聚会以及情侣约会。

As one of the global chain steakhouses, its signature steaks are favored by numerous diners for its excellent meat quality, perfect cooking techniques and delicate tastes, which are must-try dishes for diners eating here. It has an elegant environment and can provide a top view of the Pearl River scenery, which is suitable for gatherings and datings.

帕戈意大利餐厅
Prego

无限卡特权

意大利菜
Italian Cuisine

7.9 必应搜索热度
Search priority

电话 /Tel
+86 20 2886 6968

地址 /Address
广州市天河区林和中路 6 号 40 层
40F, No.6, Linhe Central Road, Tianhe
District, Guangzhou

营业时间 Opening Hours
午餐 Lunch 11:30 – 14:00
晚餐 Dinner 18:00 – 22:00
着装要求 Dress Code
优雅便服 Smart Casual
人均消费 Per Capita Consumption
280 元 280 RMB

帕戈意大利餐厅坚持采用进口食材，以独特的意式烹调方式，结合不同地区的传统和时尚菜色，带你踏上全新的美食之旅。

Prego insists on using imported ingredients, produces dishes through its special Italian culinary arts and brings diners a feast of delicacies combining various styles of traditional and fashionable cuisine.

无限卡特权

侨美食家
Qiao Mei Shi Jia

粤菜
Cantonese Cuisine

必应 搜索热度 Search priority 3.2

电话 /Tel
+86 20 8121 7168

地址 /Address
广州市荔湾区沙面南街 52 号
No.52, Shamian South Street, Liwan District, Guangzhou

营业时间 Opening Hours
早茶 Yum Cha 07:30 – 10:30
午餐 Lunch 10:30 – 14:30
晚餐 Dinner 17:00 – 21:30
夜宵 Midnight Snack 21:30 – 03:00
着装要求 Dress Code
优雅便服 Smart Casual
人均消费 Per Capita Consumption
80 元 80 RMB

侨美食家诞生于白鹅潭畔的沙面岛上，30 多年来一直很有人气。餐厅以彩色玻璃和字画装饰，环境具有老西关风情。乳鸽是这里的看家菜，外皮金灿灿的，咬下去鲜嫩多汁。

Lying on the Shamian Island by White Goose Bay, Qiao Mei Shi Jia keeps its popularity for over 30 years. Decorated with colorful glass and paintings, the space demonstrates the old Guangzhou glamour. The most famous Roasted Suckling Pigeon has a piece of golden skin wrapping the tender and juicy meat.

无限卡特权

松宫日本料理
Matsumiya

日本料理
Japanese Cuisine

必应 搜索热度 Search priority 2.6

电话 /Tel
+86 757 2927 0806

地址 /Address
广东省佛山市顺德区乐从河滨南路 3 号
佛山罗浮宫索菲特酒店 7 层
7F Sofitel Foshan 3 Hebin Road South, Lecong, Shunde District, Foshan, Guangdong Province

营业时间 Opening Hours
午餐 Lunch 11:30 – 14:30
晚餐 Dinner 17:30 – 22:00
着装要求 Dress Code
优雅便服 Smart Casual
人均消费 Per Capita Consumption
500 元 500 RMB

宫日本料理是一家优质的高端日本料理餐厅，巧妙地将正宗的日本料理与现代化氛围融合在一起。餐厅运用“少即是多”的极简主义理念和先进的设计，内饰采全木设计。餐厅提供一流的高品质寿司、刺身和铁板烧，食材均采用日本进口。

s a premium Japanese cuisine restaurant that skillfully blends authentic panese cooking with a modern environment. Insisting on the minimal of "less is more", this restaurant adopts advanced design ideas and corated entirely in wood. It offers first-class high quality sushi, sashimi and panyaki; all food materials of these dishes are imported from Japan.

松月自慢料理
Song Yue

西餐
Western Cuisine

3.6 必应搜索热度 Search priority

电话 /Tel
+86 20 8911 4777

地址 /Address
广州市珠江西路 15 号珠江城大厦商业 4 层
4F, Business Zone, Pearl River Tower,
No.15, Zhujiang West Road, Guangzhou

营业时间 Opening Hours
午餐 Lunch 11:00 – 14:00
晚餐 Dinner 17:00 – 21:30
着装要求 Dress Code
时尚休闲 Fashion Leisure
人均消费 Per Capita Consumption
350 元 350RMB

松月自慢料理是悦港琴湾集团旗下的匠心力作，拥有日式的优雅与温暖，主营刺身、手卷和锅物等日式料理。松月追求优越与匠心，选用全球公认最好产区的精品食材，主张用合适的料理方式呈现食材本味。

It is a masterwork of Yuegang Qinwan Group, and presents a Japanese elegant and warm atmosphere. It mainly provides Japanese cuisine, such as Sashimi, Temaki and Hotpot. It pursues excellence and ingenuity, selecting the best quality food materials from the world's recognized production areas, and presenting the original tastes of food materials with appropriate cooking methods.

素会
Vegetarian Club

素食
Vegetarian Cuisine

3.9 必应搜索热度 Search priority

电话 /Tel
+86 20 8174 8631

地址 /Address
广州市黄沙大道 15-17 号
No.15-17, Huangsha Road, Guangzhou

营业时间 Opening Hours
午餐 Lunch 11:00 – 15:00
晚餐 Dinner 17:00 – 22:00
着装要求 Dress Code
商务休闲 Business Casual
人均消费 Per Capita Consumption
200 元 200 RMB

素会面对珠江的一线江景，环境清幽且通透大气，内里典雅幽静，设有各式富禅意的摆设物。餐厅以素食为基础，不断创新，在尽量不改变原材料的基础上用橄榄油或菜籽油精工细烹，做出令人惊艳的素食味道。

In front of the beautiful scenery of Pearl River, it has a quiet and generou environment with elegant and marvel decoration characterized by mar Zen style furnishings. Based on a vegetarian diet, it has committed continuous innovating and producing amazing vegetarian flavors throu olive oil or canola oil without changing the ingredients as much as possibl

宋·川菜
Song Chinese Cuisine

川菜
Sichuan Cuisine

必应 搜索热度 Search priority 3.6

电话 /Tel
+86 20 8741 2345
+86 20 8621 2345

地址 /Address
广州市花城大道珠江新城高德置地冬广场 4 层 417 号
Room 417, 4F, Gaode Zhidi Square, Zhujiang New Town, Huacheng Road, Guangzhou

营业时间 Opening Hours
午餐 Lunch 11:30 – 14:30
晚餐 Dinner 17:30 – 22:00
着装要求 Dress Code
时尚休闲 Fashion Leisure
人均消费 Per Capita Consumption
250 元 250 RMB

宋·川菜拥有广州数一数二的用餐环境，餐厅门口羽毛翅膀状的巨大装饰物给所有来到这里用餐的客人以惊艳的美感，既灵动，又营造出客人用餐的私密空间。餐厅招牌菜有：蒜泥白肉、沸腾老虎斑和开水白菜等。

It has one of the best dining environments in Guangzhou. The large feather wings at the entrance of restaurant give all diners who come here an amazing sense of beauty, which are not only attractive but also building a private dining space for diners. Its signature dishes are: Sliced Boiled Pork with Garlic Sauce, Boiling Tiger Grouper, Chinese Cabbage in Soup and so on.

天和割烹料理
Zenho

日本料理
Japanese Cuisine

必应 搜索热度 Search priority 3.6

电话 /Tel
+86 20 3720 9797

地址 /Address
广州市花城大道 665 号
翡丽商务大厦 104 单元
Unit 104, Feili Commerce Building, No.665, Huacheng Road, Guangzhou

营业时间 Opening Hours
午餐 Lunch 11:00 – 14:00
晚餐 Dinner 17:00 – 22:00
着装要求 Dress Code
商务休闲 Business Casual
人均消费 Per Capita Consumption
500 元 500 RMB

天和割烹料理的创立源于对日本料理执着追求的管理层，他们遵循料理的五色、五味、五法，致力于表达人、食材与自然的和谐统一。他们将食材、环境、氛围优质融合，旨在制作出真正的料理。

This restaurant is established based on the pursuit of Japanese cuisine by its management leaders who follow the five colors, five tastes and five methods of cuisine, and are committed to expressing the harmony and unity of human, food and nature. They combine the ingredients, environment and atmosphere perfectly to create authentic cuisine.

田舍家（天汇广场店）
Inakaya(IGC)

日本料理
Japanese Cuisine

5.3 必应搜索热度 Search priority

电话 /Tel
+86 20 3727 7193

地址 /Address
广州市珠江新城兴民路 222 号天汇广场 L504 和 L602
L504&L602, IGC, No.222, Xingmin Road, Zhujiang New Town, Guangzhou

营业时间 Opening Hours
午餐 Lunch 11:30 - 14:30
晚餐 Dinner 17:00 - 22:30
着装要求 Dress Code
时尚休闲 Fashion Leisure
人均消费 Per Capita Consumption
650 元 650 RMB

田舍家分为春夏秋冬四个主题，带你感受日本四季变化。热闹的炉端烧和充满日式禅意的铁板烧，闹静结合。严选食材，确保每一道菜细致精巧。餐厅位置远眺小蛮腰，近望珠江水，厨师即席制作，美味直达唇齿。

It has four themes: spring, summer, autumn and winter, which take diners feel seasonal changes in Japan. The robatayaki and teppanyaki which is full of Japanese Zen style are not only delicate and delicious, but also made with strictly selected food materials. From here, diners can overlook the Canton Tower, appreciate the Pearl River, and enjoy delicacies with chef cooking at the spot.

藤鹤割烹
Fujitsuru Kappo

日本料理
Japanese Cuisine

2.9 必应搜索热度 Search priority

电话 /Tel
+86 20 8928 7784

地址 /Address
广州市海明路广粤天地北门 1 层 82 铺
Shop 82, 1F, Canton Place North Gate, Haiming Road, Guangzhou

营业时间 Opening Hours
午餐 Lunch 11:30 - 14:00
晚餐 Dinner 17:30 - 22:00
着装要求 Dress Code
商务休闲 Business Casual
人均消费 Per Capita Consumption
750 元 750 RMB

藤鹤割烹是广州首家怀石料理店。在日本，怀石料理是宴请重要客人时吃的料理。餐厅极其重视打造正宗日式氛围，所有的食材都是当天从日本空运而来，在最大程度上保证食材的新鲜。

It is the first Kaiseki Japanese cuisine restaurant in Guangzhou. Kaiseki is a kind of food serving for important guests in Japan. This restaurant pays great attention to creating an authentic Japanese atmosphere. All the ingredients are transported from Japan on the day by air to ensure the freshness as far as possible.

无限卡特权

万豪中餐厅
Man Ho

中餐
Chinese Cuisine

必应 搜索热度 Search priority 4.7

电话 /Tel
+86 20 6102 8380

地址 /Address
广州市天河区天河路 228 号
广州正佳广场万豪酒店 6 层
6F, Marriott Guangzhou Tianhe, No.228, Tianhe Road, Tianhe District, Guangzhou

营业时间 Opening Hours
午餐 Lunch 11:00 – 14:00
晚餐 Dinner 17:00 – 22:30
着装要求 Dress Code
优雅便服 Smart Casual
人均消费 Per Capita Consumption
200 – 300 元 200 – 300 RMB

餐厅推出多道古代宫廷菜，其烹饪团队已充分掌握粤菜的细腻之处，亦备有选择丰富的饮品选单，罗列 80 多款由专业泡茶师挑选的上等中国茶，以及来自全国著名产区的罕有葡萄酒及烈酒。

There are several classic imperial dishes revealing the quality of the chef team. Moreover, many kinds of beverages are offered, including over 80 kinds of the best Chinese tea selected by tea specialists, as well as the rare and famous wines and spirits across China.

无国界
Wu Guo Jie

粤菜
Cantonese Cuisine

必应 搜索热度 Search priority 3.7

电话 /Tel
+86 20 3879 1687

地址 /Address
广州市天河区体育西路 101 号
维多利广场 6 层
6F, Victoria Plaza, No.101, Tiyu West Road, Tianhe District, Guangzhou

营业时间 Opening Hours
午餐 Lunch 10:00 – 15:00
晚餐 Dinner 17:00 – 22:30
着装要求 Dress Code
优雅便服 Smart Casual
人均消费 Per Capita Consumption
100 元 100 RMB

正如其店名一样，无国界餐厅引领起广州的一股饮食新潮流，让食客的味蕾冲破了国家和民族的界限。餐厅地处繁华的都市，环境大气而静逸，让人能安心享用美食。

Just like its name, Wu Guo Jie is leading a new dining trend in Guangzhou, breaking the boundary between countries and ethnicities. Grand and quiet, this restaurant creates a good place for gourmets in the busy city.

喜贺极上烧肉
Kika Japanese Bar Becue Restaurant

日本料理
Japanese Cuisine

2.6 必应搜索热度 Search priority

电话 /Tel
+86 20 8330 8820

地址 /Address
广州市环市东路 367 号丽柏广场 4 层
4F, La Perle Plaza, No. 367, Huanshi East Road, Guangzhou

营业时间 Opening Hours
午餐 Lunch 11:00 – 14:30
晚餐 Dinner 17:00 – 22:00
着装要求 Dress Code
无特别着装要求 Non-specified
人均消费 Per Capita Consumption
350 元 350 RMB

喜贺极上烧肉取“喜庆欢贺”之意，秉承对日本传统美学的推崇，餐厅布局结构及装饰布置显得神韵十足。餐厅的日式烤肉讲究原汁原味，挑选上等好肉，鲜嫩的肉质，可看到均匀分布的脂肪纹理。

Its name meaning "joyous and happy" reflects the admiration of traditional Japanese aesthetics. It has an attractive layout and decoration style. The Japanese-style roast meat gives diners the original taste of ingredients by selected tender meats which diners can see the uniform texture of fat.

夏宫
Summer Palace

无限卡特权

粤菜
Cantonese Cuisine

7.5 必应搜索热度 Search priority

电话 /Tel
+86 20 8917 6498
+86 20 8917 6428

地址 /Address
广州市会展东路 1 号香格里拉大酒店 2 层
2F, Shangri-La Hotel Guangzhou, No. 1, Huizhan East Road, Guangzhou

营业时间 Opening Hours
午餐 Lunch
周一至周五 Mon. – Fri. 11:30 – 14:30
周六、周日 Sat. – Sun. 08:00 – 14:30
晚餐 Dinner
周一至周五 Mon. – Fri. 17:30 – 22:30
周六、周日 Sat. – Sun. 17:30 – 22:30
着装要求 Dress Code
无特别着装要求 Non-specified
人均消费 Per Capita Consumption
300 元 300 RMB

在夏宫中餐厅优雅别致的环境中，宾客可品味正宗粤菜精髓及中国各地区的珍馐佳肴，开启特色美食精品之旅。其 18 间极具中式风格的豪华包房，为亲友聚会或正式的商务宴请提供了精致的用餐体验。

In its elegant and desirable environment, diners will enjoy the essences of authentic Cantonese cuisine and regional delicacies in China, and step on a journey of distinctive and featured delicacies. It has 18 luxurious private rooms with unique Chinese styles, providing exquisite dining experience for friends and relatives gatherings or formal business banquets.

小蟹哥
Crab Brother Restaurant

海鲜
Seafood

必应 搜索热度 Search priority 2.6

电话 /Tel
+86 20 3788 9333

地址 /Address
广州市珠江东路 16 号
高德置地广场冬广场 3 层 327 号
Room 327, 3F, Gaode Zhidi Square, No.16, Zhujiang East Road, Guangzhou

营业时间 Opening Hours
午餐 Lunch 11:00 – 15:00
晚餐 Dinner 17:00 – 22:00
着装要求 Dress Code
无特别着装要求 Non-specified
人均消费 Per Capita Consumption
300 元 300 RMB

小蟹哥是南海渔村集团精心打造的以蟹为主题的餐厅，致力于将“蟹食”文化推向另一个全新的高度。餐厅内有国际化的新颖设计与独具时代气息的装饰，巨型的专业养殖展示池可容纳近 1500 千克蟹供顾客挑选。

As a crab-themed restaurant elaborately established by the South Sea Fishing Village Group, it devotes to lifting the 'crab food' culture to a new higher level. With a unique international design and strong era sense decorations, it has a large professional aquaculture pond which can accommodate nearly 1500kg crabs for diners to select.

徐博馆岭南养生菜
Dr. Xu's Wellbeing Branch

岭南菜
South of the Five Ridges Cuisine

必应 搜索热度 Search priority 2.8

电话 /Tel
+86 20 3807 8889

地址 /Address
广州市珠江新城临江大道 57 号中和广场 7 层
7F, Concord Center, No.57, Linjiang Road, Zhujiang New Town, Guangzhou

营业时间 Opening Hours
午餐 Lunch 11:00 – 15:00
晚餐 Dinner 17:00 – 22:00
着装要求 Dress Code
无特别着装要求 Non-specified
人均消费 Per Capita Consumption
350 元 350 RMB

博馆岭南养生菜是隶属于广州渔民新村旗下的高端品牌，餐厅善制岭南菜，最大便是用料广博奇杂、配料多而巧，让食客能够大快朵颐，是广州难得的岭南养餐厅。

a high-end subordinate brand of Guangdong Fisherman Residential arter Food and Drink Co., Ltd., it is expert in making South of the Five ges cuisine characterized by its complex materials, abundant styles, erse and ingenious ingredients, making diners enjoy their feasts. Such of healthy South of the Five Ridges cuisine is hard to find in Guangzhou.

雅歌餐厅
Alkie & Vivian's Restaurant

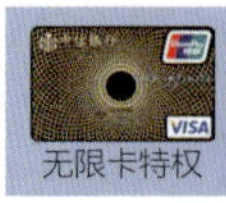

东西美食
Eastern Western Cuisine

2.6 必应搜索热度 Search priority

电话 /Tel
+86 20 3902 2569

地址 /Address
广州市西里路西里广场 4 层
4F, Xili Plaza, Xili Road, Guangzhou

营业时间 Opening Hours
午餐 Lunch 12:00 – 14:30
晚餐 Dinner 18:00 – 22:00
着装要求 Dress Code
无特别着装要求 Non-specified
人均消费 Per Capita Consumption
150 元 150 RMB

雅歌餐厅是一家拥有好吃的意大利和东南亚菜品的餐厅，只出品正宗的意大利那不勒斯柴火烧披萨，以及一系列的东南亚和意大利传统菜。餐厅拥有全开放式的厨房，是广州仅有的一家 A 级餐饮牌照东南亚餐厅。

It is a restaurant featured with delicious Italian and Southeast Asian cuisine, and only provides authentic Italian Naples Wood-fire Pizza and a series of Southeast Asian cuisine and Italian traditional dishes. It has an open kitchen and is the only Southeast Asian restaurant with class A restaurant license in Guangzhou.

漾中餐厅
Yang Chinese Restaurant

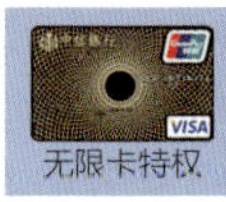

粤菜
Cantonese Cuisine

3.7 必应搜索热度 Search priority

电话 /Tel
+86 20 3695 3705

地址 /Address
广州市花都区山前大道东段北侧
广州花都合景喜来登度假酒店内
Sheraton Hotel & Resorts, North of East Section, Shanqian Road, Huadu District, Guangzhou

营业时间 Opening Hours
早餐或午餐 Breakfast or Lunch
周一至周五 Mon. – Fri. 11:30 – 14:30
周末及节假日 Weekends and Holidays
08:30 –14:30
晚餐 Dinner 17:30 – 22:00
着装要求 Dress Code
优雅便服 Smart Casual
人均消费 Per Capita Consumption
200 元 200 RMB

漾中餐厅精致放松的环境让食客享受“高雅但不高冷”的美味体验，这里的菜单由国际化的团队设计打造，注重以精致、轻松、原汁原味的形式向顾客呈现食物。

The elaborate and relaxing environment of Yang Chinese Restaurant pleases its diners by elegant and affordable dining experience. The menu is tailored by an international team focusing on presenting the dishes in an exquisite, relaxing and pure way.

无限卡特权

宜客乐西餐厅 Eatery

西餐
Western Cuisine

必应搜索热度 Search priority 7.2

宜客乐西餐厅的装潢沿袭了喜来登酒店的奢华。餐厅菜式主要以西餐及东南亚风味为主，坚持选用原产地的食品为原材料。

The interior decoration of Eatery matches with the Sheraton's luxury. And its menu features Western and Southeast Asian flavors. Eatery insists on using the local ingredients to bring out delicacies.

电话 /Tel
+86 20 3211 0720
+86 20 3211 0888

地址 /Address
广州市天河区东圃汇彩路菁映路 1 号
广州东圃合景福朋喜来登酒店 1 层
1F, Four Points by Sheraton Guangzhou Dongpu, No. 1, Jingying Road, Dongpuhuicai Road, Tianhe District, Guangzhou

营业时间 Opening Hours
午餐 Lunch 11:30 – 14:30
晚餐 Dinner 18:30 – 22:00
着装要求 Dress Code
优雅便服 Smart Casual
人均消费 Per Capita Consumption
250 元 +15% 服务费
250 RMB + 15% Service Fee

无限卡特权

意畔意大利餐厅 Il Ponte

意大利菜
Italian Cuisine

必应搜索热度 Search priority 6.1

意畔意大利餐厅展现典雅简约的异国风情，其经典的意式美食与开放式的披萨壁炉，严守正宗地道的意大利菜式烹饪法，只为让食客在享受地道意大利美味的同时拥有愉悦与舒心的体验。

Matched with an elegant, simple and exotic environment, it provides authentic Italian cuisine through classic Italian culinary arts, together with an open pizza oven, so as to provide diners with Italian delicacies and comfortable pleasure.

电话 /Tel
+86 20 6683 9999

地址 /Address
广州市林和西横路 215 号希尔顿酒店 2 层
2F, Hilton Hotel, No.215, Linhe West Side Road, Guangzhou

营业时间 Opening Hours
午餐 Lunch 11:30 – 14:30
晚餐 Dinner 18:00 – 22:00
着装要求 Dress Code
时尚休闲 Fashion Leisure
人均消费 Per Capita Consumption
250 元 250 RMB

意珍
Caffe Mondo

无限卡特权

意大利菜
Italian Cuisine

3.7 必应搜索热度 Search priority

电话 /Tel
+86 20 8883 3373

地址 /Address
广州市珠江西路 5 号
广州国际金融中心主塔楼四季酒店 72 层
72F, Four Seasons Hotel, Guangzhou International Finance Centre, No.5, Zhujiang West Road, Guangzhou

营业时间 Opening Hours
06:30 - 23:00
着装要求 Dress Code
无特别着装要求 Non-specified
人均消费 Per Capita Consumption
500 元 500 RMB

意珍餐厅坐拥一线珠江景致，内设高端江景贵宾包厢。宾客可于云端环顾花城，在美景环绕下享用精致美味的意式风味。餐厅始终坚持使用高标准的食材呈现原汁原味的意大利美食。

With the best Pearl River scenery, it sets several high-end river view VIP boxes. Diner will appreciate the Flower City from clouds and enjoy exquisite Italian flavors surrounded by beautiful scenery. This restaurant always devotes to presenting original Italian food with high standard ingredients.

意廬
Alfresco

无限卡特权

意大利菜
Italy Cuisine

8.8 必应搜索热度 Search priority

电话 /Tel
+86 20 8916 3388-6503

地址 /Address
广州市新港东路 638 号广州南丰朗豪酒店 4 层
4F, Langham Place Hotels Nanfeng Guangzhou, No.638, Xingang East Road, Guangzhou

营业时间 Opening Hours
18:00 - 22:00
着装要求 Dress Code
整齐休闲服 Neat Casual Wear
人均消费 Per Capita Consumption
330 元 330RMB

意廬餐厅的厨师以精湛的厨艺，在宽敞的开放式厨房呈献经典的意大利美馔。食客可品尝到各款时令海鲜、顶级肉排及特色美食，同时亦可于简约时尚、轻松雅致的氛围中享受畅快写意的用餐体验。

The chef of this restaurant presents classic Italian cuisine with masterful culinary arts in the spacious open kitchen. Diners can enjoy seasonal seafood, top-level steaks and featured dishes, as well as have a relaxed and enjoyable dining experience under such simple, fashionable, comfortable and elegant environment.

鱼鲜生海鲜放题（广州）
Mr.Fish(Guangzhou)

海鲜
Seafood

必应 搜索热度 Search priority 6.8

电话 /Tel
+86 20 8398 3311
+86 20 8398 3322

地址 /Address
广州市珠江新城花城大道 85 号
高德置地冬广场 5 层 507-512 铺
Shop 507-512, 5F, Gaode Zhidi Square, No.85, Huacheng Road, Zhujiang New Town, Guangzhou

营业时间 Opening Hours
18:00 – 22:00

着装要求 Dress Code
无特别着装要求 Non-specifiedl

人均消费 Per Capita Consumption
250 元 250 RMB

作为一家主营海鲜的餐厅，Mr.Fish 鱼鲜生始终坚信新鲜和优质的食材是菜式出品的保证。餐厅每日精选高品质以及高新鲜度的海鲜，在最大程度上保证食材的原汁原味，给食客带来难忘的美食享受。

As a restaurant specializing in seafood, it believes that the freshness and high-quality of ingredients are the guarantee of dishes. It selects the freshest and high quality seafood every day to ensure the original tastes and flavors of food materials and bring unforgettable delicacies to diners.

愉粤轩
Yu Yue Heen

无限卡特权

粤菜
Cantonese Cuisine

必应 搜索热度 Search priority 3.6

电话 /Tel
+86 20 8883 3371

地址 /Address
广州市珠江西路 5 号广州国际金融中心主塔楼
四季酒店 71 层
71F, Four Seasons Hotel, Guangzhou International Finance Centre, No.5, Zhujiang West Road, Guangzhou

营业时间 Opening Hours
午餐 Lunch 周一至周五 Mon – Fri.
11:00 – 14:30
周六及周日 Sat. – Sun. 10:00 – 14:30
晚餐 Dinner 17:30 – 22:00

着装要求 Dress Code
时尚休闲 Fashion leisure

人均消费 Per Capita Consumption
500 元 500 RMB

愉粤轩是一家正宗的粤菜餐厅。精致点心、特色粤菜不胜枚举，高级食材，时令海鲜，应有尽有。配合充满创意的精湛厨艺、心思灵巧的烹制手法，为食客呈献至臻完美的饕餮新体验，是用餐的理想场所。

As an authentic Cantonese cuisine restaurant, it provides delicate desserts, abundant featured Cantonese cuisine, high quality ingredients, and seasonal seafood. This restaurant is an ideal place for diners to enjoy a new glorious feast with its creative and exquisite cooking techniques.

玉堂春暖餐厅
Jade River

粤菜
Cantonese Cuisine

3.4 必应搜索热度
Search priority

电话 /Tel
+86 20 8188 6968

地址 /Address
广州市沙面南街 1 号白天鹅宾馆 3 层
3F, White Swan Hotel, No. 1, Shamian South Street, Guangzhou

营业时间 Opening Hours
周一至周五 Mon. – Fri.
11:30 – 15:00 17:30 – 22:00
周六及周日 Sat. – Sun.
08:00 – 15:00 17:30 – 22:00
着装要求 Dress Code
无特别着装要求 Non-specified
人均消费 Per Capita Consumption
350 元 350 RMB

玉堂春暖作为一家兼具格调与幽雅的广式餐厅，装修富贵却不失雅致，服务礼貌又不失亲切，没有过于繁复的菜品，却始终保持应有的水准。来到这里定要品尝羊城鲜虾饺、香茅乳鸽和酥皮叉烧包等招牌菜式。

It is a Cantonese cuisine restaurant with a combination of luxurious style and elegance, providing considerate and cordial services, as well as simple and high level dishes. Diners must try its signature dishes when coming here, such as Yangcheng Shrimp Dumplings, Lemongrass Pigeon and Crispy Barbecued Pork Buns.

郁金香中餐厅
Tulip

无限卡特权

中餐
Chinese Cuisine

6.3 必应搜索热度
Search priority

电话 /Tel
+86 20 3991 9666

地址 /Address
广州市万顷沙镇新垦 16 号
百万葵园之恋酒店 2 层
2F, Million Sunflowers Hotel, No.16, Xinken Road, Wanqingsha Town, Guangzhou

营业时间 Opening Hours
午餐 Lunch 11:30 – 14:00
晚餐 Dinner 18:00 – 21:00
着装要求 Dress Code
无特别着装要求 Non-specified
人均消费 Per Capita Consumption
200 元 200RMB

在百万葵园附近的郁金香中餐厅，吸引了许多慕名而来的食客。餐厅招牌菜为：咸香葵花鸡、绿豆酿莲藕、盐焗立鱼等。其中咸香葵花鸡是几乎每桌必点的名菜，鸡是从小吃葵花籽长大的，鸡肉爽滑，入口有韧性却不柴，让人回味无穷。

Located near the Sunflower Garden, it attracts numerous diners. Its signature dishes include: Salty Sunflower Chicken, Green Beans Stuffed Lotus Root, Salt Baked Tilapia, etc. Among them, the Salty Sunflower Chicken is a must-try dish for each table. The chicken has grown up by eating sunflower seeds; therefore, the chicken meat is smooth and flexible, which makes diners memorable.

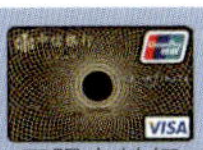

悦轩
Dining Room

意大利菜
Italian Cuisine

必应 搜索热度 Search priority 6.8

电话 /Tel
+86 20 3769 1234 - 7858

地址 /Address
广州市天河区珠江新城华夏路 16 号
No.16, Huaxia Road, Zhujiang New Town, Tianhe District, Guangzhou

营业时间 Opening Hours
早餐 Breakfast 06:30 - 10:30
午餐 Lunch 11:30 - 14:00
晚餐 Dinner 17:30 - 22:00
着装要求 Dress Code
优雅便服 / 商务正装
Smart Casual / Business Attire
人均消费 Per Capita Consumption
570 元 570 RMB

悦轩传递出异国料理的无限风情，尤其擅长地中海风味和意大利南部特色美食的制作。餐厅景观开阔，并有宽敞舒适的半私密式就餐空间，以及可容纳 12 位客人的 2 间包房。

Dining Room expresses a kind of borderless glamour by its exotic delicacies, especially the Mediterranean and Southern Italian specialties. With breathtaking views of the city, this all-day dining restaurant has cozy semi-private seating and 2 VIP rooms, each of which can seat 12 guests.

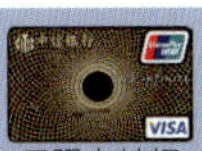

悦景轩
Yue Jing Xuan

粤菜
Cantonese Cuisine

必应 搜索热度 Search priority 3.1

电话 /Tel
+86 20 3769 1234

地址 /Address
广州市珠江新城华夏路 16 号
No. 16, Huaxia Road, Zhujiang New Town, Guangzhou

营业时间 Opening Hours
午餐 Lunch 11:30 - 14:00
晚餐 Dinner 17:30 - 22:00
着装要求 Dress Code
时尚休闲 Fashion Leisure
人均消费 Per Capita Consumption
600 元 600 RMB

悦景轩中餐厅深谙粤菜精髓并时常推陈出新，为食客精心设计各种专属的美味菜单。此外，餐厅不仅能俯瞰城市风光，宽敞的开放式厨房贯穿整个中餐厅，食客可观赏到精彩的厨艺表演，私享愉悦的用餐时光。

As a Chinese restaurant, it is familiar with the essence of Cantonese cuisine and constantly brings forth the new in order to provide well-designed and exclusive dishes to diners. In addition, this restaurant can not only overlook the city scenery, but also present a wonderful cooking show through the spacious open kitchen, so as to make diners enjoy a pleasant dining time.

御宝轩（天汇广场店）
Imperial Treasure(IGC)

粤菜
Cantonese Cuisine

6.7 必应搜索热度
Search priority

电话 /Tel
+86 20 3885 6382
+86 20 3885 6383

地址 /Address
广州市珠江新城兴民路 222 号天汇广场 L514B
L514B, IGC, No.222, Xingmin Road,
Zhujiang New Town, Guangzhou

营业时间 Opening Hours
午餐 Lunch 11:00 – 14:30
晚餐 Dinner 17:30 – 22:00
着装要求 Dress Code
商务休闲 Business Casual
人均消费 Per Capita Consumption
400 元 400 RMB

御宝轩中国风的装修，将餐厅环境打造得高雅且幽静。餐厅的服务也十分热情，能够及时满足食客的需要。来到御宝轩必点名菜：金网脆皮虾肠粉、女儿红蒸河鳗、白松露油西施虾球等。

It has an elegant and quiet environment with Chinese-style decoration, and provides warm and enthusiastic services to satisfy the needs of diners in time. Its famous must-try dishes are: Golden Crispy Shrimp Rice Roll, Nv'erhong Wine Steamed Eel and White Truffle Oil Shrimp Balls.

月色西餐厅（保利店）
Café Aqua(Baoli)

无限卡特权

东西美食
Eastern and Western Cuisine

2.7 必应搜索热度
Search priority

电话 /Tel
+86 20 2200 9999

地址 /Address
广州市黄埔区科学城揽月路 99 号
No. 99, Lanyue Road, Science City,
Huangpu District, Guangzhou

营业时间 Opening Hours
午餐 Lunch 11:30 – 14:00
晚餐 Dinner 17:30 – 21:00
着装要求 Dress Code
优雅便服 Smart Casual
人均消费 Per Capita Consumption
150 元 150 RMB

月色西餐厅以引人入胜的时尚风格、琳琅满目的饕餮美味，吸引着来自世界各地的食客。餐厅提供自助与零点服务，云集欧式、东南亚、日本、印度等各种风格的特色菜品。

Café Aqua has a unique appeal to the diners across the world by its fashionable style and abundant delicacies. Both buffet and a la carte are available here, and you can find a great variety of tasteful food from Europe, Southeast Asia, Japan and India.

月色西餐厅（增城保利店）
Café Aqua(Zengcheng Baoli)

无限卡特权

西餐
Western Cuisine

必应 搜索热度 Search priority 2.6

电话 /Tel
+86 20 3289 8888-6909

地址 /Address
广州市增城区新塘镇沿江大道 18 号
广州增城保利皇冠假日酒店
Crowne Plaza Guangzhou Zengcheng, No.18, Yanjiang Road, Xintang Town, Zengcheng District, Guangzhou

营业时间 Opening Hours
早餐 Breakfast 06:30 - 10:30
午餐 Lunch 12:00 - 14:30
晚餐 Dinner 18:00 - 21:00
着装要求 Dress Code
优雅便服 Smart Casual
人均消费 Per Capita Consumption
128 元 + 15% 服务费
128 RMB + 15% Service Fee

餐厅设计新颖别致，空间宽阔，荟萃世界美食与本地佳肴，提供美味丰盛的自助大餐。各式新鲜海鲜、美味热盘、精致甜点、缤纷水果等美食，全天候的服务，让食客大快朵颐，充分享受美妙的盛宴。

It has a modern design and spacious environment, collecting the delicacies across the world and local areas and providing delicious and abundant buffets. The fresh seafood, delicious hot dishes, exquisite desserts and various fruits bring diners a wonderful feast.

悦铂尼
Ebony

无限卡特权

西餐
Western Cuisine

必应 搜索热度 Search priority 9.0

电话 /Tel
+86 20 3808 8884

地址 /Address
广州市天河路 389 号广州文华东方酒店 4 层
4F, Mandarin Oriental Guangzhou, No.389, Tianhe Road, Guangzhou

营业时间 Opening Hours
早餐 Breakfast 06:30 - 10:30
午餐 Lunch 12:00 - 14:30
晚餐 Dinner 18:00 - 22:00
着装要求 Dress Code
商务休闲 Business Casual
人均消费 Per Capita Consumption
400 元 400 RMB

悦铂尼是一家时尚的半自助餐厅，以其上等牛排而著称。充满活力的餐厅供应半自助午餐及半自助晚餐，厨师们使用法式设计的火炉及玻璃幕墙备餐间，在开放式厨房中一展精湛技艺。是享用美食的理想去处。

It is a fashionable and semi-buffet restaurant known for its superior steaks. Half-buffet lunch and half-buffet dinner are served in a vibrant environment where chefs show their culinary arts with French-designed stoves in an open kitchen. It is a good place for enjoying delicacies.

云居
Kumoi

无限卡特权

日本料理
Japanese Cuisine

7.4 必应搜索热度
Search priority

电话 /Tel
+86 20 8883 3372

地址 /Address
广州市珠江西路 5 号
广州国际金融中心主塔楼四季酒店 72 层
72F, Four Seasons Hotel, Guangzhou International Finance Centre, No.5, Zhujiang West Road, Guangzhou

营业时间 Opening Hours
午餐 Lunch 11:30 – 14:30
晚餐 Dinner 17:30 – 22:30
（最迟点餐时间为 22:00）
着装要求 Dress Code
优雅便服 Smart Casual
人均消费 Per Capita Consumption
800 元 800 RMB

别具一格的云居提供刺身、寿司和铁板烧等一系列正宗和风料理，是一家正宗的日本料理餐厅。餐厅装潢玲珑雅致，温馨怡人，此外，在这里还可俯视繁华都市的美丽景致，分外惬意舒怀。

It is a stylish and authentic Japanese restaurant which offers a range of authentic Japanese cuisine including Sashimi, Sushi and Teppanyaki. It has exquisite decoration, warm and pleasant environment, and beautiful scenery of the bustling city from the top view, which will make diners cozy and comfortable.

深圳

SHENZHEN

1881
1881

无限卡特权

中餐
Chinese Cuisine

9.2 必应搜索热度
Search priority

电话 /Tel
+86 755 2218 7338

地址 /Address
深圳市宝安南路 1881 号君悦酒店 1 层
1F, Grand Hyatt Hotel, No.1881, Baoan South Road, Shenzhen

营业时间 Opening Hours
午餐 Lunch 11:00 – 14:00
晚餐 Dinner 17:00 – 22:00
着装要求 Dress Code
优雅便服 Smart Casual
人均消费 Per Capita Consumption
320 元 320 RMB

1881 餐厅提供地道的西北菜和四川菜，包括北京烤鸭、宫保虾球等。富有质感的内部装饰和充满艺术气息的灯饰，营造出餐厅生动、有活力的氛围，非常适合家庭或朋友聚会。享受美食的同时，搭配精选的红酒或白酒别有一番风味。

It mainly serves authentic Northwest Cuisine and Sichuan dishes, including Peking Duck and Kung Pao Prawns. The textured interior decoration and artistic lighting create a lively, vibrant atmosphere in this restaurant. It is suitable for family or friends gatherings. Diners can enjoy delicious food with selected red or white wines for different flavors.

1949 全鸭季
Duck de Chine by 1949

中餐
Chinese Cuisine

3.8 必应搜索热度
Search priority

电话 /Tel
4008 77 1949
+86 133 9218 1949

地址 /Address
深圳市南山区白石路东 8 号
欢乐海岸购物中心蓝楹坊 3 号
No.3, Lanyingfang, OPLAZA, No.8, Baishi Road East, Nanshan District, Shenzhen

营业时间 Opening Hours
午餐 Lunch 11:00 – 14:30
晚餐 Dinner 17:00 – 22:00
着装要求 Dress Code
优雅便服 Smart Casual
人均消费 Per Capita Consumption
500 元 500 RMB

深圳 1949 全鸭季融合了东方意境与西方餐饮精髓，以烤鸭配香槟就是一大亮点。餐厅招牌菜品自然是其屡获殊荣的烤鸭，餐厅也呈现出一系列融合了京、鲁、粤精选菜式的创新佳肴。

Duck de Chine by 1949 integrates the oriental glamour with Western cuisine essence, such as the innovative combination of Roast Duck with champagne. Its signature dish is doubtlessly the award-winning Roast Duck, and some creative dishes which are originated from Beijing cuisine, Shandong cuisine and Cantonese cuisine.

傲廬
Altitudes

自助餐
Buffet

必应 搜索热度 Search priority 6.0

电话 /Tel
+86 755 8271 8726

地址 /Address
深圳市益田路 5033 号
平安金融中心 117-118 层
117-118F, Pingan International Financial Center, No.5033, Yitian Road, Shenzhen

营业时间 Opening Hours
11:30 - 23:30
着装要求 Dress Code
时尚休闲 Fashion Leisure
人均消费 Per Capita Consumption
400 元 400 RMB

廬位于平安金融中心 117 层，不仅坐拥无敌风景，能 360 度俯瞰深圳全貌，而且
十私密，适合朋友聚会、商务谈判、私人派对等。在这里，你可以尽情释放味蕾神经，
金精致的自助午餐和下午茶，感受温馨的用餐氛围。

cated at the 117th floor of Ping'an International Financial Center, it not only
s unparalleled scenery and can overlook the whole picture of Shenzhen
360 degrees, but also has privacy designs which is suitable for friends
therings, business negotiations and private parties. Here diners can enjoy
citing delicacies such as exquisite buffet lunch and refined afternoon tea,
d feel the warm dining atmosphere at the same time.

碧桃时尚餐厅
Better Fashion Restaurant

创意菜
Creative Cuisine

必应 搜索热度 Search priority 2.6

电话 /Tel
+86 755 8268 6865

地址 /Address
深圳市罗湖区人民南路金光华广场 6 层
6F, King Glory Plaza, Renmin South Road, Luohu District, Shenzhen

营业时间 Opening Hours
11:00 - 22:00
着装要求 Dress Code
优雅便服 Smart Casual
人均消费 Per Capita Consumption
120 元 120 RMB

整体风格带有几分童话色彩的碧桃时尚餐厅，不仅在空间设计上颇具颠覆性，在菜式设计上同样新意十足。其创新融合菜系包括新派粤菜、公馆湘菜、精致杭帮菜，以及时尚下午茶。

Better Fashion Restaurant gives a fairy tale touch to its entire style, which is really an overthrow in both its interior and dish design. Its creative cuisine blends with new Cantonese, Mansion Hunan and refined Hangzhou dishes as well as trendy high-tea.

二十二象泰国餐厅
Soi 22

无限卡特权

泰国菜
Thai Cuisine

3.6 必应搜索热度 Search priority

电话 /Tel
+86 755 8891 4337

地址 /Address
深圳市海田路 32 号
No.32, Haitian Road, Shenzhen

营业时间 Opening Hours
周一至周五 Mon. - Fri.
11:30 - 14:00 17:30 - 22:00
周六、周日 Sat. - Sun. 11:30 - 22:00
着装要求 Dress Code
无特别着装要求 Non-specified
人均消费 Per Capita Consumption
120 元 120 RMB

二十二象是一家主营泰国菜的餐厅，整体环境简约明快，颇得年轻人的欢心，是个探寻东南亚美食的好去处。在菜品方面，餐厅的糯米芒果饭、传统冬阴功和咖喱皇大虾是不得不尝的美味。

It is a restaurant specializing in Thai cuisine. The overall environment is simple and lively, which is quite popular among young diners. It is a good place to explore Southeast Asian cuisine. In terms of dishes, this restaurant has some must-try dishes, such as Mango Sticky Rice, Traditional Tom Yum Kung and Curry King Prawns.

馥餐厅
FOO Restaurant

无限卡特权

自助餐
Buffet

3.7 必应搜索热度 Search priority

电话 /Tel
+86 755 8826 8700
+86 755 8826 8632

地址 /Address
深圳市福田区福华三路 138 号
四季酒店 6 层
6F, Four Seasons Hotel, No.138, Third Fuhua Road, Futian District, Shenzhen

营业时间 Opening Hours
早餐 Breakfast 06:30 - 10:30
午餐 Lunch 12:00 - 14:30
晚餐 Dinner 18:00 - 23:00
着装要求 Dress Code
优雅便服 Smart Casual
人均消费 Per Capita Consumption
418 元 + 15%服务费
418 RMB + 15%Service Fee

馥餐厅，顾名思义，汇聚了美食的馥郁芬芳。无论是在室内低调奢华、极具品位的环境用餐，还是在户外的餐桌旁边欣赏水景边品尝美食，餐厅独特的多元化空间都能满足客人的不同需求。

FOO Restaurant, as its name, gathers appealing scents from delicacies. Thanks to its diverse seating layout, the diners' different demands can be well satisfied, from the tasteful and exquisite indoor environment to the water-view outdoor tables.

观海酒家（山顶店）
Guan Hai(Shanding)

中餐
Chinese Cuisine

必应 搜索热度 Search priority 2.6

电话 /Tel
+86 755 2683 7999
+86 755 2685 7999

地址 /Address
深圳市观海路 1 号
No.1, Guanhai Road, Shenzhen

营业时间 Opening Hours
11:00-22:30
着装要求 Dress Code
时尚休闲 Fashion Leisure
人均消费 Per Capita Consumption
350 元 350 RMB

观海酒家始终致力于还原食材的原味，并给食客带去优质的菜品。餐厅拥有绝佳景观，食客可边享受美食边欣赏山顶的景致。其中，餐厅的两大皇牌菜分别为观海片片鸭和麻辣虾蛄肉。

This restaurant has always committed to restoring the original flavors of ingredients and brought high-quality dishes to diners. With a wonderful landscape, diners can enjoy delicacies while appreciating the scenery from the summit. In terms of dishes, the "Sea View Duck Slices" and "Spicy Squillid Meat" are signature dishes.

花舞印象
Art by team Lab

日本料理
Japanese Cuisine

必应 搜索热度 Search priority 3.8

电话 /Tel
+86 755 2641 9016

地址 /Address
深圳市香山东街华侨城
文化创意园北区 B1 栋 101 室
Room 101, Building B1, North Zone, OCT-LOFT, Xiangshan East Street, Shenzhen

营业时间 Opening Hours
午餐 Lunch 12:00 - 14:00
晚餐 Dinner 19:30 - 21:30
着装要求 Dress Code
商务休闲 Business Casual
人均消费 Per Capita Consumption
2300 元 2300 RMB

花舞印象餐厅致力于强化现代人与食物的直接接触，以数字影像艺术互动连接食物、自然和未来。餐厅精选全球优质食材，精心诚意烹饪，每一道菜品都被打造成可以入口的艺术品。

This restaurant is dedicated to strengthening the direct contact between modern people and food, and connecting the food, nature and future with digital video art. It selects high-quality ingredients all over the world, and carefully makes each dish an edible artwork.

蚝门九式（海上世界店）
Oyster King(Sea World)

无限卡特权

潮汕菜
Chaoshan Cuisine

3.3 必应搜索热度 Search priority

电话 /Tel
+86 755 8827 7466

地址 /Address
深圳市南山区蛇口海上世界船前广场 C-204
C-204, Front Square, Shekou Sea World, Nanshan District, Shenzhen

营业时间 Opening Hours
午餐 Lunch 11:30 – 14:00
晚餐 Dinner 17:30 – 22:30
着装要求 Dress Code
优雅便服 Smart Casual
人均消费 Per Capita Consumption
120 元 120 RMB

蚝门九式海上世界店把地方美食上升为一种对文化的追求。餐厅引进世界各地多种高端进口生蚝，并将经典蚝门九式与日式刺身、国际顶级葡萄酒结合，是生蚝爱好者的天堂。

Oyster King has elevated the local cooking to a culture pursuit, importing various top oysters from all over the world and presenting in the classic Oyster King way. Oyster and Sashimi with a sip of world-class wine constitute a heaven for oyster-lovers.

虎喰烧肉 · 酒场（购物公园店）
Hu Can(Shopping Mall)

烧烤
Barbecue

2.6 必应搜索热度 Search priority

电话 /Tel
+86 755 2394 0521

地址 /Address
深圳市购物公园北园 B 区 1 区
Zone 1, Area B, Shopping Mall North Zone, Shenzhen

营业时间 Opening Hours
11:30–23:30
着装要求 Dress Code
无特别着装要求 Non-specified
人均消费 Per Capita Consumption
350 元 350 RMB

虎喰烧肉 · 酒场餐厅秉持着“大口吃肉、大口喝酒”的理念，精心挑选澳洲进口的各部位牛肉及内脏，坚持手工切肉，并以炭火铜网无烟烧烤的方式呈现。这是一个放肆吃喝、轻松享受，将一切美好收进眼里的好去处。

Upholding the concept of "Drink liquor with big bowl, and eat big piece meat", it carefully selects all parts of beef and guts imported from Australia, and barbecues the meat through charcoal fire and brass wire mesh after cutting manually. It is a good place to eat, drink, relax and enjoy all good things.

江户前怀石料理（华侨城店）
Rdomae Kaiseki(OCT-LOFT)

日本料理
Japanese Cuisine

必应 搜索热度 Search priority 2.6

电话 /Tel
+86 755 8670 9699

地址 /Address
深圳市开平街华侨城创意园 F1-102
F1-102, OCT-LOFT, Kaiping Street, Shenzhen

营业时间 Opening Hours
午餐 Lunch 11:30 – 14:00
晚餐 Dinner 17:30 – 22:00
着装要求 Dress Code
时尚休闲 Fashion Leisure
人均消费 Per Capita Consumption
1000 元 1000 RMB

江户前怀石料理严选食材、追求本味，为食客提供纯正的日本料理。餐厅打破传统怀石上菜流程，只为更加适应国人的饮食习惯，将所有菜品盛于京瓷美器之中，以怡人的就餐格调征服了食客。

It strictly selects ingredients, pursues the original flavors and provides diners with authentic Japanese cuisine. This restaurant breaks traditional serving process of Kaiseki to better adapt to the dietary habits of Chinese people, and presents all dishes in beautiful porcelain ware to make diners pleasant during eating, which has won affection of numerous diners.

无限卡特权

爵廊
Duke's

西餐
Western Cuisine

必应 搜索热度 Search priority 6.1

电话 /Tel
+86 755 8828 9888-8922

地址 /Address
深圳市福田区深南大道 7888 号
No.7888, Shennan Road, Futian District, Shenzhen

营业时间 Opening Hours
周日至周四 Sun. – Thur. 18:00 – 01:00
周五及周六 Fri. – Sat. 18:00 – 02:00
着装要求 Dress Code
优雅便服 Smart Casual
人均消费 Per Capita Consumption
600 ~ 700 元 600 ~ 700 RMB

位于深圳东海朗廷酒店 3 层的爵廊餐厅，有着精致的欧陆式美馔和深圳规模最大的私藏酒窖，令人心生向往。餐厅陈列有大量现代艺术品，使其尽展欧式经典高端餐厅气息。

At 3F of the Langham, Shenzhen, Duke's offers exquisite Continental delicacies and owns the largest private wine cellar in Shenzhen. A great many contemporary artworks are displayed, creating a high-end European dining atmosphere.

老干杯（平安金融中心店）
Kanpai Classic(Ping'an Financial Center)

烧烤
Broil

6.5 必应搜索热度
Search priority

电话 /Tel
+86 755 6182 2987
+86 138 2324 9884

地址 /Address
深圳市益田路 5033 号
No.5033, Yitian Road, Shenzhen

营业时间 Opening Hours
午餐 Lunch 11:30 – 15:00
晚餐 Dinner 17:00 – 24:00
着装要求 Dress Code
时尚休闲 Fashion Leisure
人均消费 Per Capita Consumption
750 元 750 RMB

老干杯作为当地最受欢迎的烤肉店，不仅环境时尚，充满了现代气息，而且各类
质也是颇受好评。来到这里，一定要品尝招牌菜品：澳洲和牛 5 种烧肉组合、现
纽约客牛排、牛舌，以及北极贝奶油釜饭。

As the most popular local barbecue restaurant, it not only is fashionable a
modern, but also has a good reputation for its various superior meats. T
must-try signature dishes here include: 5 combinations of Australian Wag
Fresh-cut New Yorker Steak, Beef Tongue, and Geoduck Creamed Rice.

利宝阁
Libao Ge

粤菜
Cantonese Cuisine

4.0 必应搜索热度
Search priority

电话 /Tel
+86 755 8383 1666

地址 /Address
深圳市福田区中心四路嘉里建设广场 3 座 2 层
2F, Building 3, Kerry Plaza Tower, Fourth
Zhongxin Road, Futian District, Shenzhen

营业时间 Opening Hours
午餐 Lunch 10:30 – 15:00
（节假日 Holidays 09:30 – 15:00）
晚餐 Dinner 17:00 – 22:00
着装要求 Dress Code
优雅便服 Smart Casual
人均消费 Per Capita Consumption
300 ~ 500 元 300 ~ 500 RMB

源自香港的老牌粤菜餐厅利宝阁，深圳店同样口碑极佳。餐厅环境优雅别致，主
打高级粤菜，主张保留食材的原汁原味和天然营养成分。厨师选料上乘，烹制
巧高超，菜肴口味出众。

This old-brand Cantonese restaurant roots in Hong Kong and shares the sam
popularity as the same one in Hong Kong. With a chic space, the restaura
features high-end Cantonese cuisine and stays true to the original flavor an
natural nutrition of the ingredients. Superior ingredients are chosen by chefs wi
the addition of their unique cooking skills, the dishes here are really tasty.

里外
Inout

粤菜
Cantonese Cuisine

必应 搜索热度 Search priority **6.5**

电话 /Tel
+86 755 8221 1288

地址 /Address
深圳市南山区蛇口海上世界船尾广场
B 区 1 层 109-110 铺
Shop 109-110, 1F, Zone B, Chuanwei Square, Shekou Sea World, Nanshan District, Shenzhen

营业时间 Opening Hours
午餐 Lunch 11:00 – 14:00
晚餐 Dinner 17:00 – 22:00
着装要求 Dress Code
优雅便服 Smart Casual
人均消费 Per Capita Consumption
150 元 150 RMB

里外餐厅为顾客提供精致的粤菜、甜品和精选饮品，是一家专注地道粤厨美食与西点融合的概念餐厅。餐厅的设计围绕工业时代的印迹展开，颇具LOFT风格。

Inout is a fusion concept restaurant offering authentic Cantonese cuisine, western desserts and superior drinks. Inspired by Industrial Age, Inout is quite at LOFT style.

无限卡特权

Paletto 意大利餐厅
Paletto

意大利菜
Italian Cuisine

必应 搜索热度 Search priority **4.9**

电话 /Tel
+86 755 2222 2222

地址 /Address
深圳市福田区福华三路 116 号
深圳星河丽思卡尔顿酒店 2 层
2F, Ritz-Carlton Shenzhen, No.116, Third Fuhua Road, Futian District, Shenzhen

营业时间 Opening Hours
午餐 Lunch 12:00 – 14:30
晚餐 Dinner 17:30 – 22:00
着装要求 Dress Code
优雅便服 Smart Casual
人均消费 Per Capita Consumption
780 ~ 1680 元 780 ~ 1680 RMB

餐厅秉承原汁原味的意式烹饪技法，包括丰富的开胃前菜、风味浓郁的意大利面、现烤海鲜、牛排、经典甜品提拉米苏等。

Paletto stays true to the Italian culinary method and offers diverse appetizers, tasty Italian pasta, freshly-grill seafood, steaks and classic desserts such as Tiramisu.

莆田（平安金融中心店）
PuTien(Ping'an Financial Center)

福建菜
Fujian Cuisine

6.8 必应搜索热度
Search priority

电话 /Tel
+86 755 8323 5006

地址 /Address
深圳市益田路 5033 号 6 层 N603-a 号
No.N603-a, 6F, No.5033, Yitian Road, Shenzhen

营业时间 Opening Hours
午餐 Lunch 周一至周五 Mon. - Fri.
11:30 - 14:30
周六、周日 Sat. - Sun. 11:00 - 14:30
晚餐 Dinner 周一至周五 Mon. - Fri.
17:30 - 22:00
周六、周日 Sat. - Sun. 17:00 - 21:30
着装要求 Dress Code
优雅便服 Smart Casual
人均消费 Per Capita Consumption
150 ~ 200 元 150 ~ 200 RMB

作为一家在海内外拥有多家连锁店的知名餐饮品牌，莆田极其重视餐厅环境的营造，餐厅团队倾心设计室内环境布局，只为让食客获得满意的用餐体验。来到莆田餐厅，一定要尝试店内的九转小肠、酥炒芋头、芋香鸭等精美佳肴。

As a well-known restaurant brand with many chain stores both at home and abroad, it focuses on the construction of restaurant environment which is carefully designed by the restaurant team, so as to provide diners with a satisfactory dining experience. When coming to this restaurant, diners must try its delicacies, such as Braised Intestines in Brown Sauce, Crispy Fried Taro and Taro Duck.

鮨一日本料理
Sushi Yi Qi

日本料理
Japanese Cuisine

2.6 必应搜索热度
Search priority

电话 /Tel
+86 755 8322 9857
+86 135 2889 5843

地址 /Address
深圳市深南路大中华国际金融中心 C 座 1 层
1F, Building C, International Finance Centre, Shennan Road, Shenzhen

营业时间 Opening Hours
午餐 Lunch 11:30 - 14:00
晚餐 Dinner 17:30 - 22:00
着装要求 Dress Code
商务休闲 Business Casual
人均消费 Per Capita Consumption
1500 元 1500 RMB

鮨一日本料理自开业以来就受到无数食客老饕的喜爱。店内拥有正宗的日式环境与装修，采用无菜单料理形式，厨师根据应季食材挑选并制作前菜、刺身、料理、碗汁、甜品等餐品，以保证菜品的最大新鲜度。

This restaurant has been favored by countless customers and diners since its opening. It has an original Japanese-style environment and decoration, and provides cuisine in a non-menu form. Chefs select seasonal ingredients to produce appetizer, sashimi, dish, juice, desserts and other dishes so as to ensure the maximum freshness of dishes.

无限卡特权

鮨青岚
Aoarashi

日本料理
Japanese Cuisine

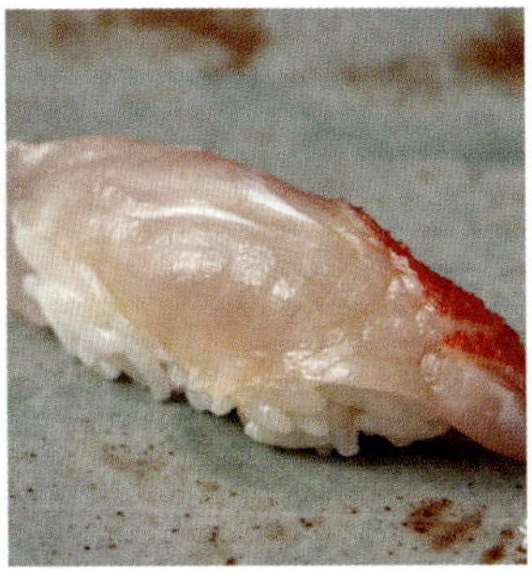

必应 搜索热度 Search priority 2.7

电话 /Tel
+86 135 1058 8866

地址 /Address
深圳市福华一路大中华喜来登酒店东翼 2 层
2F, Sheraton Shenzhen Futian Hotel, East Wing, First Fuhua Road, Shenzhen

营业时间 Opening Hours
午餐 Lunch 10:00 – 14:00
晚餐 Dinner 18:00 – 22:00
着装要求 Dress Code
商务休闲 Business Casual
人均消费 Per Capita Consumption
1800 元 1800 RMB

不出深圳也可以吃到水平高超的怀石料理，鮨青岚就是这样一家拥有纯正日式风格的日本料理店。餐厅的装修风格全部精心设计而成，所有的餐具均为日本进口。从食材的选用到上菜的顺序，都十分讲究。

It is a pure Japanese-style restaurant providing authentic Japanese cuisine, bringing diners to enjoy high-level Kaiseki in Shenzhen. This restaurant has a meticulously designed decoration with all tableware imported from Japan. Its material selection and sequence of service are also fastidious.

晴空
Seiku

日本料理
Japanese Cuisine

必应 搜索热度 Search priority 9.8

电话 /Tel
+86 755 2690 7826

地址 /Address
深圳市粤海街道科苑南路 2888 号
深圳湾万象城 L413
L413, MIXC, No.2888, Keyuan South Road, Yuehai Street, Shenzhen

营业时间 Opening Hours
午餐 Lunch 12:00 – 14:00
晚餐 Dinner 18:00 – 22:00
着装要求 Dress Code
优雅便服 Smart Casual
人均消费 Per Capita Consumption
2200 元 2200 RMB

晴空日本料理餐厅始终致力于为食客展现更好的怀石料理，晴空的主厨都以当季最优秀的食材为食客定制菜单，不设单点。餐厅菜品新鲜美味且富有创意，叠加层次丰富的食材，让各种味道逐层打开食客的味蕾。

It is always committed to providing the best Kaiseki to diners. Chefs select the best seasonal ingredients to customize the menu for diners without a la carte. Its dishes are fresh, delicious and creative with rich layers of ingredients superimposed, opening the diners' taste buds layer-by-layer.

寿司大（宝安店）
Sushi Da(Baoan)

日本料理
Japanese Cuisine

4.1 必应搜索热度 Search priority

电话 /Tel
+86 755 2349 0789

地址 /Address
深圳市海秀路熙龙湾一期 5-110 号
No.5-110, Phase I, Xilongwan, Haixiu Road, Shenzhen

营业时间 Opening Hours
午餐 Lunch 11:30 - 14:00
晚餐 Dinner 17:30 - 22:00
着装要求 Dress Code
优雅便服 Smart Casual
人均消费 Per Capita Consumption
350 元 350 RMB

寿司大环境幽静私密，所有食材均搜罗自日本北海道、长崎、鹿儿岛等地。宛若凝脂的珍珠米饭，色彩艳丽的各类鱼生，恰到好处的捏制弧度，显示出食物的原味，让食客在品尝时有惊艳之感。

With quiet and private environment, it selects all ingredients from Hokkaido, Nagasaki, kagoshima and other places. The rice like a creamy pearl with colorful raw fish under appropriate molding gives the original tastes of food, and surprises diners after eating.

四叶寿司
Sushi Yotsuba

日本料理
Japanese Cuisine

3.8 必应搜索热度 Search priority

电话 /Tel
+86 755 8966 7866

地址 /Address
深圳市南山区深南大道 9001-1 号
No.9001-1, Shennan Road, Nanshan District, Shenzhen

营业时间 Opening Hours
午餐 Lunch 11:30 - 14:00
晚餐 Dinner 17:30 - 22:00
着装要求 Dress Code
优雅便服 / 商务正装
Smart Casual/Business Attire
人均消费 Per Capita Consumption
800 元 800 RMB

四叶寿司餐厅秉持将日本传统寿司带到中国的质朴信念，从原材料、制作方法到店内设计、服务理念，均保持日本正统高端寿司店的本真特色。

With the pure faith of bringing Japanese conventional sushi to China, Sushi Yotsuba always maintains the typical feature of an authentic and premium Japanese sushi restaurant in ingredients selection, culinary art, interior design and service philosophy.

无限卡特权

唐阁
T'ang Court

粤菜
Cantonese Cuisine

必应 搜索热度 Search priority **5.3**

电话 /Tel
+86 755 8828 9888-8923

地址 /Address
深圳市深南大道 7888 号
深圳东海朗廷酒店 3 层
3F, The Langham Shenzhen, No.7888, Shennan Road, Shenzhen

营业时间 Opening Hours
午餐 Lunch 11:30 - 14:30
晚餐 Dinner 17:30 - 22:00
着装要求 Dress Code
优雅便服 Smart Casual
人均消费 Per Capita Consumption
731 元 731 RMB

唐阁餐厅进驻深圳朗廷酒店，以其时尚的格调、华丽高雅的装潢与精心炮制的正宗地道粤菜互相辉映，将一贯贴心周到的服务与地道佳肴带到这个活力之都。唐阁将新派创意与传统中餐巧妙融合，为宾客呈献令人耳目一新的正宗地道粤菜。

Located at Langham Hotel Shenzhen, it brings the fashionable, gorgeous and elegant decoration, elaborately cooked authentic Cantonese cuisine, and considerate services to this vibrant city. It skillfully combines new ideas with Chinese traditional dishes to provide refreshing authentic Cantonese cuisine to diners.

王品牛排（益田假日广场店）
Wang Steak(Yitian Holiday Plaza)

西餐
Western Cuisine

必应 搜索热度 Search priority **4.5**

电话 /Tel
+86 755 8629 8729

地址 /Address
深圳市深南大道 9028 号益田假日广场 3 层
3F, Yitian Holiday Plaza, No.9028, Shennan Road, Shenzhen

营业时间 Opening Hours
午餐 Lunch 11:30 - 14:00
晚餐 Dinner 17:30 - 21:00
着装要求 Dress Code
优雅便服 Smart Casual
人均消费 Per Capita Consumption
395 元 395 RMB

王品牛排以“一头牛仅供六客”的特色台塑牛排为大家熟知，用数十种中西香料腌浸两天两夜，高温烘烤一个半小时，全熟且鲜嫩多汁。王品以精美的菜色、优雅的环境和贴心的服务，打造高端餐饮体验。

Upholding the concepts of "one cow can only serve six diners", the well-known featured Wang Steak is marinated with dozens of Chinese and Western spices for 2 days and 2 nights, and then baked at high temperature for one and a half hours, which is well-done, tender and juicy. This restaurant creates high-end dining experience with exquisite dishes, elegant environment and considerate services.

万豪中餐厅
Man Ho Chinese Restaurant

无限卡特权

粤菜
Cantonese Cuisine

4.2 必应搜索热度
Search priority

电话 /Tel
+86 755 2269 8200

地址 /Address
深圳市深南大道 6005 号
金茂 JW 万豪酒店 2 层
2F, JW Marriott Hotel Shenzhen, No.6005, Shennan Road, Shenzhen

营业时间 Opening Hours
午餐 Lunch 11:00 - 14:00
晚餐 Dinner 17:00 - 22:30
着装要求 Dress Code
优雅便服 Smart Casual
人均消费 Per Capita Consumption
220 元 220 RMB

万豪中餐厅位于酒店 2 层，装修风格典雅，却又处处体现着简约的时尚元素。用餐区域被充满浓郁中国风情的镂空图纹屏风分隔成几个错落有致的空间，配以前卫灯具的点缀。这里是家宴、公司聚餐、商务宴请的优选场所。

Located at the second floor of the Hotel, it has an elegant decoration with simple and fashion elements everywhere. The dining area is divided into several well-proportioned spaces by Chinese-style hollow graph screens, matching with modern lamps and lanterns. It is the best place for family feasts, company dinners, business banquets, etc.

梧桐 Plus(万象城店)
Wish Plus(MIXC)

无限卡特权

中餐
Chinese Cuisine

2.9 必应搜索热度
Search priority

电话 /Tel
+86 755 8669 1686
+86 755 8665 1686

地址 /Address
深圳市宝安南路 1881 号万象城华润大厦 3 层
3F, MIXC Huarun Building, No.1881, Baoan South Road, Shenzhen

营业时间 Opening Hours
周一至周五 Mon. - Fri.
11:00 - 14:30 17:00 - 22:00
周六、周日 Sat. - Sun. 11:00 - 22:00
着装要求 Dress Code
优雅便服 Smart Casual
人均消费 Per Capita Consumption
390 元 390 RMB

幽雅的餐厅设计，为美食增添了自然的意境。这里出品中西合璧创意菜，听名字很普通，但端上来却总能给你惊喜。梧桐能将巧妙的摆盘设计注入到菜品中，即便是再经典的菜式，也能带给你意外惊喜。

It has an elegant environment with a natural artistic atmosphere. Here provides creative cuisine combined Chinese and Western dishes, which sound ordinary but will surprise diners when appear. This restaurant presents classic dishes innovatively to bring surprise to diners.

无限卡特权

粤菜
Cantonese Cuisine

香乐园
Shang Garde

必应 搜索热度 Search priority 3.9

电话 /Tel
+86 755 2151 3838

地址 /Address
深圳市福田区益田路 4088 号
深圳福田香格里拉大酒店 1 层
1F, Futian Shangri-La Hotel, No.4088, Yitian Road, Futian District, Shenzhen

营业时间 Opening Hours
午餐 Lunch 11:30 - 14:30
晚餐 Dinner 17:30 - 22:30
着装要求 Dress Code
优雅便服 Smart Casual
人均消费 Per Capita Consumption
150 ~ 200 元 150 ~ 200 RMB

香乐园旨在以口味纯正的菜品、亲切友善的服务、超值的定价和雅致的氛围为宾客打造轻松闲适的欧洲 Bistro（当地菜，风味小馆）概念餐厅。这里拥有一个可供 80 位宾客就餐的大厅，及 6 间共可容纳 58 位宾客的典雅包间。
As a restaurant with the leisure European Bistro concept, it provides authentic cuisine, considerate service and affordable price with elegant atmosphere. The dining area has 80 seats and 6 VIP rooms which can accommodate 58 diners.

法国菜 浙江菜
French Cuisine and Zhejiang Cuisine

香舍会
Belle Époque

必应 搜索热度 Search priority 7.8

电话 /Tel
+86 755 8608 8278

地址 /Address
深圳市南山区华侨城天鹅堡会所
Swan Castle Club, OCT, Nanshan District, Shenzhen

营业时间 Opening Hours
午餐 Lunch 11:00 - 14:30
晚餐 Dinner 17:30 - 22:30
着装要求 Dress Code
优雅便服 Smart Casual
人均消费 Per Capita Consumption
200 元 200 RMB

由香港名厨主理的中、西式美食值得一试。西式名菜包括香煎法式鹅肝、烤澳洲和牛肋骨伴红酒烩牛胸腺等；中式菜品有龙皇西施泡鸳鸯饭、黄金小米烩辽参等。
The famous Hong Kong chef brings in both eastern and western delicacies including Fried Foie Gras, Grilled Australian Wagyu Beef Rib with Red Wine Braised Beef Thymus, Egg White and Seafood in Rice Soup as well as Braised Liao Sea Cucumber in Millet Soup.

乡约音乐美食餐厅
Xiang Yue Music Restaurant

湘菜
Hunan Cuisine

2.6 必应搜索热度
Search priority

电话 /Tel
+86 755 2844 5522

地址 /Address
深圳市龙岗区坂田贝尔路
本丰商务酒店 1 层停车场院内
Parking Lot, 1F, Benfeng Business Hotel, Bantian Beier Road, Longgang District, Shenzhen

营业时间 Opening Hours
午餐 Lunch 11:00 – 14:30
晚餐 Dinner 17:30 – 23:00
着装要求 Dress Code
优雅便服 Smart Casual
人均消费 Per Capita Consumption
150 元 150 RMB

餐厅致力于让就餐者得到高品质而又健康的美食体验，所有食材均为绿色无污染，来自湖南常德的大厨以拿手的常德特色菜等经典湖南美味，让喜爱美食与音乐的人们在这里得到双重满足。

The restaurant dedicates to providing high-quality and healthy delicacies for every diner with green and pollution-free food materials. The chef from Changde brings in authentic regional flavors. It is a good place for those who love gourmets and music.

新粤
Xinyue Restaurant

中餐
Chinese Cuisine

2.7 必应搜索热度
Search priority

电话 /Tel
+86 755 2587 0699

地址 /Address
深圳市福田区东园路滨江新村 53 号
No.53, Binjiang New Town, Dongyuan Road, Futian District, Shenzhen

营业时间 Opening Hours
午餐 Lunch 11:00 – 14:00
晚餐 Dinner 17:00 – 21:30
着装要求 Dress Code
优雅便服 Smart Casual
人均消费 Per Capita Consumption
51 元 51 RMB

新粤餐厅坚持回归传统的中式烹调方式，对食物进行精细处理后，再采用传统中式烹调手法，将新疆菜与南方的饮食习惯相结合，形成了兼容并包的独特风格。

Xinyue Restaurant stays true to the traditional Chinese culinary methods after the elaborate treatment to ingredients. Combining Xinjiang cuisine with southern dietary customs, this restaurant forms a unique eclectic style.

秀 · 自助餐厅
Silk

无限卡特权

中西美馔和自助餐
Chinese and Western dishes and buffets

必应 搜索热度 Search priority 8.9

电话 /Tel
+86 755 8828 9888 ext.8921

地址 /Address
深圳市福田区深南大道 7888 号
深圳东海朗廷酒店 2 层
2F, The Langham Shenzhen, No.7888, Shennan Road, Futian District, Shenzhen

秀 · 自助餐厅装潢时尚，秉承朗廷一贯的挚诚服务，供应泛亚风味佳肴和中西特色美馔。秀 · 自助餐厅汇聚环球新鲜海鲜，从寿司、三文鱼、贝类到大虾，一应俱全。更备有单点菜单，由专业餐饮团队主理，为食客缔造一场味觉飨宴。
Following the sincere serves of Langham, it has a fashionable decoration and serves Pan-Asian delicacies and food with Chinese and Western characteristics. It provides all kinds of fresh seafood from around the world, such as sushi, salmon, shellfish and prawns. It also has a la carte menu, which is produced by a professional catering team to create a delicious feast for diners.

营业时间 Opening Hours
周一至周六 Mon. - Sat. 06:30-23:00
着装要求 Dress Code
优雅便服 Smart Casual
人均消费 Per Capita Consumption
560 元 560 RMB

秀餐厅
Social

无限卡特权

西餐
Western Cuisine

必应 搜索热度 Search priority 8.9

电话 /Tel
+86 755 8828 9888-8921

地址 /Address
深圳市深南东路 5016 号
京基 100 大厦 A 座瑞吉酒店 95 层
95F, St. Regis Hotel, Building A, KK 100, No. 5016, Shennan East Road, Shenzhen

简洁明快的线条和温暖宜人的灰褐色色调，使得秀餐厅的环境十分温馨。餐厅采用开放式厨房，可向食客展示烹饪技艺，还可为食客精心制作包括著名海鲜菜品和特色国际自助餐在内的可口美食。
The simple and lively decoration with warm and pleasant taupe tone makes its environment comfortable and cozy. It features an open kitchen to show culinary skills to diners, and cooks carefully selected ingredients for diners, including famous seafood products and international buffets.

营业时间 Opening Hours
午餐 Lunch 12:00 - 14:30
晚餐 Dinner 18:00 - 21:30
着装要求 Dress Code
时尚休闲 Fashion Leisure
人均消费 Per Capita Consumption
326 元 326 RMB

逸谷
Perch

西餐
Western Cuisine

7.8 必应搜索热度
Search priority

电话 /Tel
+86 755 8828 9888

地址 /Address
深圳市深南大道 7888 号东海缤纷天地 3 层
3F, East China Sea, No.7888, Shennan Road, Shenzhen

营业时间 Opening Hours
17:00 - 01:00
着装要求 Dress Code
优雅便服 Smart Casual
人均消费 Per Capita Consumption
344 元 344 RMB

餐厅拥有闲适的露天环境，仿佛林立高楼之间的清心之谷，有宽敞的沙发区以及休闲的藤椅区。舒适的环境当然要搭配美味的菜品，店内除了外焦里嫩的牛排，还有海鲜拼盘、地中海吞拿鱼沙拉、鲜尝鱼子酱等可供选择。
It has a leisure and comfortable open environment with capacious sofa area and recreational cane chairs area, like a refreshing valley between tall buildings. In addition to comfortable environment, there are many delicious dishes for selection, such as tender steak, seafood platter, Mediterranean tuna fish salad, and fresh caviar.

印象清迈
Chiengmai Impression

泰国菜
Thai Cuisine

2.6 必应搜索热度
Search priority

电话 /Tel
+86 755 8882 8211

地址 /Address
深圳市南山区海岸城东座 1 层
162-164 号
No.162-164, 1F, East Building, Costal City, Nanshan District, Shenzhen

营业时间 Opening Hours
午餐 Lunch 11:00 – 17:00
晚餐 Dinner 17:00 – 22:00
着装要求 Dress Code
优雅便服 Smart Casual
人均消费 Per Capita Consumption
120 元 120 RMB

印象清迈餐厅的食物在口味上具备了独特的异香，所用调料不但符合健康科学的饮食原则，同时也具备很好的排毒、降血脂、美容等保健功能。
Chiengmai Impression's dishes have very special exotic flavors. Its seasoning not only emphasizes on the healthy diet principle, but also helpful in detoxification, lowering blood lipid and maintaining beauty.

悦蚝
Pyramid

西餐
Western Cuisine

必应 搜索热度 Search priority 8.1

电话 /Tel
+86 755 2691 2232

地址 /Address
深圳市南山区文昌街香山东街 4-3 号
No.4-3, Xiangshan East Street, Wenchang Street, Nanshan District, Shenzhen

营业时间 Opening Hours
午餐 Lunch 11:30 – 14:30
晚餐 Dinner 17:30 – 01:00
着装要求 Dress Code
优雅便服 Smart Casual
人均消费 Per Capita Consumption
600 元 600 RMB

悦蚝集酒吧和餐厅为一体，营造西式浪漫的设计风格。菜品主打时令生蚝，味道鲜嫩可口。每一道菜上桌之后，店员会为之做一番简单的介绍，让食客在品尝味道的同时，还能了解菜品的来历。

Integrating the bar and restaurant as one, it has a western romantic decoration style. Its dishes feature seasonal oysters which are tender and tasty. After each dish is served, the waiter will make a brief introduction, so that diners can understand the origin of dishes while enjoying delicacies.

无限卡特权

悦景扒房
Belle-Vue

西餐
Western Cuisine

必应 搜索热度 Search priority 6.2

电话 /Tel
+86 755 2218 7338

地址 /Address
深圳市宝安南路 1881 号君悦酒店 37 层
37F, Grand Hyatt Hotel, No.1881, Baoan South Road, Shenzhen

营业时间 Opening Hours
周二至周日 Tue. – Sun. 18:00 – 22:00
着装要求 Dress Code
时尚休闲 Fashion Leisure
人均消费 Per Capita Consumption
750 元 750 RMB

悦景扒房以厨师席间烹饪进口优质牛扒和生猛海鲜为特色，丰富的精选葡萄酒以及优雅的深圳美景，都为食客提供了难忘的用餐体验。无论是美食饕客，还是亲朋聚餐，这里都能满足所有食客的用餐需要。

It is characterized by imported high-quality steaks and fresh seafood cooked by chefs on the spot. The abundant selection of wines and elegant Shenzhen scenery will leave diners an unforgettable dining experience. This restaurant can meet the needs of all diners, no matter foodies or friends and relatives gatherings.

植庭·怀石料理
Teng

日本料理
Japanese Cuisine

7.4 必应搜索热度 Search priority

电话 /Tel
+86 755 8665 6789
+86 136 0961 5678

地址 /Address
深圳市深南大道 9001 号锦绣桃源内会古轩
Huiguxuan, Jinxiu Taoyuan, No.9001, Shennan Road, Shenzhen

营业时间 Opening Hours
周二、周四至周六 Tue. Thur. - Sat.
18:00 - 22:00
周日 Sun. 12:00 - 14:00
着装要求 Dress Code
优雅便服 Smart Casual
人均消费 Per Capita Consumption
2000 元 2000 RMB

为还原日本庭院式禅院风格，植庭用两年时间走遍日本做开业筹备；为确保菜品优质，餐厅每天从原产地空运食材。一方庭院，一方天地，隔绝外界的喧嚣与浮华，只为食客打造静谧安然的环境。

In order to restore the Japanese courtyard in Zen style, it spent two years traveling throughout Japan to prepare the opening of this restaurant; this restaurant airlifts the ingredients from origin places every day to ensure the quality of dishes. The courtyard creates a new world isolated from the outside noise and vanity to build a quiet environment for diners.

卓粤轩
Zhuo Yue Xuan

无限卡特权

粤菜
Cantonese Cuisine

3.0 必应搜索热度 Search priority

电话 /Tel
+86 755 8826 8800
+86 755 8826 8668

地址 /Address
深圳市福田区福华三路 138 号
四季酒店 3 层
3F, Four Seasons Hotel, No.138, Third Fuhua Road, Futian District, Shenzhen

营业时间 Opening Hours
午餐 Lunch 11:30 - 14:30
晚餐 Dinner 17:30 - 22:30
着装要求 Dress Code
无特别着装要求 Non-specified
人均消费 Per Capita Consumption
395 元 395 RMB

卓粤轩的高级粤菜厨师们选用顶级时鲜食材结合中国传统中餐厅的技艺与创新理念，细致演绎每一道菜式，让客人充分体验到尚品粤菜一丝不苟的精致创意。

To fully express the sophistication and innovation of superior Cantonese cuisine, its senior Cantonese cuisine chefs select the finest seasonal ingredients and combine the conventional Chinese culinary art with innovative ideas to express each dish for diners.

无限卡特权

自助餐
Buffet

棕榈园
The Plam Court

必应 搜索热度 Search priority 2.6

棕榈园是一家特色西餐厅，美轮美奂的建筑设计让您体验舒适、高雅的生活情趣。食客可尽享自助三餐中的玉盘珍馐。无论是亲友聚会、商务宴请还是浪漫追求，这里都是餐饮的不二之选，是让食客大快朵颐的所在。

It is a featured western cuisine restaurant with beautiful architectural design, bringing diners comfortable and elegant life-style experience. Diners can enjoy the delicious buffets here. It is the best choice for friends and relatives gatherings, business dinners, or romantic datings, and will provide diners a delicious feast.

电话 /Tel
+86 755 8350 0888-88605

地址 /Address
深圳市深南大道竹子林东方银座美爵酒店 1 层
1F, Grand Mercure Oriental Ginza Hotel, Bamboo Forest, Shennan Road, Shenzhen

营业时间 Opening Hours
早餐 Breakfast 6:30 - 10:30
午餐 Lunch 12:00 - 14:30
晚餐 Dinner 18:00 - 21:30

着装要求 Dress Code
优雅便服 Smart Casual

人均消费 Per Capita Consumption
180 元 180 RMB

香港

HONG KONG

8½ Otto e Mezzo BOMBANA
8½ Otto e Mezzo BOMBANA

意大利菜
Italian Cuisine

必应 搜索热度 Search priority 4.6

电话 /Tel
+852 2537 8859

地址 /Address
香港中环遮打道 16-20 号
置地历山大厦 2F 202 号铺
Shop 202, 2F, Landmark Alexandra House,
No. 16-20, Chater Road,
Hong Kong Central

营业时间 Opening Hours
周一至周六 Mon. - Sat.
午餐 Lunch 12:00 - 14:30
晚餐 Dinner 18:30 - 22:30

着装要求 Dress Code
优雅便服 Smart Casual

人均消费 Per Capita Consumption
午餐 440 元 +10% 服务费
Lunch 440RMB+10% Service Fee
晚餐 1250 元 +10% 服务费
Dinner 1250RMB+10% Service Fee

每年，由被称为“白松露大王”的主厨推出的白松露菜单都会吸引不少食客。其烹饪主旨并非炫技，而是用新鲜的食材调制出“妈妈的味道”。鱼子、帝王蟹、牛肉是这家餐厅经常使用的食材。

The white truffles menus provided by the chef named after "The King of White Truffles" attract numerous guests each year, as its cooking concept is to concoct "the mom-made taste" with fresh ingredients. Caviar, king crab and beef are the usual ingredients for cuisine here.

Amber
Amber

法国菜
French Cuisine

必应 搜索热度 Search priority 8.5

电话 /Tel
+852 2132 0188

地址 /Address
香港中环皇后大道中 15 号置地广场
Landmark Plaza, No.15, Queen's Road
Central, Hong Kong Central

营业时间 Opening Hours
午餐 Lunch
周一至周五 Mon. - Fri. 12:00 - 14:30
周末及节假日 Weekends and Holidays
12:00 - 14:00
晚餐 Dinner 18:30 - 22:30

着装要求 Dress Code
优雅便服 Smart Casual

人均消费 Per Capita Consumption
1350 元 + 10% 服务费
1350RMB + 10% Service Fee

Amber 餐厅洋溢着巴黎般的浪漫气息。这里主打的是创新法国菜，餐饮总监理查德·埃克布斯熟知法国传统菜式，同时将东方风味融合到法餐之中。菜式以海鲜为主。

Amber soaks in the Paris romance and features with creative French cuisine. Its F&B director Richard Ekkebus knows well about conventional French cuisine. Meanwhile, he gives a touch of eastern flavor into his works. Seafood is the major material.

Akrame
Akrame

法国菜
French Cuisine

5.8 必应搜索热度
Search priority

电话 /Tel
+852 2528 5068

地址 /Address
香港湾仔船街 9 号地下 B 铺
Shop B, Underground, No.9, Ship Street, Wan Chai, Hong Kong

营业时间 Opening Hours
周二至周日 Tue. – Sun.
午餐 Lunch 12:00 – 15:00
晚餐 Dinner 18:00 – 23:00
着装要求 Dress Code
优雅便服 Smart Casual
人均消费 Per Capita Consumption
850 元 850 RMB

Akrame 餐厅致力于将餐厅的厨艺风格毫无保留地呈现给每一位食客。店内提供精心挑选的新鲜食材，让食客在简洁舒适的氛围中享用由星级大厨精心设计的新派法式佳肴。

This restaurant is dedicated to presenting the culinary arts to all diners without reservation. Under simple and comfortable environment, it carefully selects fresh ingredients and provides new French cuisine exquisitely designed by the Michelin-starred chef to diners.

Beef Bar
Beef Bar

无限卡特权

西餐
Western Cuisine

5.8 必应搜索热度
Search priority

电话 /Tel
+852 2110 8853

地址 /Address
香港中环雪厂街 16 号 Club Lusitano 2 层
2F, Club Lusitano, No.16, Ice House Street, Hong Kong Central

营业时间 Opening Hours
周一至周六 Mon. – Sat. 17:00 – 22:00
着装要求 Dress Code
优雅便服 Smart Casual
人均消费 Per Capita Consumption
900 元 900 RMB

作为极具现代风格的牛肉专门店，餐厅设计使用高贵建筑材料，缔造出和谐优雅的气氛，餐厅为食客严选源自美国、澳洲和日本等地的顶级牛肉，让食客享受优质牛肉带来的不一般的用餐体验。

As a professional beef restaurant, it is decorated with modern and expensive building materials to create a harmonious and elegant environment. This restaurant strictly selects the top beef from the United States, Australia, Japan and other places and provides diners with extraordinary dining experience brought by high-quality beef.

Blue Butcher
Blue Butcher

西餐
Western Cuisine

必应 搜索热度 Search priority 4.3

电话 /Tel
+852 2613 9286

地址 /Address
香港中环荷李活道 108 号
No.108, Hollywood Road, Hong Kong
Central

营业时间 Opening Hours
午餐 Lunch 12:00 – 15:00
晚餐 Dinner 18:00 – 24:00
着装要求 Dress Code
优雅便服 Smart Casual
人均消费 Per Capita Consumption
午餐 260 元 + 10% 服务费
Lunch 260 RMB + 10% Service Fee
晚餐 520 元 + 10% 服务费
Dinner 520 RMB + 10% Service Fee

Blue Butcher 的环境是鲜明的纽约风，其一大亮点是铺满了喜马拉雅粉红盐砖的步入式醒肉库，所有牛肉都会在这个醒肉库里干熟至少 25 天。
This vibrant NYC-style restaurant, Blue Butcher, has a distinctive walk-in meat room finished by Himalaya pink salt bricks. Every piece of beef must be stayed in this room for at least 25 days for dry-aged.

Bo Innovation
Bo Innovation

创意菜
Creative Cuisine

必应 搜索热度 Search priority 5.2

电话 /Tel
+852 2850 8371

地址 /Address
香港湾仔庄士敦道 60 号嘉荟轩 2 层 13 号铺
Shop 13, No.2, J Residence, No.60,
Johnston Road, Wan Chai, Hong Kong

营业时间 Opening Hours
午餐 Lunch
周一至周五 Mon. – Fri. 12:00 – 15:00
晚餐 Dinner
周一至周五 Mon. – Fri. 19:00 – 24:00
周六 Sat. 18:00 – 24:00
周日不营业 Closed on Sunday
着装要求 Dress Code
优雅便服 Smart Casual
人均消费 Per Capita Consumption
1760 元 + 10% 服务费
1760 RMB + 10% Service Fee

餐厅以创始人梁经伦擅长的创意美食和分子料理著称，并将各国元素或西式食材融入中餐，或反过来组合，招牌菜品包括分子小笼包、鹅肝点心、黑松露肠粉、“叫花”法式鹌鹑等。
Bo Innovation wins huge fame for the Demon Chef Alvin Leung, featuring Alvin's masterpieces of creative dishes and molecular gastronomy. The signature covers Molecular Small Steamed Bun, Foie Gras Pastry, Black Truffle Rice Roll, Beggar's French Quail, etc.

北京楼（中环店）
Peking Garden(Central)

中餐
Chinese Cuisine

2.6 必应搜索热度
Search priority

电话 /Tel
+852 2845 8452

地址 /Address
香港金钟道 88 号太古广场 LG005 号
No.LG005, Pacific Place, No.88, Queensway, Hong Kong

营业时间 Opening Hours
午餐 Lunch 11:30 – 16:30
晚餐 Dinner 17:30 – 23:00
着装要求 Dress Code
优雅便服 Smart Casual
人均消费 Per Capita Consumption
1000 元 1000 RMB

北京楼以皮脆肉嫩的北京填鸭闻名海外，屡获殊荣。除此之外，正宗的北京楼富贵鸡也别具风味，点此菜品可近距离观赏到大厨精湛的片鸭技巧以及拉面表演，使食客在用餐时感到热闹非凡。

Its Peking Duck is known overseas for crispy skin and tender meat, and has won numerous awards. In addition, the authentic Steamed Chicken with Stuffing also has unique flavors, matching with exquisite slicing skills and hand-pulled noodles performance provided by the chef, making diners feel pleasant during eating.

柏屋香港
Kashiwaya Hong Kong

无限卡特权

日本料理
Japanese Cuisine

4.8 必应搜索热度
Search priority

电话 /Tel
+852 2520 5218

地址 /Address
香港中环安兰街 18 号 8 层
8F, No.18, On Lan Street, Hong Kong Central

营业时间 Opening Hours
午餐 Lunch 12:00 – 13:30
晚餐 Dinner 18:30 – 21:00
着装要求 Dress Code
整洁体面 Clean and Decent
人均消费 Per Capita Consumption
1700 元 1700 RMB

在香港，如果想要品味地道的日式料理，位于中环安兰街的柏屋香港不容错过。这里最出名的是怀石料理，总厨及店主松尾英明亲自设计每季菜单，新鲜的食材每天从日本运到香港，以保证最佳饮食体验。

In Hong Kong, any Japanese cuisine lover won't miss Kashiwaya Hong Kong in On Lan Street in Central. It's famous for Kaiseki. Its Chef and owner Matsuo Hideaki designs the menu in person every season. The fresh ingredients are delivered to Hong Kong from Japan every day by flight to ensure the best dining experience.

Café Gray Deluxe

Café Gray Deluxe

法国菜
French Cuisine

Café Gray Deluxe 的灵感源自旧巴黎的豪华咖啡厅，它利用天然素材、独特的雕刻品及原创艺术品，打造融合东方风格的当代法式情怀，L 形的窗户外是迷人的海景。

Inspired by the old Paris luxury cafe, Café Gray Deluxe makes good use of natural ingredients, characteristic sculptures and original artwork to bring out a sense of contemporary French complex blending oriental style. The L-shape window draws in marvelous sea view.

必应 搜索热度 Search priority 3.8

电话 /Tel
+852 3968 1106

地址 /Address
香港金钟道 88 号太古广场奕居 49 层
49F, Upper House, Pacific Place, No.88, Queensway, Hong Kong

营业时间 Opening Hours
早餐 Breakfast 06:30 – 10:30
午餐 Lunch
周一至周六 Mon. – Sat. 12:00 – 14:30
晚餐 Dinner 18:00 – 22:30
着装要求 Dress Code
优雅便服 Smart Casual
人均消费 Per Capita Consumption
260 元以上 More than 260 RMB

Caprice

Caprice

法国菜
French Cuisine

位于香港四季酒店 6 层的 Caprice 是一家流露着优雅高贵气息的法国餐厅。餐厅备有近千种来自波尔多和勃艮第地区的精选美酒，以及窖藏手工法式奶酪。

Caprice is a French restaurant with an elegant atmosphere on the sixth floor of the Four Seasons Hotel. It offers an extensive selection of wines from the Bordeaux and Burgundy regions, along with a cellar full of artisanal French cheeses.

必应 搜索热度 Search priority 7.9

电话 /Tel
+852 3196 8860

地址 /Address
香港中环金融街 8 号四季酒店 6 层
6F, Four Seasons Hotel, No.8, Finance Street, Hong Kong Central

营业时间 Opening Hours
18:30 – 22:30
着装要求 Dress Code
优雅便服 Smart Casual
人均消费 Per Capita Consumption
880 ~ 1760 元 + 10% 服务费
880 ~ 1760 RMB + 10% Service Fee

都爹利会馆
Duddell's

中餐
Chinese Cuisine

5.0 必应搜索热度 Search priority

电话 /Tel
+852 2525 9191

地址 /Address
香港中环都爹利街 1 号上海滩 3 至 4 层
3F and 4F, The Bund, No.1, Duddell Street, Hong Kong Central

营业时间 Opening Hours
周一至周六 Mon. – Sat. 12:00 – 15:00
18:00 – 23:00
周日 Sun. 12:00 – 15:00 18:00 – 22:00
着装要求 Dress Code
优雅便服 Smart Casual
人均消费 Per Capita Consumption
700 元 700 RMB

都爹利会馆将艺术与精致的餐饮概念融合，在香港中心雕琢出一个独特的空间。餐厅内中国传统水墨画与主厨萧显志的特色菜肴相得益彰，这里同时供应传统菜色和深受艺术空间影响的主题菜肴。

It combines the art and exquisite dining concepts to build a unique space in the Hong Kong Center. The traditional Chinese ink-wash paintings complement with Chef Xiao Zhixian's signature dishes; it also provides traditional dishes and themed dishes influenced by the art space.

Epure
Epure

无限卡特权

法国菜
French Cuisine

6.3 必应搜索热度 Search priority

电话 /Tel
+852 3185 8330

地址 /Address
香港尖沙咀广东道 5 号
海港城海洋中心 4 层 403 号铺
Shop 403, 4F, Ocean Centre, Harbour City, No.5, Canton Road, Tsim Sha Tsui, Hong Kong

营业时间 Opening Hours
午餐 Lunch 12:00 – 14:30
晚餐 Dinner 18:00 – 22:00
着装要求 Dress Code
优雅便服 Smart Casual
人均消费 Per Capita Consumption
650 元 650 RMB

Epure 餐厅严选优质的阿尔巴白松露入馔，精心炮制出各款佳肴，把时令珍馐的细腻风味带给所有食客。设计高贵典雅，紫红色玻璃酒窖、弧形厢座和神秘森林手绘壁画，尽显法国宫廷气派。

This restaurant strictly selects high-quality Alba truffle to produce various delicacies, and brings fine flavors of seasonal food to all diners. It has noble and elegant decoration, fuchsia glass cellar, arc box seats and mysterious forest hand-painted murals, which all give a feeling of French court.

Felix
Felix

西餐
Western Cuisine

必应 搜索热度 Search priority 8.0

电话 /Tel
+852 2696 6778

地址 /Address
香港九龙梳士巴利道香港半岛酒店 28 层
28F, Peninsula Hong Kong, Salisbury Road, Kowloon, Hong Kong

营业时间 Opening Hours
晚餐 Dinner 18:00 – 22:30
（最后点单 Last Order 22:30）
小吃供应时间 Snacks 18:00 – 24:00
（最后点单 Last Order 24:00）
饮品供应时段 Drinks 17:30 – 01:30
（最后点单 Last Order 01:00）
夜宵供应时间 Midnight Snack 22:30 – 24:00
（最后点单 Last Order 24:00）
着装要求 Dress Code
优雅便服 Smart Casual
人均消费 Per Capita Consumption
350 ~ 880 元（套餐 960 ~ 1488 元）
350 ~ 880RMB
（Set Course 960 ~ 1488 RMB）

Felix 展现了一个奇幻世界，将多样化的环境融合在一起，幻化成视觉和味觉的盛宴。从标志性的高档干酪刨丝器和开瓶器等精品餐具，到富有特色的椅子，餐厅处处彰显着设计师菲利 · 普斯塔克独树一帜的风格。

Felix presents a fantastic world and creates a visual and palate feast by blending various environments. Its delicate dishware, from the signature exclusive cheese grater to wine opener, and its characteristic chairs reveal the extraordinary style of its designer, Philippe Starck.

国福楼
Guo Fu Lou

粤菜
Cantonese Cuisine

必应 搜索热度 Search priority 4.4

电话 /Tel
+852 3141 8888

地址 /Address
香港中环红棉路 22 号
No.22, Cotton Tree Drive, Hong Kong Central

营业时间 Opening Hours
午餐 Lunch 11:30 – 15:00
晚餐 Dinner 18:00 – 23:00
着装要求 Dress Code
优雅便服 Smart Casual
人均消费 Per Capita Consumption
680 元 680 RMB

国福楼以红和紫的色调设计，展现餐厅的优雅华贵。主厨选用优质的食材，以娴熟的技艺烹饪出传统风味的精致粤菜。松脆可口的烤乳猪和鲜嫩细腻的蟹肉桂花炒虾丝，都是此地不可错过的极品美食。

It has an elegant and luxurious decoration in red and purple tones. The chef selects high-quality ingredients to produce delicate Cantonese cuisine with traditional flavors through skilled culinary arts. The crispy Roast Suckling Pig and tender Crab Meat Fried Shrimp with Osmanthus are the best food that must try here.

吉地士餐厅
Gaddi's

法国菜
French Cuisine

3.6 必应搜索热度
Search priority

电话 /Tel
+852 2696 6763

地址 /Address
香港九龙梳士巴利道香港半岛酒店 1 层
1F, Peninsula Hong Kong, Salisbury Road, Kowloon, Hong Kong

营业时间 Opening Hours
午餐 Lunch 12:00 – 14:30
晚餐 Dinner 19:00 – 22:30
着装要求 Dress Code
商务休闲 Business Casual
人均消费 Per Capita Consumption
1760 元 + 10% 服务费
1760 RMB + 10% Service Fee

这家供应精美欧陆佳肴的餐厅装饰华丽、品位非凡，堪称香港最奢华的餐厅之一。如果想享用丰盛一餐，可试试“品尝菜单”，或者主厨特别推荐的季节性特选。
This delicate and tasteful restaurant features continental delicacies and is regarded as the most deluxe restaurant in Hong Kong. Taste Menu and the Chef's seasonal specialties are worth trying.

酒锅
The Drunken Pot

无限卡特权

火锅
Hotpot

3.6 必应搜索热度
Search priority

电话 /Tel
+852 2323 7098

地址 /Address
香港铜锣湾登龙街 18 号 V Point 27 层
27F, V Point, No.18, Tang Lung Street, Causeway Bay, Hong Kong

营业时间 Opening Hours
周日至周四 Sun. – Thur. 12:00 – 01:00
周末及节假日 Weekends and Holidays
12:00 – 02:00
着装要求 Dress Code
优雅便服 Smart Casual
人均消费 Per Capita Consumption
午餐 68 元起
Lunch Starting from 68 RMB
晚餐 250 元起
Dinner Starting from 250 RMB

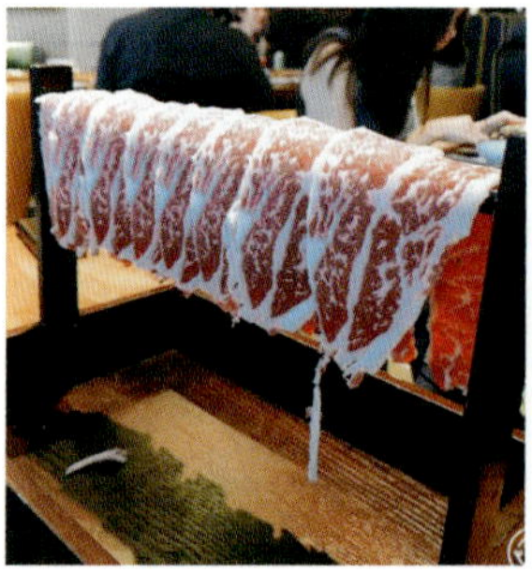

酒锅是一家在香港十分有人气的火锅店，餐厅环境优美，富有格调，精致主题装潢。餐厅的菜品新鲜，全部使用活鱼，滋味十足。这里更有超过 18 款的汤底及多款首创汤底，包括“走火入锅”，令食客回味无穷。
It is a popular hot pot restaurant in Hong Kong with beautiful and exquisite environment in delicate themes. The dishes of this restaurant are very fresh and delicious, which all made of live fishes. There are more than 18 kinds of soup base and numerous original soup bases, including the "Cross Pot", making diners memorable.

嘉麟楼
Spring Moon

粤菜
Cantonese Cuisine

必应 搜索热度 Search priority 4.9

电话 /Tel
+852 2696 6760

地址 /Address
香港九龙梳士巴利道香港半岛酒店 1 层
1F, Peninsula Hong Kong, Salisbury Road, Kowloon, Hong Kong

营业时间 Opening Hours
午餐 Lunch
周一至周六 Mon. – Sat. 11:30 – 14:30
周日及节假日
Sunday and Holidays 11:00 – 14:30
晚餐 Dinner 18:00 – 22:30

着装要求 Dress Code
优雅便服 Smart Casual

人均消费 Per Capita Consumption
午餐 440 元 + 10% 服务费
Lunch 440 RMB + 10% Service Fee
晚餐 700 ~ 880 元 + 10% 服务费
Dinner 700 ~ 880 RMB + 10% Service Fee

琳琅满目的各类粤式佳肴美点，让来到这里的食客大呼过瘾，包括经典的水晶虾饺、烧卖、烧味、奶黄月饼等。由专人介绍及冲泡的 25 种以上上等茗茶，也为食客增加了饮食闲趣。

A great variety of Cantonese dim sums, including Crystal Shrimp Dumpling, Shaomai, Chinese BBQ Plate, and Custard Moon Cake, will satisfy diners. Besides, there are over 25 kinds of top-class teas brew and made by special personnel, which improves the dinning pleasure.

Kaiseki Den by Saotome
Kaiseki Den by Saotome

日本料理
Japanese Cuisine

必应 搜索热度 Search priority 2.6

电话 /Tel
+852 2851 2820

地址 /Address
香港湾仔活道 28 号铺
Shop 28, Wood Road, Wan Chai, Hong Kong

营业时间 Opening Hours
周一至周六 Mon. – Sat. 18:30 – 23:00

着装要求 Dress Code
优雅便服 Smart Casual

人均消费 Per Capita Consumption
2242 元 2242 RMB

想要体验正宗的怀石料理，那就来 Kaiseki Den by Saotome。传统典雅的日式风格为餐厅增色不少，食材和颜色的搭配摆盘都很有艺术感，仿佛每一道菜品都在书写属于自己的故事。

If you want to try an authentic Kaiseki cuisine, you must visit this restaurant. It has a traditional elegant Japanese-style decoration and provides dishes with artistic presentation and collocation of materials and colors, as if every dish is writing its own story.

立体派
Ramen Cubism

日本料理
Japanese Cuisine

4.5 必应搜索热度 Search priority

电话 /Tel
+852 2399 0811

地址 /Address
香港中环威灵顿街 27-29 号元益大厦地库
Basement, Yuanyi Building, No.27-29, Wellington Street, Hong Kong Central

营业时间 Opening Hours
周一至周四、周日 Mon. - Thur. Sun. 11:00-23:00
周五至周六 Fri. - Sat. 11:00-00:00
着装要求 Dress Code
优雅便服 Smart Casual
人均消费 Per Capita Consumption
77 元 77 RMB

立体派拉面馆是由日本冠军级拉面厨师林隆臣同大阪厨艺界领袖人物松村贵大于香港创立的拉面品牌。两位日本拉面界的厨师合力将位于香港中环的餐厅打造成独一无二的时尚拉面空间，并力求将立体派塑造成城中餐饮热点。
It is a ramen brand founded by the Japanese ramen champion chef Lin Longchen and Osaka culinary leader Matsumura Takashio in Hong Kong. These two Japanese ramen chefs have transformed the restaurant in Central Hong Kong into a unique fashionable ramen space, and are striving to make it become a dining hotspot in this city.

利苑酒家（北角店）
Lei Garden(North Point)

粤菜
Cantonese Cuisine

3.6 必应搜索热度 Search priority

电话 /Tel
+852 2806 0008

地址 /Address
香港北角城市花园 9 至 10 座 1 层
1F, Building 9 and Building 10, City Garden Hotel, North Point, Hong Kong

营业时间 Opening Hours
午餐 Lunch 11:30 - 15:00
晚餐 Dinner 18:00 - 23:00
着装要求 Dress Code
商务休闲 Business Casual
人均消费 Per Capita Consumption
300 元 300 RMB

利苑酒家一贯保持香港酒楼特有的风格，店内宽敞明亮，装修优雅大气，十分考究。琳琅满目的粤式佳肴美点让食客大呼过瘾，包括经典的肠粉、叉烧、虾饺、杨枝甘露等，为食客奉献精致优雅的菜式。
Keeping a unique style of Hong Kong restaurant, it has a spacious and bright environment with elegant and fastidious decoration. It provides a variety of delicious Cantonese cuisine, including classic rice noodles roll, roast pork, shrimp dumplings, chilled mango sago cream with pomelo, etc., and other exquisite and elegant dishes for diners.

六福菜馆
Loaf On

海鲜
Seafood

必应 搜索热度 Search priority 3.0

电话 /Tel
+852 2792 9966

地址 /Address
香港西贡市场街 49 号铺
Shop 49, Market Street, Sai Kung, Hong Kong

营业时间 Opening Hours
周一至周六 Mon. – Sat. 11:00 – 22:00
着装要求 Dress Code
优雅便服 Smart Casual
人均消费 Per Capita Consumption
341 元 341 RMB

环境低调的六福菜馆，菜品上一点也不低调。窗明几净，一尘不染，干净整洁，坐下来只想美美地吃上一顿。招牌菜椒盐鲍鱼，个个肥厚鲜美；海鲜鱼汤，精心熬制浓郁鲜厚，喝上一口回味无穷。

It has a common environment and fabulous delicacies. Under the bright, clean and tidy environment, diners just want to sit down and eat a delicious meal. Signature dishes include Pepper Salt Aabalone which is fat and delicious, and Seafood Soup that is carefully boiled with rich and fresh flavors, leaving endless wonderful feelings aftertaste.

龙景轩
Lung King Heen

粤菜
Cantonese Cuisine

必应 搜索热度 Search priority 4.0

电话 /Tel
+852 3196 8880

地址 /Address
香港中环金融街 8 号四季酒店 4 层
4F, Four Seasons Hotel, No. 8, Financial Street, Hong Kong Central

营业时间 Opening Hours
午餐 Lunch
周一至周五 Mon. – Fri. 12:00 – 14:30
周末及节假日 Weekends and Holidays
11:30 – 15:00
晚餐 Dinner 18:30 – 22:00
着装要求 Dress Code
优雅便服 Smart Casual
人均消费 Per Capita Consumption
880 ~ 1760 元 + 10% 服务费
880 ~ 1760 RMB + 10% Service Fee

远近闻名的龙景轩以海鲜和点心最为著名，菜单上的各款菜肴均出自行政总厨陈恩德师傅的灵感创意，加上本地最新鲜高级食材的选用，口感与质感俱佳。

Seafood and dim sum are the specialties of Lung King Heen. All dishes are the creative works of Executive Chef Chan Yan Tak, made of the freshest local upscale ingredients, their tastes and textures are superb.

利苑酒家（尖沙咀店）
Lei Garden(Tsim Sha Tsui)

无限卡特权

粤菜
Cantonese Cuisine

2.9 必应搜索热度 Search priority

电话 /Tel
+852 2722 1636

地址 /Address
香港尖沙咀么地道 63 号好时中心地库 2 层
B2, Hershey Centre, No.63, Mody Road, Tsim Sha Tsui, Hong Kong

营业时间 Opening Hours
午餐 Lunch 11:30 – 15:00
晚餐 Dinner 18:00 – 23:00
着装要求 Dress Code
优雅便服 Smart Casual
人均消费 Per Capita Consumption
300 元 300 RMB

利苑开业至今一直备受食客好评。挑高的空间，桌与桌之间宽敞明亮，空间分配合理，加上清澈的水族箱，活灵活现。冰火三层肉一直是这里的招牌菜，第一层皮脆，第二层入口即化，第三层香嫩，口感变幻莫测。

It has been well praised by diners since its opening. It has a tall space with reasonable allocation, and is capacious between tables, together with clear aquariums, creating a vivid atmosphere. The Fire and Ice Pork Belly is the signature here, giving unpredictable tastes: the first layer is crispy, the second layer is melted in the mouth, and the third layer is tender.

利苑酒家（旺角店）
Lei Garden(Mong Kok)

无限卡特权

粤菜
Cantonese Cuisine

3.6 必应搜索热度 Search priority

电话 /Tel
+852 2392 5184

地址 /Address
香港旺角洗衣街 121 号铺
Shop 121, Sai Yee Street, Mong Kok, Hong Kong

营业时间 Opening Hours
午餐 Lunch 11:30 – 15:00
晚餐 Dinner 18:00 – 23:30
着装要求 Dress Code
优雅便服 Smart Casual
人均消费 Per Capita Consumption
300 元 300 RMB

地处旺角四十多年的老店利苑酒家，无论菜品还是装修，都是其在此立足如此之久的依据。经典的港式酒楼风格，低调中尽显大气。作为一间好的粤菜馆，厨师对烧味、炖汤、小炒、海鲜驾轻就熟，得心应手。

As an old restaurant with more than 40-year history, it is located at Mong Kok. Its typical Hong Kong restaurant decoration and dishes support its popularity. It is an authentic Cantonese cuisine restaurant with chefs proficient in barbecue, stewed soup, fried dishes and seafood.

MIC Kitchen
MIC Kitchen

西餐
Western Cuisine

必应 搜索热度 Search priority 4.1

电话 /Tel
+852 3758 2239

地址 /Address
香港士丹利街 11 号 26 层
26F, No.11, Stanley Street, Hong Kong

营业时间 Opening Hours
周一至周六 Mon. - Sat.
19:00 - 23:00
着装要求 Dress Code
优雅便服 Smart Casual
人均消费 Per Capita Consumption
815 元 815 RMB

餐厅凭借独特的分子料理名声远扬，开放式厨房让食客直观感受到分子料理的魅力。菜式品相优美，七彩番茄、西藏黑牦牛芝士、豆腐花等各具特色。豆腐花是饱含浓郁豆腐味道的分子泡沫，中西合璧碰撞出不一样的火花。

Known for its unique molecular cuisine, it has an open kitchen to let diners directly feel the charm of molecular cuisine. Its dishes are beautiful and distinctive, such as Colorful Tomatoes, Tibetan Black Yak Cheese and Beancurd Jelly. The Beancurd Jelly is full of rich flavors of tofu molecular foam made through the combination of Chinese and Western techniques.

无限卡特权

名人坊
Celebrity Cuisine

粤菜
Cantonese Cuisine

必应 搜索热度 Search priority 5.9

电话 /Tel
+852 3650 0066

地址 /Address
香港中环九如坊 3 号中环兰桂坊酒店 1 层
1F, Lan Kwai Fong Hotel Hong Kong, No.3, Kau U Fong, Hong Kong Central

营业时间 Opening Hours
午餐 Lunch 11:30 - 15:00
晚餐 Dinner 18:00 - 23:30
着装要求 Dress Code
无特别着装要求 Non-specified
人均消费 Per Capita Consumption
530 元 530 RMB

名人坊主营各种正宗地道粤菜，餐厅对各种菜品的把控极为严格，每道菜的每一个步骤皆不容丝毫马虎，始终认真对待每一位食客。餐厅虽然不大，但是胜在精巧，小小的天地就可尽显粤菜之中的经典。

It mainly provides authentic Cantonese cuisine, and controls the quality of each dish strictly without any error during each process in order to provide the best services to each diner. Although the restaurant is not large, it has a delicate environment where presents authentic Cantonese cuisine in such a small world.

明阁
Ming Court

无限卡特权

粤菜
Cantonese Cuisine

5.5 必应搜索热度
Search priority

电话 /Tel
+852 3552 3028

地址 /Address
香港旺角上海街 555 号香港康得思酒店 6 层
6F, Cordis Hotel, No.555, Shanghai Street,
Mong Kok, Hong Kong

营业时间 Opening Hours
周一至周五 Mon. – Fri.
11:00 – 14:30 18:00 – 22:30
着装要求 Dress Code
优雅便服 Smart Casual
人均消费 Per Capita Consumption
520 元 520RMB

餐厅采用雅致自然的深色调，低调中尽显气派；玻璃窗外，美景尽收眼底。松露金菇虫草花，金菇处理得恰到好处，没有菇类独有的泥味，同时又不失口感，还能隐约吃到芹香，可见主厨的细致和用心。

It has an elegant and natural environment in dark luxurious tone, and beautiful scenery outside of glass windows. Its Truffle Enoki Mushroom Cordyceps Flowers is very delicious with chef's ingenuity, the mushroom is tasty with no mushroom mud flavors after processing, and has a touch of celery fragrance.

ON
ON

西餐
Western Cuisine

9.1 必应搜索热度
Search priority

电话 /Tel
+852 2174 8100

地址 /Address
香港中环安兰街 18 号 29 层
29F, No.18, On Lan Street, Hong Kong
Central

营业时间 Opening Hours
周一至周四 Mon. – Thur.
12:00–14:30 18:30–22:30
周五至周六 Fri. – Sat.
12:00–14:30 18:30–23:00
着装要求 Dress Code
优雅便服 Smart Casual
人均消费 Per Capita Consumption
900 元 900 RMB

坐在 29 层的 ON 餐厅窗边，可以透过落地窗欣赏窗外的美景；而在餐厅内，可以近距离看到厨师制作美食的过程。生牛肉塔塔、焦糖鹅肝炖蛋、蜜瓜火腿都是餐厅的招牌菜品，是来店不容错过的美食。

Sitting by the window of this restaurant located at the 29th floor, diners can enjoy beautiful scenery through the French windows, and closely appreciate the cooking process of delicious food provided by chefs. Raw Beef Tower, Caramelized Goose Liver Stewed Egg, Melon Harm are all the signature dishes that you must try.

Pierre
Pierre

法国菜
French Cuisine

必应 搜索热度 Search priority 7.5

电话 /Tel
+852 2825 4001

地址 /Address
香港中环干诺道中 5 号
香港文华东方酒店 25 层
25F, Mandarin Oriental Hong Kong, No.5, Connaught Road Central, Hong Kong Central

营业时间 Opening Hours
周一至周五 Mon. – Fri. 12:00 – 24:00
周六 Sat. 19:00 – 24:00
周日及节假日休息
Closed on Sunday and Holidays

着装要求 Dress Code
商务休闲 Business Casual

人均消费 Per Capita Consumption
1300 元 + 10% 服务费
1300 RMB + 10% Service Fee

集摩登与瑰丽于一身的法式餐厅 Pierre，2006 年开业后就一直深受食客欢迎，而每到法国名厨皮埃尔 · 加涅尔四个月一次的造访时间，餐厅内必定座无虚席。Pierre 的菜式充满诗情画意，且具田园风味。

It is a restaurant of modern beauty and magnificence. The restaurant is popular ever since it's opening in 2006. Every time the French chef Pierre Gagnaire makes his once-in-four-months visit here, it would be fully seated. The dishes made by Pierre are described as "poetic and idyllic like a Chinese ink and wash painting".

鮨鲁山
Rozan

日本料理
Japanese Cuisine

必应 搜索热度 Search priority 5.2

电话 /Tel
+852 2574 1333

地址 /Address
香港湾仔活道 18 号萃峰地下 2 号店
Shop 2, Oakhill Underground, No.18, Wood Road, Wan Chai, Hong Kong

营业时间 Opening Hours
午餐 Lunch
周三至周日 Wed. – Sun. 12:00 – 14:30
晚餐 Dinner
周二至周日 Tue. – Sun. 18:30 – 22:30

着装要求 Dress Code
优雅便服 Smart Casual

人均消费 Per Capita Consumption
午餐 700 ~ 1400 元 + 10% 服务费
Lunch 700 ~ 1400 RMB + 10% Service Fee
晚餐 1400 ~ 2100 元 + 10% 服务费
Dinner 1400 ~ 2100 RMB + 10% Service Fee

高级寿司店鮨鲁山自开业以来便备受赞誉，菜单每天更新，因此客人每一次光顾都会有不一样的独特体验。所用食材均从日本空运而来，经过厨师的细心处理，达到最佳食用状态。

Rozan, a high-end sushi restaurant, wins tons of praises since its opening. Its everyday-updated menu refreshes the diners eachtime they come. All the ingredients are from Japan by air, and reach its upmost taste in the chef's hands.

呇（湾仔店）
Qi(Wan Chai)

中餐
Chinese Cuisine

7.3 必应搜索热度
Search priority

电话 /Tel
+852 2527 7117

地址 /Address
香港湾仔庄士敦道 60 号
J Senses 2 层 12 号铺
Shop 12, 2F, J Senses, No.60, Johnston Road, Wan Chai, Hong Kong

营业时间 Opening Hours
午餐 Lunch 12:00 – 14:30
晚餐 Dinner 18:00 – 22:00
着装要求 Dress Code
优雅便服 Smart Casual
人均消费 Per Capita Consumption
350 元 350 RMB

进门后便可看到巨幅的川剧脸谱画，深黑的墙体和餐台配以大红灯笼，风格上与传统川菜馆不同。厨师是香港人，曾深修川菜，将香港口味和川菜融合，做出鲜辣却不油腻的口感。

There is a Sichuan opera face painting at the entrance, black walls and tables with red lanterns, which is different from traditional Sichuan restaurant styles. The chef comes from Hong Kong and has deeply studied Sichuan cuisine. He has combined Hong Kong tastes with Sichuan cuisine to create fresh and spicy flavors without greasy taste.

乔尔 · 卢布松美食坊
L'Atelier de Joël Robuchon

西餐
Western Cuisine

6.0 必应搜索热度
Search priority

电话 /Tel
+852 2166 9000

地址 /Address
香港中环德辅道中 12–16 号置地广场
告罗士打大厦 4 层 401 号
Room 401, 4F, Gloucester Building, Landmark, No.12–16, Des Voeux Road Central, Hong Kong Central

营业时间 Opening Hours
午餐 Lunch
周一至周五 Mon. – Fri. 12:00 – 14:30
晚餐 Dinner 18:30 – 22:30
着装要求 Dress Code
商务休闲 Business Casual
人均消费 Per Capita Consumption
1760 元 1760 RMB

L'Atelier 是"工作坊"的意思，设计理念是开放式厨房。在餐厅幽暗的灯光效果中，厨师们好似舞台剧的幕后工作人员，静静地在 U 形吧台后做即兴表演。

L'Atelier means the workshop, with a theme of opening kitchen in design. The chefs in the dim lighting just like staff working behind stage, quietly performs improvisation behind the U-shape counter.

Rech by Alain Ducasse

Rech by Alain Ducasse

法国菜
French Cuisine

必应 搜索热度 Search priority 4.1

电话 /Tel
+852 2313 2323

地址 /Address
香港九龙尖沙咀梳士巴利道 18 号
香港洲际酒店大堂
Lobby, InterContinental Hong Kong, No.18, Salisbury Road, Tsim Sha Tsui, Kowloon, Hong Kong

营业时间 Opening Hours
周一至周五 Mon. - Fri. 18:00-23:00
周六至周日 Sat. - Sun.
12:00-14:30 18:00-23:00
着装要求 Dress Code
优雅便服 Smart Casual
人均消费 Per Capita Consumption
1200 元 1200 RMB

餐厅主打从法国空运而来的新鲜生蚝和鱼类，还选用优质鲜鱼和贝壳类海产，为食客呈现顶级法式海鲜体验。细腻的菜式及酒单突显品位。餐厅简约时尚的设计流露出法国风情，在维多利亚港美景的烘托下更显特别。

This restaurant provides fresh oysters and fish transported by air from France, as well as superior fresh fish and shellfish to bring the best French seafood experience for diners. The exquisite dishes and wine list demonstrate its taste. Its simple and fashionable design shows a French style, which is more special under the beautiful scenery of Victoria Harbor.

无限卡特权

肉匠
Nikushou

日本料理
Japanese Cuisine

必应 搜索热度 Search priority 5.7

电话 /Tel
+852 2387 2878

地址 /Address
香港铜锣湾耀华街 38 号 Zing！大厦 22 层
22F, Zing!, No.38, Yaohua Street, Causeway Bay, Hong Kong

营业时间 Opening Hours
18:30-01:00
着装要求 Dress Code
优雅便服 Smart Casual
人均消费 Per Capita Consumption
1400 元 1400 RMB

作为香港知名的日式烤肉餐厅，肉匠餐厅以正宗的日本和牛出名。餐厅环境充满了日式简约温馨的格调，适合朋友或者家人聚餐。餐厅的食材都是由日本空运而来的，招牌肉酱烧、七品和牛、和牛刺身都是不得不点的美味。

As a famous Japanese barbecue restaurant in Hong Kong, it is well-known for its authentic Japanese Wagyu beef. It has a comfortable Japanese-style environment, which is suitable for friends or family gatherings. The food materials of this restaurant are transported from Japan by air. Its signature dishes include Featured Barbecue Meat, Seven Grade Wagyu Beef and Wagyu Sashimi.

Sushi Tokami
Sushi Tokami

无限卡特权

日本料理
Japanese Cuisine

4.9 必应搜索热度 Search priority

电话 /Tel
+852 2771 3938

地址 /Address
香港海港城海洋中心二阶 216A 号铺
Shop 216A, Phase II, Ocean Centre, Harbour City, Hong Kong

营业时间 Opening Hours
午餐 Lunch 12:00 – 15:00
晚餐 Dinner 18:00 – 22:30
着装要求 Dress Code
优雅便服 Smart Casual
人均消费 Per Capita Consumption
1200 元 1200 RMB

Sushi Tokami 的三文鱼感动了无数食客，店主是日本筑地市场一家三文鱼店的创办人，因此每天都可以获得新鲜优质的食材。精心烹煮的寿司饭，配以天然发酵的赤醋，展现出江户前传统寿司的文化。

Its salmon has won the praise of numerous diners. The owner is a founder of a salmon restaurant in Tsukiji fish market; therefore, this restaurant has fresh and high-quality ingredients every day. The carefully prepared sushi rice with naturally fermented red vinegar presents the traditional Edomae Chirashi Sushi culture.

Sushi Wadatsumi
Sushi Wadatsumi

日本料理
Japanese Cuisine

3.7 必应搜索热度 Search priority

电话 /Tel
+852 2619 0199

地址 /Address
香港上环皇后大道中 181 号新纪元广场 2 层
2F, Grand Millennium Plaza, No.181, Queen's Road Central, Sheung Wan, Hong Kong

营业时间 Opening Hours
周一至周六 Mon. – Sat.
12:00–14:30 18:30–22:00
着装要求 Dress Code
优雅便服 Smart Casual
人均消费 Per Capita Consumption
1100 元 1100 RMB

Sushi Wadatsumi 是由来自东京米其林寿司店铃木厨师创立的品牌，新鲜的食材、精湛的厨艺和充满日式风格的用餐空间，使食客尽情享受原汁原味的日本料理。

It is a brand founded by Chef Suzuki from a Michelin-starred Sushi restaurant in Tokyo. The fresh ingredients, exquisite cooking skills and Japanese-style dining space bring diners to enjoy the original and authentic Japanese cuisine.

卅二公馆
Mott 32

中餐
Chinese Cuisine

必应 搜索热度 Search priority 7.0

电话 /Tel
+852 2885 8688

地址 /Address
香港中环德辅道中 4-4A 号渣打银行大厦地库
Basement, Standard Chartered Bank Tower, No.4-4A, Des Voeux Road Central, Hong Kong Central

营业时间 Opening Hours
午餐 Lunch 12:00 – 15:00
晚餐 Dinner 18:00 – 24:00
着装要求 Dress Code
优雅便服 Smart Casual
人均消费 Per Capita Consumption
午餐 442 元 + 10% 服务费
Lunch 442 RMB + 10% Service Fee
晚餐 700 元 + 10% 服务费
Dinner 700 RMB + 10% Service Fee

卅二公馆的名字源自美国纽约唐人街 Mott Street 32 号，唐人街便是在该处逐步形成的。餐厅在呈现现代香港用餐体验的同时，不忘展示传统文化最美好的一面。

Mott 32 was named after Mott Street No.32 in Chinatown in New York City of America, which was also the birthplace of Chinatown. Mott 32 not only showcases a modern Hong Kong dining experience but also demonstrates the essence of the traditional culture.

苏浙汇（湾仔店）
Jardin de Jade(Wan Chai)

中餐
Chinese Cuisine

必应 搜索热度 Search priority 5.7

电话 /Tel
+852 3528 0228

地址 /Address
香港湾仔港湾道 30 号
新鸿基中心地下 G3 - 4 铺
Shop G3 - 4, Sun Hung Kai Centre Underground, No.30, Harbour Road, Wan Chai, Hong Kong

营业时间 Opening Hours
午餐 Lunch 11:30 – 15:30
晚餐 Dinner 18:00 – 22:00
着装要求 Dress Code
优雅便服 Smart Casual
人均消费 Per Capita Consumption
1000 元 1000 RMB

苏浙汇中餐厅传承中华烹饪的精华，开创健康、美味的中式特色美食，菜品不仅食材新鲜、有质感，而且香、色、味俱全。设计以黑金的主色调映衬着雅致的灯光，使其熠熠生辉。

This restaurant inherits the essences of Chinese cuisine and provides healthy and delicious Chinese dishes. Its dishes are not only fresh and delicious, but also good in taste, color and flavors. It is decorated in black and gold tones against elegant lamps, making the whole restaurant sparkling.

The Ocean
The Ocean

西餐
Western Cuisine

7.1 必应搜索热度 Search priority

电话 /Tel
+852 2889 5939

地址 /Address
香港浅水湾海滩道 28 号
No.28, Beach Road, Repulse Bay, Hong Kong

营业时间 Opening Hours
周二至周五 Tue.– Fri. 18:00 – 23:00
周六、周日 Sat. – Sun. 12:00 – 15:30
18:00 – 23:00
着装要求 Dress Code
优雅便服 Smart Casual
人均消费 Per Capita Consumption
750 元 750 RMB

The Ocean 餐厅的设计充满海洋元素，店内随处可见装有水母和珊瑚的水族箱，透过面向大海一侧的落地窗，更可将浅水湾海景尽收眼底。餐厅主打海鲜菜肴，法式海鲜料理是这里的当家菜。

It is designed with ocean elements. Aquarium boxes containing jellyfish and coral can be seen everywhere in this restaurant. The French window facing the sea offers a panoramic view of Repulse Bay. It mainly provides seafood dishes, among which the French seafood is the signature dish here.

Tosca
Tosca

意大利菜
Italian Cuisine

电话 /Tel
+852 2263 2270

8.4 必应搜索热度 Search priority

地址 /Address
香港九龙柯士甸道西 1 号环球贸易广场
香港丽思卡尔顿酒店 102 层
102F, Ritz-Carlton Hong Kong, Hong Kong International Commercial Center, No.1, Austin Road West, Kowloon, Hong Kong

营业时间 Opening Hours
午餐 Lunch
周一至周五 Mon. – Fri. 12:00 – 14:30
周末及节假日
Weekends and Holidays 11:30 – 15:00
晚餐 Dinner 18:00 – 22:30
着装要求 Dress Code
优雅便服 Smart Casual
人均消费 Per Capita Consumption
午餐 440 ~ 700 元 + 10% 服务费
Lunch 440 ~ 700 RMB + 10% Service Fee
晚餐 1060 ~ 1320 元 + 10% 服务费
Dinner 1060 ~ 1320 RMB + 10% Service Fee

名字源自世界著名歌剧的 Tosca 意大利餐厅，挑高的空间，流露出高雅气息，更备有开放式厨房，大厨在这里精心设计和烹调意大利特色美食。

Tosca is an Italian restaurant, getting its name from a well-known opera. The high volume of space and the open kitchen bring in elegance. The chef's carefully designed menu and the Italian delicacies are rather appealing.

Takumi by Daisuke Mori
Takumi by Daisuke Mori

创意菜
Creative Cuisine

必应 搜索热度 3.9
Search priority

电话 /Tel
+852 2574 1299

地址 /Address
香港湾仔活道 16 号萃峰地下 1 号店
Shop 1, Oakhill Underground, No.16, Wood Road, Wan Chai, Hong Kong

营业时间 Opening Hours
周一至周六 Mon. - Sat.
12:00-14:30 18:00-22:30
着装要求 Dress Code
优雅便服 Smart Casual
人均消费 Per Capita Consumption
2000 元 2000 RMB

餐厅致力于将法国烹饪传统与日本优质食材相结合，创造出独特的法日融合菜。餐厅内的开放式厨房让食客既可以欣赏到大厨烹调，又可以和大厨交流互动。
It aims to create distinctive French-Japanese fusion cuisine by combining French culinary arts with Japanese high-quality ingredients. The open kitchen allows diners to enjoy chefs' cooking process and interact with chefs.

TATE Dining Room
TATE Dining Room

法国菜
French Cuisine

必应 搜索热度 4.1
Search priority

电话 /Tel
+852 2555 2172

地址 /Address
香港上环荷里活道 210 号
No.210, Hollywood Road, Sheung Wan, Hong Kong

营业时间 Opening Hours
周一至周六 Mon. - Sat. 19:00 - 22:00
着装要求 Dress Code
优雅便服 Smart Casual
人均消费 Per Capita Consumption
1600 元 1600 RMB

TATE Dining Room 餐厅会随四季时令供应不同的菜式，主厨 Vicky Lau 是平面设计师出身，后深造烹饪技巧，她将设计灵感融入到菜肴的口感和摆盘当中，与其说是食物，不如说更像一件独一无二的艺术品。
It provides different dishes in different seasons. Chef Vicky Lau, a former graphic designer, has acquired advanced culinary skills, and integrates the design inspiration into the tastes and presentation of dishes to make the delicacy of dishes more like a unique artwork than food.

唐阁
T'ang Court

无限卡特权

粤菜
Cantonese Cuisine

5.3 必应搜索热度 Search priority

电话 /Tel
+852 2132 7898

地址 /Address
香港尖沙咀北京道 8 号香港朗廷酒店 1 层及 2 层
1F and 2F, Langham Hong Kong, No.8, Peking Road, Tsim Sha Tsui, Hong Kong

营业时间 Opening Hours
周一至周五 Mon. – Fri.
12:00 – 15:00 18:00 – 23:00
周六、周日 Sat. – Sun.
11:00 – 15:00 18:00 – 23:00
着装要求 Dress Code
优雅便服 Smart Casual
人均消费 Per Capita Consumption
800 元 800 RMB

粤菜食府唐阁设计格调典雅。餐厅厨师以无出其右的手艺，用最新鲜的食材烹调出各种珍馐佳肴，展现唐朝盛世的气派。招牌菜有三葱爆龙虾、酿焗鲜蟹盖和金钱鲜虾球等。

It is a Cantonese cuisine restaurant with elegant and splendid decoration. Based on the unrivalled culinary skill, the restaurant's chefs produce numerous delicacies with the freshest ingredients to show the glorious of Tang dynasty. Signature dishes include Fried Lobster with Scallion, Braised Oysters in Port Wine and Shrimp Balls.

天空龙吟
Tenku RyuGin

日本料理
Japanese Cuisine

3.8 必应搜索热度 Search priority

电话 /Tel
+852 2302 0222

地址 /Address
香港九龙柯士甸道西 1 号环球贸易广场 101 层
101F, International Commerce Center, No.1, Austin Road West, Kowloon, Hong Kong

营业时间 Opening Hours
晚餐 Dinner 18:00 – 21:30
着装要求 Dress Code
商务休闲 Business Casual
人均消费 Per Capita Consumption
2100 元 + 10% 服务费
2100 RMB + 10% Service Fee

天空龙吟九成的食材取自日本，每天从日本空运到店内。餐厅精选时令食材，如鱼肝、樱花季节时令的樱花虾、樱花叶、樱鲷（暖鱼）、九州鲍鱼等，并选用高级新潟米。

Almost 90% of the ingredients are transported from Japan by air every day. This restaurant strictly selects seasonal ingredients, including fish liver, sakura shrimp during the blooming season of cherry blossom, cherry leaves, sakura bream, abalone from Kyushu and quality rice of last harvest.

天龙轩
Tin Lung Heen

粤菜
Cantonese Cuisine

在位于香港丽思卡尔顿酒店 102 层的天龙轩内，客人可以透过大幅落地玻璃窗将香港大都会的醉人景色尽收眼底。主厨刘秉雷师傅拥有超过 36 年的经验，是香港顶级的粤菜厨师。

The guests in Tin Lung Heen at the 102F of The Ritz-Carlhon Hong Kong can enjoy the awesome scene of Hong Kong through the massive floor-to-ceiling glass windows. The Chef Liu Binglei has over 36 years of culinary background and is listed one of the best Cantonese chefs in Hong Kong.

必应 搜索热度 Search priority 3.9

电话 /Tel
+852 2263 2270

地址 /Address
香港九龙柯士甸道西 1 号环球贸易广场香港丽思卡尔顿酒店 102 层
102F, Ritz-Carlton Hong Kong, Hong Kong International Commercial Center, No.1, Austin Road

营业时间 Opening Hours
午餐 Lunch
周一至周五 Mon. - Fri. 12:00 - 14:30
周末及节假日 Weekends and Holidays
11:30 - 15:00
晚餐 Dinner 18:00 - 22:30

着装要求 Dress Code
优雅便服 Smart Casual

人均消费 Per Capita Consumption
午餐 440 ~ 700 元 + 10% 服务费
Lunch 440 ~ 700 RMB + 10% Service Fee
晚餐 1060 ~ 1320 元 + 10% 服务费
Dinner 1060 ~ 1320 RMB + 10% Service Fee

VEA Restaurant and Lounge
VEA Restaurant and Lounge

法国菜
French Cuisine

来自香港的获奖调酒师 Antonio Lai 与来自英国的 Amir Javaid 合作，将米其林厨师 Vicky Cheng 制作的亚洲风味小吃与每种饮品搭配享用，一场美食和畅饮的极致味觉体验从这里开始。

It provides an ultimate delicacies and drinking experience by award-winning bartender Antonio Lai from Hong Kong collaborated with Amir Javaid from the UK, and Michelin chef Vicky Cheng who produces Asian snacks to eat with drinks.

必应 搜索热度 Search priority 4.2

电话 /Tel
+852 2711 8639

地址 /Address
香港中环威灵顿街 198 号
No.198, Wellington Street, Hong Kong Central

营业时间 Opening Hours
周一至周六 Mon. - Sat.
17:00 - 01:00

着装要求 Dress Code
优雅便服 Smart Casual

人均消费 Per Capita Consumption
1550 元 1550 RMB

Wagyu Takumi
Wagyu Takumi

法日料理
French and Japanese Cuisine

3.6 必应搜索热度 Search priority

电话 /Tel
+852 2574 1299

地址 /Address
香港湾仔活道 16 号萃峰地下 1 号店
Shop 1, Oakhill Underground, No.16, Wood Road, Wan Chai, Hong Kong

营业时间 Opening Hours
午餐 Lunch 12:00 – 14:30
晚餐 Dinner 18:30 – 22:30
着装要求 Dress Code
优雅便服 Smart Casual
人均消费 Per Capita Consumption
午餐 700 ~ 1060 元 + 10% 服务费
Lunch 700 ~ 1060 RMB + 10% Service Fee
晚餐 1840 元 + 10% 服务费
Dinner 1840 RMB + 10% Service Fee

Wagyu Takumi 以法国料理为基础，加入日式食材和做法，是全新概念的创意餐厅。主厨 Daisuke MoRi 擅长将主要来自日本、法国的新鲜昂贵食材融汇，以法、日烹调方式创制出独具匠心的美食。

Wagyu Takumi is a creative restaurant which is based on French cuisine and blends with Japanese ingredients and culinary methods. Its Executive Chef Daisuke MoRi is good at cooking the top ingredients mainly from Japan and France through the innovative French and Japanese culinary skills.

文华扒房 & 酒吧
Mandarin Grill & Bar

酒吧
Bar

3.7 必应搜索热度 Search priority

电话 /Tel
+852 2825 4004

地址 /Address
香港中环干诺道中 5 号香港文华东方酒店 1 层
1F, Mandarin Oriental Hong Kong, No.5, Connaught Road Central, Hong Kong Central

营业时间 Opening Hours
周一至周五 Mon. – Fri. 07:30 – 10:00
12:00 – 14:30 18:30 – 22:00
周六至周日 Sat. – Sun. 18:30–22:00
着装要求 Dress Code
休闲正装 Casual Dress
人均消费 Per Capita Consumption
1400 元 1400 RMB

文华扒房由 Terence Conran 亲自设计，整体显得精美活泼。在餐厅内可以一览皇后像广场与遮打花园。菜品采用当令有机食材，为传统扒房融入全新的灵感。

It is designed by Terence Conran, presenting an overall elegant and lively environment. The restaurant has a panoramic view of the Statue Square and Chater Garden. The dishes are made with seasonal organic ingredients, providing a new inspiration for traditional steakhouse.

文华厅
Wan Wah

粤菜
Cantonese Cuisine

必应 搜索热度 Search priority 2.9

电话 /Tel
+852 2825 4003

地址 /Address
香港中环干诺道中 5 号
香港文华东方酒店 25 层
25F, Mandarin Oriental Hong Kong, No.5, Connaught Road Central, Hong Kong Central

营业时间 Opening Hours
周一至周五 Mon. – Fri.
12:00–14:30 18:30–22:00
周六至周日 Sat. – Sun.
11:30–15:00 18:30–22:00
着装要求 Dress Code
优雅便服 Smart Casual
人均消费 Per Capita Consumption
1200 元 1200 RMB

文华厅环境优雅，可将维多利亚港与香港的繁华市景尽收眼底。在城市的星光下享用浪漫晚餐，惬意品尝在香港家喻户晓的午餐精选点心，都是文华厅带来的完美饕餮体验。

With an elegant decoration, it has a panoramic view of Victoria Harbor and the bustling city view of Hong Kong. Eating under romantic city stars, diners will enjoy delicacies and selected lunch dim sum which is well known in this city leisurely.

夏宫
Summer Palace

粤菜
Cantonese Cuisine

必应 搜索热度 Search priority 7.6

电话 /Tel
+852 2820 8552

地址 /Address
香港金钟法院道太古广场二座
港岛香格里拉酒店 5 层
5F, Hong Kong Island Shangri-La Hotel, Building II, Pacific Place, Supreme Court Road, Queensway, Hong Kong

营业时间 Opening Hours
周一至周六 Mon. – Sat.
11:30 – 14:30 18:30 – 22:30
周日 Sun. 11:00 – 15:00 18:00 – 22:30
着装要求 Dress Code
优雅便服 Smart Casual
人均消费 Per Capita Consumption
580 元 580 RMB

夏宫是一家屡获殊荣的中餐厅，以传统广东佳肴久负盛名，其菜谱包罗各式正宗广东名菜及时令佳肴。餐厅装潢富含中国传统文化气息。

It is an award-winning Chinese restaurant with a long history of traditional Cantonese cuisine. It has a menu gathering authentic Cantonese cuisine and seasonal dishes, and a traditional decoration rich in Chinese culture.

铁板烧 · 铸
IM Teppanyaki & Wine

日本料理
Japanese Cuisine

3.6 必应搜索热度
Search priority

电话 /Tel
+852 2570 7088

地址 /Address
香港大坑铜锣湾道 134 号地下
Underground, No.134, Tung Lo Wan Road, Tai Hang, Hong Kong

营业时间 Opening Hours
午餐 Lunch 12:00 – 14:30
晚餐 Dinner 18:00 – 22:30
着装要求 Dress Code
优雅便服 Smart Casual
人均消费 Per Capita Consumption
1300 元 1300 RMB

作为香港为数不多的米其林星级铁板烧餐厅，日式风格的设计加上精美的欧式餐具，还有空运而来的新鲜食材，无处不体现着餐厅的高级感。就餐时还可近距离观赏大厨料理，为食客带来美食和视觉的双重享受。

As one of few Michelin-starred teppanyaki restaurants in Hong Kong, it has a Japanese-style decoration, exquisite European tableware, and fresh food materials transported by air, reflecting the high-level of this restaurant everywhere. Chefs will put on culinary arts performances to bring diners with delicacies and visual enjoyment.

香宫
Shang Palace

粤菜
Cantonese Cuisine

4.4 必应搜索热度
Search priority

电话 /Tel
+852 2733 8754

地址 /Address
香港九龙尖沙咀东部么地道 64 号
No.64, Mody Road, Tsim Sha Tsui East, Kowloon, Hong Kong

营业时间 Opening Hours
午餐 Lunch
周一至周五 Mon. – Fri. 12:00 – 15:00
周末及节假日 Weekends and Holidays
10:30 – 15:00
晚餐 Dinner 18:30 – 23:00
着装要求 Dress Code
优雅便服 Smart Casual
人均消费 Per Capita Consumption
530 元 + 10% 服务费
530 RMB + 10% Service Fee

九龙香格里拉大酒店的香宫以正宗粤菜闻名遐迩，餐厅主厨莫杰强曾为摩洛哥国王穆罕默德六世、俄罗斯总统以及全球诸多达官贵人和社会名流掌勺。

Shang Palace is famous for its authentic Cantonese cuisine in Kowloon Shangri-La Hotel. Its Executive Chef Mo Jieqiang ever cooked for many celebrities and socialites, like the Russian President and King Mohammed VI of Morocco.

欣图轩
Yan Toh Heen

粤菜
Cantonese Cuisine

必应 搜索热度 Search priority 4.9

电话 /Tel
+852 2313 2323

地址 /Address
香港九龙梳士巴利道 18 号香港洲际酒店地下
Underground, InterContinental Hong Kong, No.18, Salisbury Road, Kowloon, Hong Kong

营业时间 Opening Hours
午餐 Lunch
周一至周六 Mon. - Sat. 12:00 - 14:30
周日 Sunday 11:30 - 15:00
晚餐 Dinner 18:00 - 23:00
着装要求 Dress Code
优雅便服 Smart Casual
人均消费 Per Capita Consumption
1060 元 + 10% 服务费
1060 RMB + 10% Service Fee

欣图轩最出色的是粤菜和精致点心，传统粤菜的烹调方法、上乘的时令新鲜食材，配合入时的摆盘，色、香、味俱全。雀龙造型的玛瑙屏风和古董高柜等装饰，为餐厅营造出家的氛围。

Yan Toh Heen features Cantonese cuisine and exquisite snacks. It connects the best and fresh seasonal ingredients and traditional Cantonese cuisine culinary art as well as great dish presentation, offering dishes with great color, flavor and taste. Dragon-shaped agate screens, antique high cabinet and other decoration create a home atmosphere.

新同乐鱼翅酒家（尖沙咀店）
Sun Tung Lok(Tsim Sha Tsui)

粤菜
Cantonese Cuisine

必应 搜索热度 Search priority 2.6

电话 /Tel
+852 2152 1417

地址 /Address
香港尖沙咀广东道 3 号马哥孛罗香港酒店 6 层
6F, Marco Polo Hong Kong Hotel, No.3, Canton Road, Tsim Sha Tsui, Hong Kong

营业时间 Opening Hours
午餐 Lunch 11:30 - 15:00
晚餐 Dinner 18:00 - 22:00
着装要求 Dress Code
优雅便服 Smart Casual
人均消费 Per Capita Consumption
900 元 900 RMB

闻名业界的鱼翅是新同乐的招牌，餐厅会先让食客尝试汤汁的咸淡再烹饪，因此每一位食客都可以品尝到最适应自己口味的鱼翅。精致的摆盘和鲜美的菜品使食客们流连忘返。

As its signature dish, the shark's fin, which is famous among the industry, will be prepared after diner tasting the soup, so as to adjust the taste according to each diner's preference. Exquisite presentation and delicious dishes make diners indulge in pleasures without stop.

夜上海（尖沙咀店）
Ye Shanghai(Tsim Sha Tsui)

中餐
Chinese Cuisine

6.7 必应搜索热度 Search priority

电话 /Tel
+852 2376 3322

地址 /Address
香港尖沙咀广东道 3 号马哥孛罗香港酒店 6 层
6F, Marco Polo Hong Kong Hotel, No.3, Canton Road, Tsim Sha Tsui, Hong Kong

营业时间 Opening Hours
午餐 Lunch 11:00 – 15:00
晚餐 Dinner 18:00 – 23:00
着装要求 Dress Code
优雅便服 Smart Casual
人均消费 Per Capita Consumption
460 元 460 RMB

餐厅门前招牌处有一幅老式上海壁画，餐厅内设计为暗色系，时尚典雅。晚餐时在落地窗旁就餐，可以感受香港的浪漫夜景。招牌菜有松子黄鱼和干烧虾球等。
There is an old Shanghai mural in front of the entrance signboard. It has an elegant and glorious decoration in dark colors. Diners can enjoy the romantic night view of Hong Kong during dining sitting by a French window. Signature dishes include Yellow-Fin Tuna with Pine Nuts and Dry-Braised Prawn.

逸东轩（佐敦店）
Yat Tung Heen(Jordan)

粤菜
Cantonese Cuisine

2.7 必应搜索热度 Search priority

电话 /Tel
+852 2710 1093

地址 /Address
香港佐敦弥敦道 380 号逸东酒店 B2
B2, Eaton Hotel, No.380, Nathan Road, Jordan, Hong Kong

营业时间 Opening Hours
午餐 Lunch 11:00–15:00
晚餐 Dinner 18:00–23:00
着装要求 Dress Code
优雅便服 Smart Casual
人均消费 Per Capita Consumption
390 元 390 RMB

食客一步入逸东轩餐厅，便会被强烈的中式风格环绕，内部木质墙面和细节装饰也颇具特色。菜品选用上等新鲜的食材，加上厨师的精心制作，使每位食客都能品尝到正宗的粤菜。
Upon entering the restaurant, diners will be surrounded by strong Chinese style decoration with featured interior wooden walls and detailed furnishings. The dishes are made with superior fresh ingredients with skilled chef's culinary arts, providing diners with authentic Cantonese cuisine.

营致会馆
Ying Jee Club

中餐
Chinese Cuisine

必应 搜索热度 Search priority 5.0

电话 /Tel
+852 2801 6882

地址 /Address
香港中环干诺道中 41 号
盈置大厦地下 G05,107 及 108 号铺
Shop G05, 107 and 108, Underground,
Nexxus Building, No.41, Connaught Road
Central, Hong Kong Central

营业时间 Opening Hours
午餐 Lunch 11:30 – 15:00
晚餐 Dinner 18:00 – 23:00
着装要求 Dress Code
优雅便服 Smart Casual
人均消费 Per Capita Consumption
750 元 750 RMB

营致会馆被誉为“粤菜之巅，仍在香江”。餐厅由米其林星级粤菜总厨萧显志掌舵，每道菜式均以新鲜食材入馔，加上萧师傅独门的烹饪功夫，匠心铸制出一道道令人回味无穷的粤式美馔，将传统粤菜之精粹展现得淋漓尽致。

Honored as "The best Cantonese cuisine is still in Hong Kong", it is led by the Michelin-starred chef Xiao Xianzhi. Each dish is made with fresh ingredients through Chef's unique cooking skills. This restaurant creates a series of delicious Cantonese dishes that are memorable and bring out the essences of traditional Cantonese cuisine.

御宝轩
Imperial Treasure Fine Shanghai Cuisine

粤菜
Cantonese Cuisine

必应 搜索热度 Search priority 4.5

电话 /Tel
+852 2663 9919

地址 /Address
香港铜锣湾皇冠假日酒店 2 层
2F, Crowne Plaza, Causeway Bay,
Hong Kong

营业时间 Opening Hours
午餐 Lunch 11:30 – 15:00
晚餐 Dinner 18:00 – 23:00
着装要求 Dress Code
优雅便服 Smart Casual
人均消费 Per Capita Consumption
500 元 500 RMB

御宝轩是一家深受当地人喜爱且极为正宗的粤菜餐厅。招牌菜式包括乳猪糯米饭、叉烧包和蟹肉蒸蛋白等。餐厅装饰高端优雅，十分适合与好友相聚。

It is a very authentic Cantonese cuisine restaurant which is popular among the locals. Signature dishes include Suckling Pig Glutinous Rice, Barbecued Pork Bun and Steamed Crab Meat with Eggs. It has a high-level and elegant decoration, and is suitable for friend gatherings.

浙江轩
Zhejiang Heen

中餐
Chinese Cuisine

3.8 必应搜索热度
Search priority

电话 /Tel
+852 2877 9011

地址 /Address
香港湾仔骆克道 300 至 306 号
侨阜商业大厦
Kiu Fu Commercial Building, No.300-306,
Lockhart Road, Wan Chai, Hong Kong

营业时间 Opening Hours
12:00 – 23:00
着装要求 Dress Code
优雅便服 Smart Casual
人均消费 Per Capita Consumption
290 元 290 RMB

浙江轩餐厅设计古典雅致，午市时间座无虚席。浙江轩连续数年获得米其林一星，招牌菜有长江熏鱼、清炒河虾仁和松仁鸡米锅巴。餐厅有三层，二层是散客，其他为包房。

It has a classic and elegant decoration and is always full of diners during lunch time. It has been awarded a Michelin star for several years, and its signature dishes include Smoked Yangtze River, Stir-fried River Shrimps and Pine Nuts Chicken Rice Crust. There are three floors, two floors are for individual diners, and the other is for private rooms.

志魂
Sushi Shikon

日本料理
Japanese Cuisine

5.1 必应搜索热度
Search priority

电话 /Tel
+852 2643 6800

地址 /Address
香港上环苏杭街 29 号尚园
Mercer Hotel, No.29, Jervois Street,
Sheung Wan, Hong Kong

营业时间 Opening Hours
周一至周六 Mon. – Sat.
12:00–14:00 18:00–20:30
着装要求 Dress Code
优雅便服 Smart Casual
人均消费 Per Capita Consumption
4000 元 4000 RMB

志魂是香港非常著名的餐厅之一，餐厅内吧台共设 8 个席位，包厢可以容纳 6 位。招牌菜是鲍鱼肝，淋上浓郁的鲍鱼肝酱，再加上腌制的米，酸中有鲜，唇齿留香。

It is a three Michelin-starred restaurant in Hong Kong. There are 8 seats in the bar counter and 6 seats in the box. The signature dish is Abalone Liver poured with rich abalone liver sauce and pickled rice, providing a fresh and sour tastes and lingering aromas.

其他

OTHER

雅舍餐厅
The Manor

无限卡特权

西餐
Western Cuisine

4.9 必应搜索热度
Search priority

电话 /Tel
+853 2882 8898

地址 /Address
澳门路氹城金沙城中心瑞吉酒店 1 层
1F, St. Regis, Cotai Central, Macao

营业时间 Opening Hours
早餐 Breakfast 06:30 – 10:30
午餐 Lunch 12:00 – 15:00
晚餐 Dinner 18:00 – 23:00
着装要求 Dress Code
无特别着装要求 Non-specified
人均消费 Per Capita Consumption
270 元 270 RMB

雅舍餐厅装潢优雅，格调雅致，是适合商务宴请、朋友小聚、情侣约会的场所。餐厅主打土生葡人下午茶，提供超过三十款精致煎炸美点、糕点及蒸点心。除澳葡式点心外，餐厅还加入了经典中式点心，如叉烧包、烧卖等小吃。

It has a comfortable and glorious environment with elegant decorations, which is suitable for business banquets, friends gathering and lovers dating. It mainly provides Macanese afternoon tea with over 30 delicately fried delicacies, cakes and steamed pastries. In addition to the Macanese dim sum, this restaurant also serves classic Chinese dim sum, such as Barbecued Pork Bun and Steamed Pork Dumplings.

班妮
Bane

意大利菜
Italian Cuisine

5.9 必应搜索热度
Search priority

电话 /Tel
+853 8113 1200

地址 /Address
澳门路氹连贯公路
澳门喜来登金沙城中心酒店 1 层
1F, Sheraton Macao Hotel, Cotai Central, Estrada do Istmo, Macao

营业时间 Opening Hours
11:30–21:00
着装要求 Dress Code
无特别着装要求 Non-specified
人均消费 Per Capita Consumption
290 元 290 RMB

班妮餐厅出品正宗的意大利美食，搭配意大利风情浓郁的环境，食客可以一边享受美食，一边探索意大利风味。餐厅的招牌菜为：香辣西西里红虾意粉、火焰波士顿龙虾意粉、温泉蛋恺撒沙拉等。

It provides authentic Italian cuisine with a rich Italian style environment. Diners can enjoy the delicacies while exploring Italian flavors. Its signature dishes include: Spicy Sicilian Red Shrimp Pasta, Flaming Boston Lobster Pasta, Hot Spring Egg Caesar Salad, etc.

香宫餐厅
Shang Palace

粤菜 湘菜
Cantonese Cuisine and Hunan Cuisine

必应 搜索热度 Search priority 4.4

香宫以红色镂空复古木质墙面与红色地毯、椅子相辉，呈现东方典雅情调。餐厅面朝宽广的北部湾海景，为客人提供优雅的用餐环境。香宫提供粤菜、湘菜及本地菜肴，每日还提供粤式早午茶、香宫经典菜肴等。

It has an elegant Oriental decoration style with red hollow vintage walls, red carpets and chairs. This restaurant faces the broad Beibu Gulf, which creates an elegant dining environment for diners. It provides Cantonese cuisine, Hunan cuisine and local dishes, as well as Cantonese brunch and signature dishes every day.

电话 /Tel
+86 779 2062 288-52

地址 /Address
北海市茶亭路 33 号
No.33, Chating Road, Beihai

营业时间 Opening Hours
早餐 Breakfast
周一至周五 Mon.- Fri. 08:30 - 11:00
周六、日及节假日 08:00 - 11:00
午餐 Lunch 11:00 - 14:30
晚餐 Dinner 17:30 - 22:00
着装要求 Dress Code
优雅便服 Smart Casual
人均消费 Per Capita Consumption
150 元 150 RMB

颐景轩中餐厅
YeeKing Chinese Resturant

无限卡特权

中餐
Chinese Cuisine

必应 搜索热度 Search priority 2.6

颐景轩中餐厅位于旅游度假区内，空气清新、景观秀丽，内部格调高雅。餐厅崇尚绿色、生态、健康的理念，主营精品淮扬菜、湘菜、粤菜菜系，并结合地方特色，形成了丰富而独特的菜品体系。

Located at the tourist resort, it has an elegant and quiet environment with fresh air and beautiful scenery. This restaurant advocates the concept of green, ecology and health, and mainly provides Huaiyang cuisine, Hunan cuisine and Guangdong cuisine, together with local characteristics, forming a rich and unique food system.

电话 /Tel
+86 519 6802 1888

地址 /Address
常州市武进区雪堰镇嬉戏路 8 号
No.8, Xixi Road, Xueyan Town, Wujin District, Changzhou

营业时间 Opening Hours
午餐 Lunch 11:00 - 13:30
晚餐 Dinner 17:00 - 20:30
着装要求 Dress Code
商务休闲 Business Casual
人均消费 Per Capita Consumption
150 元 150 RMB

PHO 东田越南粉
PHO

越南菜
Vietnamese Cuisine

7.4 必应搜索热度
Search priority

电话 /Tel
+86 23 6765 7363

地址 /Address
重庆市 IFS 1 层美食广场内
Gourmet Plaza, 1F, IFS, Chongqing

营业时间 Opening Hours
10:00–22:00
着装要求 Dress Code
无特别着装要求 Non-specified
人均消费 Per Capita Consumption
90 元 90 RMB

PHO 东田越南粉自开业以来，已经收获了大批的忠实拥趸。在有 PHO 东田越南粉的地方，你都可以吃到这碗以文火熬制 12 小时的汤头，不添加香精、不加盐，配以白嫩 Q 弹的河粉。餐厅希望将这碗粉，分享给热爱美食的人。
PHO has won numerous diners' hearts since its opening. Here, diners can enjoy this famous bowl of soup prepared 12-hour without essence or salt, and served with white tender rice noodles. This restaurant hopes to share this bowl of noodles with people who love food.

御公馆中餐厅
Royal Court Restaurant

中餐
Chinese Cuisine

2.6 必应搜索热度
Search priority

电话 /Tel
+86 23 8889 9999

地址 /Address
重庆市北部新区经开园龙怀街 1 号
No.1, Longhuai Street, Economic Development Zone, New North District, Chongqing

营业时间 Opening Hours
午饭 Lunch 11:30 – 14:00
晚饭 Dinner 17:30 – 21:30
着装要求 Dress Code
优雅便服 Smart Casual
人均消费 Per Capita Consumption
午餐 150 元 Lunch 150 RMB
晚餐 220 ~ 300 元 Dinner 220 ~ 300 RMB

御公馆中餐厅是不可多得的品味粤菜与本地特色渝菜的好去处，在这家时尚氛围与中国传统元素相结合的餐厅，不仅可以品尝到美味，还可以观赏到高尔夫球场的自然景观。
Royal Court Restaurant is a good choice if you want to taste Cantonese cuisine and local flavor in Chongqing. It combines fashion modern style with traditional Chinese elements. Dining here, you can enjoy the fabulous scene of golf course.

船中餐厅
Sampan

中餐
Chinese Cuisine

必应 搜索热度 Search priority **7.0**

电话 /Tel
+86 731 8870 8888

地址 /Address
长沙市芙蓉南路二段 128 号
现代广场长沙现代凯莱大酒店 1 层
1F, Xiandai Gloria Grand Hotel, No.128, Furong South Road Second Part, Changsha

营业时间 Opening Hours
午餐 Lunch 11:00 – 14:00
晚餐 Dinner 17:00 – 21:30
着装要求 Dress Code
优雅便服 Smart Casual
人均消费 Per Capita Consumption
大厅 60 元 Lounge 60 RMB
包厢 150 ~ 200 元
Private Room 150 ~ 200 RMB

船中餐厅环境别致、装修豪华，这里不仅有精心烹饪的传统粤菜，还有湘菜、川菜、潮州菜和一系列现代健康美食。船中餐厅从装修设计到服务都非常用心，适合朋友聚会，能够让来此品尝的食客流连忘返。

Sampan has a unique environment and luxury decoration, and serves traditional Cantonese cuisine as well as Hunan, Sichuan and Chaozhou specialties. From decoration design to service, you can feel its ingenuity and prudence. It is an ideal place for friends gathering or enjoying a fantastic meal.

金松露餐厅
Truffle's

法国菜
French Cuisine

必应 搜索热度 Search priority **2.6**

电话 /Tel
+86 731 8870 8888

地址 /Address
长沙市芙蓉南路二段 128 号
现代广场长沙现代凯莱大酒店 1 层
1F, Xiandai Gloria Grand Hotel, No.128, Furong South Road Second Part, Changsha

营业时间 Opening Hours
午餐 Lunch 11:30 – 14:30
晚餐 Dinner 17:30 – 22:00
着装要求 Dress Code
正装 Formal
人均消费 Per Capita Consumption
288 元 288 RMB

金松露的每一道菜品都经过厨师的精心烹制，融合了经典与现代元素。金松露餐厅严谨处理的食材、创意混搭的菜品、精致的就餐环境，不仅满足了宾客的饮食消费需求，而且融合了时尚艺术和创新餐饮文化。

It provides dishes carefully cooked by chefs and pays greatly attention to ingredients selection, creative dish collaboration and sophisticated creation of dining space. Truffle's not only satisfies the diners' palate but also meets their demands for trendy arts and creative dining culture.

TIVANO
TIVANO

意大利菜
Italian Cuisine

4.4 必应搜索热度
Search priority

电话 /Tel
+86 28 6297 4190

地址 /Address
成都市锦江区笔帖式街 81 号成都博舍酒店
The Temple House, No.81, Bitieshi Street, Jinjiang District, Chengdu

营业时间 Opening Hours
午餐 Lunch 11:30 – 14:30
晚餐 Dinner 18:00 – 22:00
着装要求 Dress Code
优雅便服 Smart Casual
人均消费 Per Capita Consumption
300 ~ 350 元 300 ~ 350 RMB

TIVANO 餐厅致力于把最正宗的意大利佳肴带到成都。开放式厨房是 TIVANO 的亮点之一，餐厅拥有开放式直立烤肉架、烧烤炉和薄饼石炉，客人可以即席欣赏厨师团队精心烹饪各款美食。

TIVANO dedicates to bringing the most authentic Italian cuisine to Chengdu. One of the TIVANO's features is the open kitchen with an open vertical grill, BBQ grill and stone pizza oven allowing diners to enjoy the cooking drama.

和清亚洲料理
Heqing Asian Reataurant

日本料理
Japanese Cuisine

2.6 必应搜索热度
Search priority

电话 /Tel
+86 28 8887 6666-8381

地址 /Address
成都市武侯区临江西路 1 号
成都明宇尚雅饭店内 2 层
2F, Galaxy Minyoun Chengdu Hotel, No.1, Linjiang West Road, Wuhou District, Chengdu

营业时间 Opening Hours
午餐 Lunch 11:30 – 14:00
晚餐 Dinner 17:30 – 21:00
着装要求 Dress Code
优雅便服 Smart Casual
人均消费 Per Capita Consumption
200 元 200 RMB

和清亚洲料理主打日式料理，更将亚洲美食精华融会贯通，形成特色鲜明的亚洲料理。大堂设有独立的铁板烧烤区，可邀约好友相聚于此。餐厅隐秘的私人空间、日式的榻榻米、暖色调的和风软装，惬意至极。

It mainly provides Japanese cuisine featured with a distinctive Asian style through combining the essences of different Asian food. The lobby has a separate Barbecue area which is suitable for friends gathering. It also has private rooms and Japanese tatami with warm colors and Japanese style decoration, making diners feel cozy and comfortable.

无限卡特权

廊桥
The Bridge

中餐
Chinese Cuisine

必应 搜索热度 Search priority 8.9

电话 /Tel
+86 28 8444 6888
+86 28 8444 3888

地址 /Address
成都市锦江区滨江东路 66 号
No.66, Binjiang East Road, Jinjiang District, Chengdu

廊桥为了让食客们拥有极致且独一无二的饮食体验，设计并重塑了餐厅整体空间构造和内外装潢。与此同时，廊桥与华人名厨江振诚合作，奉上川菜国际化的具象演绎，即“岁时料理”，书写川菜进化的更多可能。

In order to provide diners with ultimate and unique dining experience, it has designed and reshaped the overall spatial structure and interior and exterior decorations. Besides, cooperating with famous Chinese chef Andre Chiang, it presents the concrete interpretation of internationalized Sichuan food, namely "Season Cuisine", and develops more possibilities of Sichuan cuisine.

营业时间 Opening Hours
午餐 Lunch
周二至周日 Tue. – Sun. 11:30 – 14:00
晚餐 Dinner 17:30 – 22:00
酒吧 Bar 18:00 – 02:00
着装要求 Dress Code
休闲正装 Casual Dress
人均消费 Per Capita Consumption
500 元 500 RMB

丽轩中餐厅
Lixuan Chinese Restaurant

中餐
Chinese Cuisine

必应 搜索热度 Search priority 3.1

电话 /Tel
+86 28 8358 8888

地址 /Address
成都市青羊区顺城大街 269 号
成都富力丽思卡尔顿酒店 26 层
26F, Ritz-Carlton Hotel Chengdu, No.269, Shuncheng Street, Qingyang District, Chengdu

餐厅主打粤式佳肴，辅以特色川菜。环境设计灵感来自古蜀文明，以“芙蓉古都”和“丝绸之路”为设计主线，随处可见的蜀锦装饰、缤纷的花朵，为摩登时尚的餐厅点缀出成都特有的气息。

Lixuan features Cantonese cuisine with some Sichuan specialties. Its interior design is inspired by the old Shu Culture, with Old Lotus Capital and Silk Road as its design themes. Sichuan Brocade decorations and vibrant flowers can be found everywhere, giving a touch of Chengdu sense to this modern restaurant.

营业时间 Opening Hours
午餐 Lunch 11:30 – 14:00
晚餐 Dinner 17:30 – 22:00
着装要求 Dress Code
优雅便服 Smart Casual
人均消费 Per Capita Consumption
200 ~ 300 元 200 ~ 300 RMB

品味餐厅
Taste Restaurant

自助餐
Buffet

6.5 必应搜索热度
Search priority

电话 /Tel
+86 28 8266 6666-6608

地址 /Address
成都市温江区文化路 111 号
No.111, Wenhua Road, Wenjiang District, Chengdu

营业时间 Opening Hours
06:30 - 23:00
着装要求 Dress Code
优雅便服 Smart Casual
人均消费 Per Capita Consumption
150 ~ 200 元 150 ~ 200 RMB

品味餐厅是一个以多国风味为卖点的自助餐厅，品种繁多。厨师精选当季新鲜食材，为食客呈现最佳菜肴。餐厅不定期推出美食节，如韩国美食节、东南亚美食节，让食客充分体会到各国风味。

Taste is a buffet restaurant featuring multinational cuisine, offering a great variety of delicacies. The chefs choose fresh ingredients in season to present the best food. Besides, the irregularly-hold gourmet fairs, like Korean Fair and Southeastern Fair, are good chances to taste exotic flavors.

尚雅全日餐吧
Galaxy Bistro

自助餐
Buffet

3.3 必应搜索热度
Search priority

电话 /Tel
+86 28 8887 6666-8308

地址 /Address
成都市武侯区临江西路 1 号
成都明宇尚雅饭店内 1 层
1F, Galaxy Minyoun Chengdu Hotel, No.1, Linjiang West Road, Wuhou District, Chengdu

营业时间 Opening Hours
早餐 Breakfast
周一至周五 Mon. - Fri. 6:30 - 10:00
周六、周日 Sat. - Sun. 6:30 - 10:30
晚餐 Dinner 17:30-21:00
着装要求 Dress Code
优雅便服 Smart Casual
人均消费 Per Capita Consumption
160 元 160 RMB

餐厅提供中、西、日美食佳肴，更有丰盛海鲜晚餐自助，配上临江美景，给人带来超然浪漫的就餐回忆。餐厅装修风格时尚现代，精美布艺包裹原木家具，完美融合东西文化装饰，处处洋溢着舒适和谐的艺术气息。

With beautiful river view, it provides Chinese cuisine, Western cuisine and Japanese delicacies, as well as abundant seafood buffet dinner, leaving diners romantic eating memories. It is decorated in a fashionable and contemporary style, with elegant fabrics, wood furniture and Eastern-Western cultural articles, giving diners a comfortable and harmonious artistic feel everywhere.

莎拉泰餐厅
Sala Thai

泰国菜
Thai Cuisine

莎拉泰餐厅是一家不可多得的高档泰国菜餐厅。这里环境别致，厨师们选用时鲜食材，结合独特的技艺和创新理念，为宾客提供丰富美味的食物。

Sala Thai is an impressive high-end Thai restaurant with a beautiful space. The chefs select seasonal ingredients and take full advantages of their remarkable culinary art with creative ideas to present a great deal of delicacies for each diner.

必应 搜索热度 Search priority 7.4

电话 /Tel
+86 28 8712 6666

地址 /Address
成都市都江堰青城山镇东软大道 2 号
No.2, Dongruan Road, Qingchengshan Town, Dujiangyan, Chengdu

营业时间 Opening Hours
午餐 Lunch
周五到周日 Fri. – Sun. 11:30 – 14:30
晚餐 Dinner
周三到周日 Wed. – Sun. 17:30 – 22:00
着装要求 Dress Code
优雅便服 Smart Casual
人均消费 Per Capita Consumption
300 元 300 RMB

棠宫餐厅
Tang Restaurant

川菜 粤菜
Sichuan Cuisine and Cantonese Cuisine

精选的浓厚汤底，季节主打的当地特色食材，厨师精心烹饪的菜品，优雅精致的用餐环境，这些都使这里成为品尝成都火锅的最佳选择。

Tang Restaurant has selective soup which is rich in fragrance with local ingredients in season. The chefs carefully prepare every dish, and the dinning environment is chic and delicate, making Tang a good place to taste Chengdu hotpot.

必应 搜索热度 Search priority 2.6

电话 /Tel
+86 28 8266 6666-6620

地址 /Address
成都市温江区文化路 111 号
No.111, Wenhua Road, Wenjiang District, Chengdu

营业时间 Opening Hours
午餐 Lunch 11:30 – 14:00
晚餐 Dinner 17:30 – 21:00
着装要求 Dress Code
优雅便服 Smart Casual
人均消费 Per Capita Consumption
150 ~ 250 元 150 ~ 250 RMB

御苑餐厅
Royal Court Restaurant

无限卡特权

中餐
Chinese Cuisine

3.6 必应搜索热度
Search priority

电话 /Tel
+86 28 6633 0518

地址 /Address
成都市青羊区宽巷子 38-39 号 1 层
1F, No.38-39, Kuanxiangzi Alley, Qingyang District, Chengdu

营业时间 Opening Hours
午餐 Lunch 11:00 – 14:30
晚餐 Dinner 17:30 – 22:00
着装要求 Dress Code
优雅便服 Smart Casual
人均消费 Per Capita Consumption
780 ~ 1680 元 780 ~ 1680 RMB

御苑餐厅主打的钓鱼台菜，被誉为中华美食皇冠上的钻石。钓鱼台菜传承宫廷肴馔根脉，汇集八大菜系精髓与世界各国食材，可谓代表中华料理的殿堂级美食。

Royal Court features Diaoyutai cuisine which is regarded as the jewelry in the Chinese cuisine. Starting from the days of the ancient imperial court, Diaoyutai cuisine collects the essence of 8 major Chinese cuisines and the ingredients across Terrace Dining Private Rooms the world representing top cuisine of Chinese food.

怡品堂中餐厅（临江路店）
Yi Palace Chinese Restaurant(Linjiang Road)

无限卡特权

中餐
Chinese Cuisine

2.6 必应搜索热度
Search priority

电话 /Tel
+86 28 8553 0099

地址 /Address
成都市武侯区临江西路 1 号
No.1, Linjiang West Road, Wuhou District, Chengdu

营业时间 Opening Hours
午餐 Lunch 11:00 – 14:00
晚餐 Dinner 17:00 – 22:00
着装要求 Dress Code
便服 Casual
人均消费 Per Capita Consumption
200 元 200 RMB

怡品堂由殿堂级名厨李雪冬及其团队掌勺，除高级粤菜、新派川菜，还加入其他菜系的招牌菜与别具创意的佳肴。餐厅装修风格现代，以鲜明的暖黄、白色和复古红为主色调。

The Chef Li Xuedong and his team specialize in new Cantonese and Sichuan dishes, as well as other cuisine specialties and creative cuisine. The interior of the restaurant is modern, with warm yellow, white and retro red as main colors.

无限卡特权

宴庭中餐厅
Yan Ting Chinese Restaurant

中餐
Chinese Cuisine

必应 搜索热度 Search priority 3.3

电话 /Tel
+86 28 6283 0657

地址 /Address
成都市青羊区太升南路 88 号
成都瑞吉酒店 2 层
2F, St. Regis Chengdu, No.88, Taisheng South Road, Qingyang District, Chengdu

营业时间 Opening Hours
午餐 Lunch 11:30 – 14:30
晚餐 Dinner 17:30 – 22:30
着装要求 Dress Code
优雅便服 Smart Causal
人均消费 Per Capita Consumption
300 元 300 RMB

宴庭中餐厅的周末港式点心早午餐、清炒虾仁配花生和辣椒油、麻婆豆腐和担担面等招牌美食，让美食爱好者慕名而来。主餐厅和 3 间私人包房的设计结合了拼接瓷片等中式设计元素，时尚而典雅。

On weekends, the brunch dim sums, Fried Shrimp with Peanuts and Chilly Oil, Mapo Beancurd, and Dan Dan Noodle attract many gourmets. The main restaurant area and 3 VIP rooms adopt Chinese elements like tile inlay, making the whole restaurant fashionable and elegant.

无限卡特权

芳菲苑全日餐厅
The Lounge

中西美食
Chinese Western Cuisine

必应 搜索热度 Search priority 6.9

电话 /Tel
+86 571 8827 8888

地址 /Address
杭州市江干区五星路 65 号 1 层
1F, No.65, Wuxing Road, Jianggan District, Hangzhou

营业时间 Opening Hours
早餐 Breakfast 06:30 – 10:30
午餐 Lunch 11:30 – 14:00
晚餐 Dinner 17:00 – 22:30
着装要求 Dress Code
优雅便服 Smart Casual
人均消费 Per Capita Consumption
200 ~ 350 元 200 ~ 350 RMB

芳菲苑设有 154 个座位，外临城市绿化平台，可以享用早餐、中餐、晚餐以及下午茶。瓷片装饰的天花板诉说着杭州的瓷器文化；沿窗布置的舒适沙发与家具，既保留了中式古典韵味，又兼具西式风格。

The Lounge has 154 seats close toan urban greening zone, which is a good place to enjoy breakfast, lunch, dinner and high-tea. Its ceramic-decorated ceiling reveals the porcelain culture of Hangzhou city. The Lounge sofa and furniture are placed along the window, remaining Chinese flavor but revealing a touch of western style.

湖滨 28
28 Hubin Road

杭帮菜
Hangzhou Cuisine

无限卡特权

3.8 必应搜索热度 Search priority

电话 /Tel
+86 571 8779 1234-2828

地址 /Address
杭州市湖滨路 28 号杭州凯悦酒店 1 层
1F, Hyatt Regency Hangzhou, No. 28, Hubin Road, Hangzhou

营业时间 Opening Hours
午餐 Lunch 11:30 - 14:30
晚餐 Dinner 17:00 - 21:00
夜宵 Midnight Snack 21:30 - 03:00
着装要求 Dress Code
优雅便服 Smart Casual
人均消费 Per Capita Consumption
500 元 500 RMB

湖滨 28 环境优雅惬意，在这里可以欣赏到西湖美景。这里提供原汁原味的杭帮菜，原料上乘，大厨们刀功精湛，火候掌握得恰到好处。金牌扣肉、蟹粉豆腐、龙井虾仁等传统名菜口味地道。

28 Hubin Road is an elegant and relaxing Chinese restaurant with beautiful West Lake scenery. It stays true to the flavor of Hangzhou cuisine, makes use of top ingredients and has a remarkable chef team. Its famous classic dishes cover Signature Braised Pork, Tofu in Minced Crab Soup, Long Jing Tea Fried Shrimp.

湖光阁
Waterlight Court

西餐
Western Cuisine

无限卡特权

2.6 必应搜索热度 Search priority

电话 /Tel
+86 571 8586 0000-7210

地址 /Address
杭州市西湖区紫金港路
西溪天堂国际旅游综合体 2 号杭州西溪悦榕庄
Banyan Tree Hangzhou, No.2, West Brook International Tourist Complex, Zijingang Road, Xihu District, Hangzhou

营业时间 Opening Hours
早餐 Breakfast 06:30 - 10:30
午餐 Lunch 12:00 - 14:00
晚餐 Dinner 18:00 - 22:00
着装要求 Dress Code
无特别着装要求 Non-specified
人均消费 Per Capita Consumption
200 元 200 RMB

湖光阁掩映于国家级湿地的疏林之间，环境精致，陈设典雅。临内湖而闲坐于户外露台，四周湖光山色可以尽收眼底。餐厅主打新式西餐，以国际特选美食和当地风味为特色。

Surrounded by the national wetland park, Waterlight Court has a fabulous environment with an elegant interior decoration as an echo to such nice scenery. The outdoor terrace allows diners to enjoy delicacies under beautiful lake view environment. This restaurant features creative new Western dishes, international specialties and local flavors.

金沙厅
Jin Sha

中餐
Chinese Cuisine

必应 搜索热度
Search priority 4.0

电话 /Tel
+86 571 8113 5188

地址 /Address
杭州市西湖区灵隐路 5 号
杭州西子湖四季酒店 1 层
1F, Four Seasons Hotel Hangzhou at West Lake, No. 5, Lingyin Road, Xihu District, Hangzhou

备受食客赞誉的金沙厅坐落于美丽的杭州西子湖畔，主打高级粤菜、上海菜及多款特色杭州菜。餐厅特设户外餐饮平台，令顾客在品味美食的同时兼顾美景。
The highly-regarded Jin Sha stands by the beautiful West Lake in Hangzhou offering high-end Cantonese and Shanghai cuisines with some Hangzhou specialties. Outdoor seats are available for diners to enjoy the food in a relaxing lake-side terrace.

营业时间 Opening Hours
午餐 Lunch 11:30 - 14:00
晚餐 Dinner 17:30 - 22:00
着装要求 Dress Code
优雅便服 Smart Casual
人均消费 Per Capita Consumption
500 元 + 15% 服务费
500 RMB + 15% Service Fee

无限卡特权

静岸标帜餐厅 & 酒吧
Panorama Signature Restaurant & Bar

自助餐
Buffet

必应 搜索热度
Search priority 3.2

电话 /Tel
+86 571 2689 6317

地址 /Address
杭州市上城区望江东路 39 号
杭州尊蓝钱江豪华精选酒店 22 层
22F, The Azure Qiantang, A Luxury Collection Hotel, No.39, Wangjiang East Road, Shangcheng District, Hangzhou

与一般的自助餐厅不同，静岸标帜餐厅 & 酒吧的理念是让食客能够慢慢品味每一道美食的独具匠心和不同风味。厨师团队设计用心，菜品丰富且精致，任意一盘都称得上色香味美。
Different from the ordinary buffet restaurants, Panorama dedicates to slow each diner down to find out the characteristics and flavors of each dish. The abundant dishes are carefully designed by the chef team and each one is a combination of aesthetics and palate.

营业时间 Opening Hours
早餐 Breakfast 06:30 - 10:00
午餐 Lunch 11:30 - 14:30
晚餐 Dinner 17:30 - 21:30
着装要求 Dress Code
优雅便服 Smart Casual
人均消费 Per Capita Consumption
500 元 500 RMB

名园餐厅
MingYuan

中餐
Chinese Cuisine

4.6 必应搜索热度 Search priority

电话 /Tel
+86 571 8288 8777

地址 /Address
杭州市市心中路 818 号
杭州开元名都大酒店 3 层
3F, New Century Grand Hotel Hangzhou, No.818, Shixin Central Road, Hangzhou

营业时间 Opening Hours
午餐 Lunch 11:00 – 13:30
晚餐 Dinner 17:30 – 20:30
着装要求 Dress Code
优雅便服 Smart Casual
人均消费 Per Capita Consumption
200 元 200 RMB

名园的设计布局皆是按照古典园林亭台楼阁而来的，有种穿梭于古典园林、闲坐于花前柳下的感觉。名园擅长的菜肴，讲究的是严谨的传统配方和工艺流程，并在出品时多了一份不动声色的奢华和厨师独有的特色。
The design and layout are all originated from classical gardens, pavilions terraces and open halls. Walking and dining here place diners in the midst of historic gardens. Its dishes are produced with strictly traditional methods and techniques, and characterized by a quiet luxury and unique chef style.

牛排家（杭州店）
Steak House(Hangzhou)

西餐
Western Cuisine

7.4 必应搜索热度 Search priority

电话 /Tel
+86 571 8792 2223
+86 571 8721 1113

地址 /Address
杭州市下城区武林路 9 号
WAKE TOWN 商业街 1 栋 2 层 203
Shop 203, 2F, Building 1, WAKE TOWN Commercial Street, Wulin Road, Xiacheng District, Hangzhou

营业时间 Opening Hours
11:00–22:00
着装要求 Dress Code
优雅便服 Smart Casual
人均消费 Per Capita Consumption
350 元 350 RMB

牛排家（杭州店）位于繁华的西湖周边地段，环境舒适宜人，为旅游食客和时尚人群增添了一个享受美食的好选择。餐厅以优质湿式熟成进口牛排为主打，搭配优质进口葡萄酒，带给食客完美的就餐体验。
Located at a busy place by the West Lake, it is a good choice for tourists and fashionable people to enjoy delicious food and comfortable environment. This restaurant mainly serves high quality wet aged imported steaks, matching with superior imported wines, bringing a perfect dining experience for diners.

牛焱潮汕火锅
Niu Yan Chaoshan Beef Hotpot

潮汕菜
Chaoshan Cuisine

必应 搜索热度 Search priority 2.6

电话 /Tel
+86 571 8653 3388

地址 /Address
杭州市江干区景昙路 18-26 号庆春银泰 2 层
2F, Yintai Store Qingchun Branch, No.18-26, Jingtan Road, Jianggan District, Hangzhou

营业时间 Opening Hours
午餐 Lunch 11:00 – 14:30
晚餐 Dinner 17:00 – 22:00
着装要求 Dress Code
优雅便服 Smart Casual
人均消费 Per Capita Consumption
100 元 100 RMB

牛焱潮汕火锅主打潮汕手切牛肉，食材选择以新鲜与健康为原则，厨师于店内现场手切牛肉，保证食客吃到的都是鲜嫩、健康的牛肉。

Niu Yan features Chaoshan hand-cut tender beef, insisting in the principle of freshness and health. The chef cuts the beef in restaurant to ensure it is fresh and healthy.

PHO 东田越南粉
PHO

越南菜
Vietnamese Cuisine

必应 搜索热度 Search priority 7.4

电话 /Tel
+86 571 8692 9561

地址 /Address
杭州江汉路龙湖滨江
天街商业中心 1 栋 601-41 号
Room 601-41, Building 1, Longfor Binjiang Business Center, Jianghan Road, Hangzhou

营业时间 Opening Hours
10:00 – 21:30
着装要求 Dress Code
无特别着装要求 Non-specified
人均消费 Per Capita Consumption
90 元 90 RMB

PHO 东田越南粉作为知名造型师李东田的跨界之作，已在全国开设多家分店。餐厅的火车头牛肉河粉汤头清甜爽口，再加上大把豆芽，挤上很多青柠汁，泡在滚烫的汤碗里，挤一点甜辣酱在牛肉与河粉上，其鲜香爽滑，不言而喻。

As a crossover restaurant established by the well-known stylist Tony Lee, it has opened a number of branches among the country. The locomotive PHO is sweet and refreshing, together with a large number of bean sprouts and a lot of lime juice, soaking in a hot soup bowl and squeezing with a little sweet chili sauce on the beef and rice noodles, which is evidently fresh, fragrant and smooth.

四季轩

Four Seasons Chamber

中餐
Chinese Cuisine

2.6 必应搜索热度 Search priority

电话 /Tel
+86 571 8288 8888-8725

地址 /Address
杭州市萧山区市心中路 818 号
No.818, Shixin Central Road, Xiaoshan District, Hangzhou

营业时间 Opening Hours
午餐 Lunch 11:00-14:00
晚餐 Dinner 17:00-21:00
着装要求 Dress Code
无特别着装要求 Non-specified
人均消费 Per Capita Consumption
180 元 180 RMB

四季轩中餐厅作为杭州中餐厅的佼佼者之一，一直致力于打造让食客满意的精致中餐。餐厅的厨师团队在保留传统风味的基础上，又加入了更多的巧思创新，让中餐在四季轩展现新的光彩。此外，餐厅环境幽静，适合朋友到此小聚。

As one of the best Chinese restaurants in Hangzhou, it has been committed to producing exquisite Chinese cuisine that satisfies diners. The chef team not only retains traditional flavors, but also adds more ingenuity and innovation to make Chinese food alive. In addition, the restaurant has a quiet environment, which is suitable for friends gatherings.

溪客厅

Le Lotus

西式简餐
Western Informal Cuisine

4.6 必应搜索热度 Search priority

电话 /Tel
+86 571 8539 7677

地址 /Address
杭州市上城区长生路 57 号
No.57, Changsheng Road, Shangcheng District, Hangzhou

营业时间 Opening Hours
早午餐 Brunch 07:30 - 14:00
午餐 Lunch 11:30 - 14:00
下午茶 Afternoon Tea 14:00 - 17:00
晚餐 Dinner 17:30 - 21:00
着装要求 Dress Code
无特别着装要求 Non-specified
人均消费 Per Capita Consumption
500 元 500 RMB

溪客厅为杭州湖边邨的主要餐厅，其名源自"莲花"，因此以莲池为环境主题。优雅而古典的法式风情展现在民国时期的建筑中，颇具韵味。

Xike, also known as Le Lotus, is a major restaurant with lotus pool as its theme environment. The elegance and classic French style is presented in the building of the period of Republic of China.

无限卡特权

御苑中餐厅
Royal Court Restaurant

中餐
Chinese Cuisine

必应 搜索热度 Search priority 5.9

电话 /Tel
+86 571 8827 8888

地址 /Address
杭州市江干区五星路 65 号 18-19 层
18-19F, No.65, Wuxing Road, Jianggan District, Hangzhou

营业时间 Opening Hours
午餐 Lunch 11:30 – 14:00
晚餐 Dinner 17:30 – 22:00
着装要求 Casual
优雅便服 Smart Casual
人均消费 Per Capita Consumption
午餐 600 元 Lunch 600 RMB
晚餐 800 元 Dinner 800 RMB

御苑中餐厅的名字取自钓鱼台国宾馆的园中之园，餐厅的 2 层通过两部独立电梯连接，以保证用餐的私密性。品味钓鱼台菜，不仅能尝到精美的菜肴，更能感受到中国饮食文化与细致礼节的尊贵。

The restaurant got its name from the garden in the gardens of Diaoyutai State Guest House. 2 independent lifts connect its 2 levels to ensure the privacy of dining. Dining here is not only about the delicacies but also an exclusive experience of Chinese diet culture and exclusive service.

Fine Dining
Fine Dining

法国菜
French Cuisine

必应 搜索热度 Search priority 7.0

电话 /Tel
+86 572 805 2958

地址 /Address
湖州市德清县莫干山镇紫岭村仙人坑茶场
Xianrenkeng Tea Plantation, Ziling Village, Mohkan Shan Town, Deqing County, Huzhou

营业时间 Opening Hours
午餐 Lunch 12:00 – 14:00
晚餐 Dinner 17:00 – 22:00
着装要求 Dress Code
优雅便服 Smart Casual
人均消费 Per Capita Consumption
午餐 380 元 + 15% 服务费
Lunch 380 RMB + 15% Service Fee
晚餐 580 元 + 15% 服务费
Dinner 580 RMB + 15% Service Fee
下午茶 280 元 + 15% 服务费
Afternoon Tea 280 RMB + 15% Service Fee

Fine Dining 餐厅是隐匿于浙江莫干山的一家法国乡村式美食殿堂，坐落于连绵起伏的群山中、苍翠欲滴的茶园边。餐厅精选各地应季食材，菜单每日更新。

Le Passage Mohkan Shan's Fine Dining Restaurant is a luxury French country house restaurant, nestled in the rolling hills of an organic tea plantation and a lush bamboo forest in Mohkan Shan, Zhejiang Province. The menu changes daily according to the freshest seasonal food materials of different regions.

唐阁
T'ang Court

粤菜
Cantonese Cuisine

5.3 必应搜索热度 Search priority

电话 /Tel
+86 898 6696 9777

地址 /Address
海口市滨海大道 77 号海口朗廷酒店 43 层
43F, Langham Haikou, No.77, Binhai Road, Haikou

营业时间 Opening Hours
午餐 Lunch 11:30 – 14:30
晚餐 Dinner 17:30 – 21:30
着装要求 Dress Code
优雅便服 Smart Casual
人均消费 Per Capita Consumption
649 元 649 RMB

唐阁的装潢时尚瑰丽，设有落地大窗户，让食客在海口迷人市景的环抱下，享用精心炮制的美食。厨师致力于弘扬传统粤菜，并带来令人惊喜的正宗口味。餐厅设有玻璃酒窖和私人餐室，实为私人聚餐的理想之选。

With a fashionable and glorious decoration and large French windows, diners can taste delicacies while enjoying the charming city view of Haikou. Its chef is dedicated to promoting traditional Cantonese cuisine and providing surprising authentic flavors. It has a glass cellar and private dining rooms, which makes it an ideal choice for private dining.

日月廊
Atelier

自助餐
Buffet

7.8 必应搜索热度 Search priority

电话 /Tel
+86 898 6696 9777

地址 /Address
海口市滨海大道 77 号海口朗廷酒店 6 层
6F, Langham Haikou, No.77, Binhai Road, Haikou

营业时间 Opening Hours
全日自选美食 06:30 – 23:00
早餐 Breakfast 06:30 – 10:30
午餐 Lunch 11:30 – 14:00
晚餐 Dinner 17:30 – 21:00
着装要求 Dress Code
正式休闲 Formal Leisure
人均消费 Per Capita Consumption
320 元 320 RMB

日月廊是一家提供全日自选美食以及自助餐的餐厅，每天供应丰富的早、午、晚餐，并设有互动美食台，让客人能欣赏专业厨师即席炮制亚洲菜式和西方美食，大饱口福。海南鸡饭、新加坡肉骨茶、帝王蟹腿是餐厅的招牌菜。

It provides self-selected food and all-day buffet which has abundant breakfast, lunch and dinner, and has an interactive food table, so that diners can enjoy Asian dishes and Western food cooked by professional chefs on the spot. Its signature dishes include Hainanese Chicken Rice, Singapore Pork Bakutek and King Crab Legs.

星月廊
Star Bar And Restaurant

牛排和海鲜
Steak and Seafood

必应 搜索热度 Search priority 2.6

电话 /Tel
+86 898 6696 9777

地址 /Address
海口市滨海大道 77 号海口朗廷酒店 6 层
6F, Langham Haikou, No.77, Binhai Road, Haikou

营业时间 Opening Hours
17:00 – 23:30
着装要求 Casual
正式休闲 Formal Leisure
人均消费 Per Capita Consumption
200 元 200 RMB

星月廊是一家布置时尚、环境优雅的餐厅，是享受美酒和烤肉的理想选择。餐厅菜品方面不仅有主打的烤肉，还有滋味牛排和特色海鲜，适合与好友共享。在舒适写意的氛围下，食客可以品尝特色饮料或烧烤盛宴，尽情放松。

It has a fashionable and elegant environment which is an ideal choice for enjoying good wine and barbecue. It not only mainly provides barbecue, but also has tasteful steaks and featured seafood, suitable for sharing with friends. Under the comfortable and relaxing environment, diners can enjoy signature drinks or barbecue feast in relaxing mood.

唐阁
T'ang Court

粤菜
Cantonese Cuisine

必应 搜索热度 Search priority 5.3

电话 /Tel
+86 551 6568 8888

地址 /Address
合肥市怀宁路合肥栢景朗廷酒店 2 层
2F, Langham Hefei, Huaining Road, Hefei

营业时间 Opening Hours
午餐 Lunch 11:30 – 14:30
晚餐 Dinner 17:30 – 22:00
着装要求 Dress Code
整齐休闲 Neat and Casual
人均消费 Per Capita Consumption
820 元 820 RMB

唐阁餐厅环境雅致时尚，更有厨艺绝佳的厨师精心炮制正宗传统粤菜，让食客感受地道的美食。餐厅设有私人包厢，布置典雅惬意，适合举办小型宴会或商务晚宴。餐厅招牌菜有：蟹盖焗饭、锦绣烧味拼盘和水晶虾饺皇等。

It has an elegant and fashionable environment with masterful chefs cooking authentic traditional Cantonese cuisine, providing diners with authentic food. This restaurant has private rooms with elegant and comfortable decoration which are suitable for small banquets or business dinners. Its signature dishes include Crab Baked Rice, Assorted Barbecue Meat and Crystal Shrimp Dumplings.

季自助餐厅
Seasons Buffet

自助餐
Buffet

8.5 必应搜索热度
Search priority

电话 /Tel
+86 551 6568 8888-6770

地址 /Address
合肥市怀宁路合肥栢景朗廷酒店 2 层
2F, Langham Hefei, Huaining Road, Hefei

营业时间 Opening Hours
早餐 Breakfast
周一至周五 Mon. - Fri. 06:30 - 10:00
周六、周日 Sat. - Sun. 06:30 - 10:30
午餐 Lunch
周一至周五 Mon. - Fri. 12:00 - 14:00
周六、周日 Sat. - Sun. 12:00 - 14:30
晚餐 Dinner 17:30 - 21:30
着装要求 Dress Code
整齐休闲 Neat and Casual
人均消费 Per Capita Consumption
230 元 230 RMB

季自助餐厅汇聚各地文化和佳肴，为食客带来中西特色美馔和单点菜式。厨师会在美食站和开放式厨房即席炮制美食，加上新鲜的时令海产，让所有食客都能享受这场味觉飨宴。餐厅招牌菜有：现煎银鳕鱼、澳洲牛排、烤鸭卷等。

This restaurant integrates local cultures with delicacies, and provides diners with Western and Chinese featured dishes and a la carte dishes. Chefs cook delicacies and fresh seasonal seafood at the food station and open kitchen to present a feast for diners. Its signature dishes: Fried Cod Fish, Australian Steak, Chinese Duck Pancakes, etc.

朗豪西餐厅
The Place

中餐和西餐
Chinese and Western Cuisine

7.6 必应搜索热度
Search priority

电话 /Tel
+86 573 8789 7888

地址 /Address
海宁市文苑南路 228 号海宁朗豪酒店大堂
Lobby, Langham Haining, No.228, Wenyuan South Road, Haining

营业时间 Opening Hours
06:00 - 23:00
着装要求 Dress Code
优雅便服 Smart Casual
人均消费 Per Capita Consumption
220 元 220 RMB

朗豪西餐厅环境优雅大气，宽敞的空间可同时容纳多人用餐，为食客打造舒心的用餐环境。餐厅供应汇聚中西美食的自助餐，还有多种自选美馔。不论是悠闲午餐还是私人晚宴，都令人回味无穷。

It has an element and spacious environment which can accommodate many people dining at the same time under comfortable and relaxing atmosphere. This restaurant serves a buffet of Chinese and Western cuisines, as well as various delicacies. Both the leisure lunch and private dinner will make diners memorable.

明阁
Ming Court

粤菜
Cantonese Cuisine

必应 搜索热度 Search priority 5.5

电话 /Tel
+86 573 8789 7888

地址 /Address
海宁市文苑南路 228 号海宁朗豪酒店 2 层
2F, Langham Haining, No.228, Wenyuan South Road, Haining

营业时间 Opening Hours
午餐 Lunch 11:00 – 14:30
晚餐 Dinner 17:00 – 22:00
着装要求 Dress Codel
高级休闲 Senior Leisure
人均消费 Per Capita Consumption
470 元 470 RMB

明阁餐厅主营粤菜，以各种精品佳肴为食客打造高端的用餐环境。明阁的厨师以其精湛的厨艺，精心炮制创新且地道的顶级粤菜，再加上优雅瑰丽的布置，使餐厅成为举办商务宴会、家庭聚餐和时尚庆典的理想场地。

It mainly provides Cantonese cuisine and creates a high-end dining environment for diners with various delicacies. With chefs cooking innovative and authentic superior Cantonese cuisine through their excellent culinary arts and an elegant and magnificent environment, it becomes an ideal place for business banquets, family gatherings and fashion celebrations.

樱馆
Sakura

日本料理
Japanese Cuisine

必应 搜索热度 Search priority 9.1

电话 /Tel
+86 573 8789 7888

地址 /Address
海宁市文苑南路 228 号海宁朗豪酒店 2 层
2F, Langham Haining, No.228, Wenyuan South Road, Haining

营业时间 Opening Hours
周四至周六 Thur. – Sat.
晚餐 Dinner 17:00 – 22:00
着装要求 Dress Code
高级休闲 Senior Leisure
人均消费 Per Capita Consumption
200 元 200 RMB

樱馆提供顶级铁板烧，让食客体验精致高端的日本美食，加上殷勤周到的服务，还有清酒，缔造创新的餐饮体验。餐厅设有铁板烧餐桌，食客可在现场一边欣赏热情的铁板烧表演，一边品尝美食。

It provides Haining top Teppanyaki to bring diners experience exquisite high-end Japanese cuisine, and creates an innovative dining experience with attentive considerate services and sakes. This restaurant is equipped with a teppanyaki table, allowing diners enjoy teppanyaki performance while tasting delicious food.

钱湖渔港
Seafood House

无限卡特权

宁波菜
Ningbo Cuisine

5.2 必应搜索热度
Search priority

电话 /Tel
+86 574 2888 1234

地址 /Address
宁波市鄞州区东钱湖大堰路 188 号
No.188, Dayan Road, Dongqian Lake, Yinzhou District, Ningbo

营业时间 Opening Hours
午餐 Lunch 11:30 – 14:30
晚餐 Dinner 17:00 – 21:30
着装要求 Dress Code
优雅便服 Smart Casual
人均消费 Per Capita Consumption
300 元 300 RMB

宁波柏悦酒店内的钱湖渔港，环境静谧优雅，中式风格中流露着江南水乡的雅趣。餐厅在其他方面也充分体现出本地特色文化，比如菜式以极具宁波特色的水产美食为主。

Seafood House inside Park Hyatt Ningbo is tranquil and graceful with an interesting water-town touch in its Chinese-style settings. Other aspects of the restaurant show the local features too. For example, its dishes feature the local seafood from Ningbo.

钱湖阁
Fortune Pavilion

宁波菜
Ningbo Cuisine

3.6 必应搜索热度
Search priority

电话 /Tel
+86 574 2893 7564

地址 /Address
宁波市东钱湖旅游度假区连心路 99 号宁波东钱湖华茂希尔顿度假酒店会议中心 1 层
1F, Hilton Ningbo Dongqian Lake Resort, Convention Centre, No.99, Lianxin Road, Dongqian Lake Tourist Resort, Ningbo

营业时间 Opening Hours
早午餐 Brunch 07:30 – 14:00
午餐 Lunch 11:30 – 14:00
下午茶 Afternoon Tea 14:00 – 17:00
晚餐 Dinner 17:30 – 21:00
着装要求 Dress Code
无特别着装要求 Non-specified
人均消费 Per Capita Consumption
500 元 500 RMB

钱湖阁中餐厅临湖而居，主打宁波本帮菜及海鲜，本地厨师的精湛厨艺打造出令人垂涎的美食盛宴。无论是在充满时尚格调的大厅，还是在带有瞰湖露台的私密包厢，食客都可在品尝美味的同时，欣赏到美不胜收的湖景。

As a Chinese restaurant located near a lake, it features with Ningbo local cuisine and seafood. The exquisite culinary arts of local chefs create a mouth-watering delicacies feast. Diners will enjoy a beautiful lake view while tasting delicious food in the fashionable lobby or private boxes with balcony.

无限卡特权

明阁
Ming Court

中餐
Chinese Cuisine

必应 搜索热度 Search priority 5.5

电话 /Tel
+86 574 8911 4777

地址 /Address
宁波市中山东路 2109 号
宁波文化广场朗豪酒店 3 层
3F, Langham Place Ningbo Culture, No.2109, Zhongshan East Road, Ningbo

营业时间 Opening Hours
午餐 Lunch 11:00 – 14:00
晚餐 Dinner 17:00 – 21:00
着装要求 Casual
整齐休闲 Neat and Casual
人均消费 Per Capita Consumption
540 元 540 RMB

宁波明阁餐厅时刻秉持钻研的精神，为了完全展现香港同名食府的精髓，并展现属于宁波的独特魅力，餐厅的厨师用心挖掘珍稀特色食材，致力于为食客呈现一场精致的盛宴。此外，餐厅提供丰富多彩的商务套餐，任君选择。

This restaurant always adheres to the spirit of research to fully present the essence of Hong Kong restaurant with the same name and show the unique charm of Ningbo. Its chefs carefully select rare and local food materials to provide delicacies feasts for diners. In addition, this restaurant provides various business packages for diners to choose.

佩雷丝
The Place

自助餐
Buffet

必应 搜索热度 Search priority 7.6

电话 /Tel
+86 574 8908 9999-6610

地址 /Address
宁波市中山东路 2109 号
宁波文化广场朗豪酒店 1 层
1F, Langham Place Ningbo Culture, No.2109, Zhongshan East Road, Ningbo

营业时间 Opening Hours
早餐 Breakfast
周一至周五 Mon. – Fri. 06:30 – 10:00
周六、周日 Sat. – Sun. 06:30 – 10:30
午餐 Lunch
周一至周五 Mon. – Fri. 11:00 – 14:00
周六、周日 Sat. – Sun. 11:00 – 14:30
晚餐 Dinner 17:30–21:00
着装要求 Dress Code
整齐休闲 Neat and Casual
人均消费 Per Capita Consumption
154 元 154 RMB

佩雷丝餐厅供应各类中西佳肴，无论是享用自助餐还是照菜单点，都尽可能满足食客的需求。餐厅从意粉、意式薄饼、时令海鲜、寿司刺身到顶级牛排及烤肉，应有尽有，全天候为食客献上精彩纷呈的环球特色美馔。

It provides a wide variety of Chinese and Western cuisine, no matter the buffet or dishes ordered according to the menu will meet the needs of diners as much as possible. This restaurant serves spaghetti, tortillas, seasonal seafood, sushi and sashimi, prime steaks and barbecued meats throughout the day to bring diners experience global characteristics.

陆潮新派中餐厅
LuChao

粤菜
Cantonese Cuisine

3.7 必应搜索热度
Search priority

电话 /Tel
+86 25 5878 0888

地址 /Address
南京市建邺区邺城路 2 号
南京卓美亚酒店 40 层
40F, Jumeirah Hotel Nanjing, No.2,
Yecheng Road, Jianye District, Nanjing

营业时间 Opening Hours
午餐 Lunch 11:30-14:30
晚餐 Dinner 17:30-21:30
着装要求 Dress Code
休闲时尚 Leisure Fashion
人均消费 Per Capita Consumption
450 元 450 RMB

陆潮新派中餐厅供应各类原始风味美食以及备受欢迎的现代佳肴，菜式搭配新颖，细节考究。餐厅菜品摆盘精美，佳肴不绝，是招待特别贵宾、家人及好友的理想场地。现代粤菜包括手工点心、粤式烤鸭、鹅肝和神户牛肉等。

It provides all kinds of delicacies in original flavors and popular modern cuisine with innovative and exquisite collocation of dishes. This restaurant is an ideal place for special guests, family and friends gatherings as it presents beautiful and delicious dishes. The modern Cantonese cuisine includes handmade pastry, Cantonese roast duck, foie gras, Wagyu beef, etc.

酌鱻海鲜餐吧
ZhuoXian

海鲜
Seafood

2.6 必应搜索热度
Search priority

电话 /Tel
+86 25 5878 0888

地址 /Address
南京市建邺区邺城路 2 号南京卓美亚酒店 41 层
41F, Jumeirah Hotel Nanjing, No.2, Yecheng Road, Jianye District, Nanjing

营业时间 Opening Hours
17:30 - 01:00
着装要求 Dress Code
休闲时尚 Leisure fashion
人均消费 Per Capita Consumption
400 元 400 RMB

酌鱻海鲜餐吧采用深蓝灰色、橄榄绿和深棕色质朴色调装饰，旨在为食客呈现充满趣致而又休闲放松的环境。海鲜菜单融合各国风味，所有菜品均采用现捕海鲜烹制。餐厅的所有菜品均选用优质食材，以餐前小吃的形式供应，适合分食共享。

It is decorated in dark bluish gray, olive green and dark brown colors, aiming to establish an interesting and relaxing environment for diners. The seafood menu contains the delicacies of various countries with all seafood caught and cooked on the spot. All the dishes in this restaurant are made of high quality ingredients and are served in the form of appetizer, which are suitable for sharing.

悦庐
The Fireplace

西餐
Western Cuisine

必应 搜索热度 Search priority 2.6

电话 /Tel
+86 512 6288 1234-3430

地址 /Address
苏州市工业园区华池街 88 号
苏州凯悦酒店 3 层
3F, Hyatt Regency Suzhou, No.88, Huachi Street, Industrial Park, Suzhou

营业时间 Opening Hours
17:00 – 22:00
着装要求 Dress Code
优雅便服 Smart Casual
人均消费 Per Capita Consumption
400 元 400 RMB

悦庐是肉食者的天堂。招牌美食带骨肉眼牛排在特制的砧板盛器上呈现，烤到恰好，不老不血。将切下的一小块放进嘴里，肥瘦均匀，鲜嫩多汁。

The Fireplace is a paradise for meat-lovers. The signature Bone-in Rib Eye Steak is skillfully baked and presented on chopping board. With a bite of it, you can feel the perfect beef texture with juice.

凯宾全日制餐厅
Café K

咖啡厅
Café

必应 搜索热度 Search priority 3.7

电话 /Tel
+86 898 8865 5555

地址 /Address
三亚市海棠湾海棠北路 2 号
No.2, Haitang North Road, Haitang Bay, Sanya

营业时间 Opening Hours
早餐 Breakfast 07:00 – 10:30
午餐及晚餐 Lunch & Dinner
12:00 – 22:30
着装要求 Dress Code
优雅便服 Smart Casual
人均消费 Per Capita Consumption
300 元 300 RMB

在凯宾全日制餐厅，客人能够近距离观赏欧陆美食、时鲜佳肴与海南特色菜品的烹饪过程。这里装潢考究，环境优雅温馨，技艺精湛的西厨团队为顾客奉上地道的欧陆风情美食。

It is available to watch closely how the Continental delicacy, seasonal cuisine and Hainan-flavor cuisine are crafted in Café K. With the sophisticated decorations and elegant environment, the superb western chefs offer the authentic continental cuisine with various beverages served.

康提奇餐厅
Kon Tiki Restaurant

自助餐
Buffet

3.7 必应搜索热度 Search priority

电话 /Tel
+86 898 8875 8888

地址 /Address
三亚市海棠北路 88 号三亚香格里拉度假酒店
Shangri-La Sanya Resort & Spa Hotel, No.88, Haitang North Road, Sanya

营业时间 Opening Hours
晚餐 Dinner 17:30 – 22:30
着装要求 Dress Code
优雅便服 Smart Casual
人均消费 Per Capita Consumption
150 元 150 RMB

位于三亚香格里拉度假酒店乐蜓园 1 层的康提奇餐厅提供夏威夷和波利尼西亚式的全新用餐体验。它将最传统的配方与现代的烹饪手法相结合，用独具特色的海南本地海鲜和调味料烹饪出色味俱佳的波利尼西亚美食。
Located at 1st floor of Dragonfly of Shangri-La Sanya Resort & Spa Hotel, Kon Tiki Restaurant brings in a new Hawaii and Polynesia dining experience. It combines traditional recipes with modern cooking methods, and uses special Hainan seafood and condiment to showcase fresh Polynesia tastes.

霓湾海鲜西餐厅
Neera Seafood Restaurant

西餐
Western Cuisine

6.3 必应搜索热度 Search priority

电话 /Tel
+86 898 8863 9999

地址 /Address
三亚市亚龙湾国家旅游度假区
三亚美高梅度假酒店
Mgm Grand Sanya, Yalong Bay National Resort, Sanya

营业时间 Opening Hours
早餐 Breakfast 07:00 – 11:00
午餐 Lunch 11:30 – 14:30
晚餐 Dinner 17:30 – 22:00
着装要求 Dress Code
优雅便服 Smart Casual
人均消费 Per Capita Consumption
200 元 200 RMB

霓湾海鲜西餐厅为酒店的臻享系列目的地之一，专门为喜爱享受高品质及个性化的客人提供服务，也期待为不同的客人打造尊贵礼遇。
As one of the destinations that you cannot miss Neera Seafood Restaurant, it satisfies diners' demands with high-quality and personalized services, and looks forward to offering exclusive experience for different guests.

熹餐厅
S.E.A. Restaurant

海鲜
Seafood

必应 搜索热度 Search priority 2.7

电话 /Tel
+86 898 8875 8888

地址 /Address
三亚市海棠北路 88 号三亚香格里拉度假酒店
Shangri-La Sanya Resort & Spa Hotel, No.88, Haitang North Road, Sanya

营业时间 Opening Hours
晚餐 Dinner 17:30 - 22:30
着装要求 Dress Code
优雅便服 Smart Casual
人均消费 Per Capita Consumption
200 ~ 300 元 200 ~ 300 RMB

熹餐厅主打新加坡、马来西亚、泰国等原汁原味的东南亚美食。餐厅大厨谢嘉成来自马来西亚，经验丰富，深谙东南亚美食烹饪之道。优雅的音乐和精致的东南亚装饰为整个餐厅增色不少。

S.E.A Restaurant features authentic Southeastern delicacies such as Singapore, Malaysia and Thailand cuisines. The Malaysian chef Xie Jiacheng is a master of this regional flavor. Graceful music and delicate Southeastern-style decoration surround the whole space.

悦轩中餐厅
Yuen Court Chinese Restaurant

中餐
Chinese Cuisine

必应 搜索热度 Search priority 2.6

电话 /Tel
+86 898 8865 5555

地址 /Address
三亚市海棠湾海棠北路 2 号
No.2, Haitang North Road, Haitang Bay, Sanya

营业时间 Opening Hours
午餐 Lunch 11:30 - 14:00
晚餐 Dinner 17:30 - 21:00
着装要求 Dress Code
优雅便服 Smart Casual
人均消费 Per Capita Consumption
200 ~ 250 元 200 ~ 250 RMB

悦轩中餐厅拥有 13 间雅致包厢，餐厅烹饪精致粤菜与海南本地特色菜品。除中式菜肴外，客人也可在此品尝到进口名酒及配菜佳饮。

With 13 refined VIP rooms, Yuen Court Chinese Restaurant offers elaborate Cantonese cuisines and local Hainan-flavor dishes, including imported famous wines, side dishes and beverages.

奥西亚诺海底餐厅
Ossiano Underwater Restaurant & Bar

西餐
Western Cuisine

3.5 必应搜索热度
Search priority

电话 /Tel
+86 898 8898 6666

地址 /Address
三亚市海棠湾海棠北路 36 号
三亚 · 亚特兰蒂斯大堂 G 层
G, Lobby, Atlantis Hotel Sanya, No.36,
Haitang North Road, Haitang Bay, Sanya

营业时间 Opening Hours
午餐 Lunch 11:30 – 14:30
晚餐 Dinner 17:30 – 22:00
着装要求 Dress Code
优雅便服 Smart Casual
人均消费 Per Capita Consumption
1600 元 1600 RMB

奥西亚诺海底餐厅位于酒店花园层，在午餐及晚餐时段均提供多个套餐形式的菜单，丰富的海鲜拼盘呈现在餐桌上，紧接着是豪华的海鲜主菜，佐以精选葡萄酒或特制鸡尾酒和餐后甜点，伴以国内独一份的用餐景致，呈现独一份的浪漫。Located at the hotel's garden floor, it provides multiple lunch and dinner packages. Diners can enjoy abundant seafood platter followed by a luxurious seafood main dish, together with selected wine or special cocktails and desserts while appreciating such unique and romantic dining environment.

蟹
Crab

新加坡菜
Singapore Cuisine

7.9 必应搜索热度
Search priority

电话 /Tel
+86 898 8898 6666

地址 /Address
三亚市海棠湾海棠北路 36 号
三亚 · 亚特兰蒂斯“蟹”餐厅
“Crab”, Atlantis Hotel Sanya, No.36,
Haitang North Road, Haitang Bay, Sanya

营业时间 Opening Hours
午餐 Lunch 11:30 – 14:30
晚餐 Dinner 17:30 – 22:00
着装要求 Dress Code
无特别着装要求 Non–specified
人均消费 Per Capita Consumption
400 元 400 RMB

蟹餐厅是一家主打螃蟹料理的新加坡风味餐厅，也是三亚地区唯一专门为宾客炮制各类螃蟹料理的特色餐厅。该餐厅采用新加坡风格的烹饪方法，确保食品的新鲜度，提供如驰名辣椒蟹、金沙咸蛋黄蟹、胡椒蟹等多种蟹料理。As a Singapore cuisine restaurant, it specializes in crab cuisine and is also the only one restaurant that provides various crab food in Sanya. The Singapore chef from Atlantis incorporates Singapore flavors into the menu and provides diners a unique Tarik performance during dining.

BSK
Bread Street Kitchen & Bar

西餐
Western Cuisine

必应 搜索热度 Search priority 8.2

电话 /Tel
+86 898 8898 6666

地址 /Address
三亚市海棠湾海棠北路 36 号
No.36, Haitang North Road, Haitang Bay, Sanya

营业时间 Opening Hours
午餐 Lunch 11:30 – 14:30
晚餐 Dinner 17:30 – 22:00
着装要求 Dress Code
优雅便服 Smart Casual
人均消费 Per Capita Consumption
460 元 460 RMB

餐厅主打英伦和欧陆菜式，全部使用英国进口的食材与配料，搭配来自西南太平洋地区的优质特色食材，从而烹制出堪比其伦敦餐厅的优质菜品；除了经典之作，酒水方面还提供具有创意性的新式鸡尾酒和来自世界各地的优质葡萄酒。

This restaurant mainly provides British and European cuisine with all food materials and ingredients imported from UK, together with high-quality featured ingredients from the Southwest Pacific Area, producing high-quality dishes as good as those in London. In addition to classic dishes, it also serves innovative new cocktails and fine wines from all over the world.

心畅酒吧
Sing Ken Ken Bar

西式简餐
Western Informal Cuisine

必应 搜索热度 Search priority 3.6

电话 /Tel
+86 898 8338 9888

地址 /Address
陵水县英州镇清水湾大道
海南莱佛士酒店
Raffles Hainan, Qingshuiwan Road, Yingzhou Town, Lingshui County

营业时间 Opening Hours
午餐 Lunch 11:00 – 18:00
着装要求 Dress Code
正装、泳装 Formal Wear , Swimming Suit
人均消费 Per Capita Consumption
150 元 150 RMB

休闲写意的心畅酒吧让宾客可以一边享受舒适阳光，一边品尝新鲜调制的饮品和风味小吃。整个餐厅也营造出一种轻松愉悦、休闲写意的独特氛围——优雅舒适的背景音乐、池边的室内餐厅、特色酒水，以及得天独厚的自然环境。

This casual Sing Ken Ken Bar enables guests to enjoy an impressive array of professionally mixed drinks and fresh local flavor snack while relaxing in the sunshine. It features grace and comfortable background music, poolside indoor dinning, special drinks and advantaged natural environment.

意味海鲜餐厅
Sapori

地中海菜式
Mediterranean Cuisine

7.1 必应搜索热度
Search priority

电话 /Tel
+86 898 8338 9888-6312

地址 /Address
陵水县英州镇清水湾大道
海南莱佛士酒店
Raffles Hainan, Qingshuiwan Road,
Yingzhou Town, Lingshui County

营业时间 Opening Hours
晚餐 Dinner 17:30-22:00
着装要求 Dress Code
正装或休闲装 Foemal or Casual
人均消费 Per Capita Consumption
380 元 380 RMB

餐厅位于莱佛士酒店的白沙滩边，室内优雅精致的氛围和室外宽敞小资的露台都是享用美食的绝佳场所。餐厅主打正宗地中海风味菜品，供应各式意大利葡萄酒和佳肴，再加上壮阔的海景，令其滋味锦上添花。
It is located by the white beach of Raffles Hotel, and is a perfect place for enjoying delicacies under an elegant indoor atmosphere and in a spacious outdoor terrace. This restaurant features authentic Mediterranean-style cuisine and serves a wide range of Italian wines and delicacies, as well as possesses spectacular sea views.

羲和雅苑（天津银河店）
XIHE Ya Court(Tianjin Galaxy)

中餐
Chinese Cuisine

2.9 必应搜索热度
Search priority

电话 /Tel
+86 22 8388 7926 / 7928

地址 /Address
天津市河西区乐园道 9 号银河购物中心 3 层
3F, Galaxy Mall, No.9, Leyuan Road,
Hexi District, Tianjin

营业时间 Opening Hours
午餐 Lunch 11:00 – 14:00
晚餐 Dinner 17:00 – 21:00
着装要求 Dress Code
优雅便服 Smart Casual
人均消费 Per Capita Consumption
142 元 142 RMB

羲和雅苑（天津银河店）窗明几净，宽敞开阔。在这里，最适合的就是和三五好友一起，一边聊天叙旧，一边品尝羲和美食。当然，除了必点的特色烤鸭之外，诸如宫保虾球、糖醋青梅小排等既传统又创新的菜品，一定会让你赞不绝口。
With bright and grand space, XIHE Ya Court (Tianjin Galaxy) is a good place for friends, gathering when enjoying XIHE's specialties. Besides the signature XIHE Special Roast Duck, other creative dishes, like Superior Crab Roe , are rather impressive too.

盛宴标帜餐厅
Feast

自助餐
Buffet

必应 搜索热度 Search priority 7.5

电话 /Tel
+86 22 6528 8888-6210

地址 /Address
天津市滨海新区开发区第二大街 50 号
No.50, Second Street, Binhai New District Development Area, Tianjin

营业时间 Opening Hours
早餐 Breakfast 06:00 - 10:00
午餐 Lunch 11:30 - 14:00
晚餐 Dinner 17:30 - 22:00
着装要求 Dress Code
无特别着装要求 Non-specified
人均消费 Per Capita Consumption
200 元 200 RMB

盛宴标帜餐厅为天津滨海喜来登酒店内的自助餐厅，国际化的多品类菜肴、开放式厨房和现场烹饪的美食，能够为客人带来美好的就餐体验。

Feast is a buffet restaurant inside Tianjin Sheraton Hotel, offering various international cuisines. The open kitchen with chefs preparing food on site brings in wonderful dining experience.

羲和雅苑（北郊熙地港店）
XIHE Ya Court(City On)

中餐
Chinese Cuisine

必应 搜索热度 Search priority 2.9

电话 /Tel
+86 29 8668 9805
+86 29 8668 9806

地址 /Address
西安市未央区未央路 170 号
熙地港购物中心 4 层
4F, City On, No.170, Weiyang Road, Weiyang District, Xi'an

营业时间 Opening Hours
午餐 Lunch 11:00 - 14:30
晚餐 Dinner 17:00 - 22:00
着装要求 Dress Code
优雅便服 Smart Casual
人均消费 Per Capita Consumption
120 元 120 RMB

羲和雅苑每一位厨师都热爱美食又创意无限，不仅创新出烤鸭的创意吃法，更研制出青梅小排、拆骨肉炖白菜等菜式。同时，这里中国风浓郁的古典装修风格一定会让食客收获一段愉悦的美食体验。

XIHE Ya Court features Beijing cuisine. Every chef here has great passion for delicacy and creation. Besides the creative way to cook roast duck, they also develop Braised Spare Ribs in Green Plum Sauce and Stewed Boneless Meat and Cabbages. Dining in such a classical Chinese-style restaurant must be a joyful and beautiful culinary experience.

乐美中餐厅
Le Mei

无限卡特权

粤菜
Cantonese Cuisine

3.9 必应搜索热度
Search priority

电话 /Tel
+86 592 7709 178

地址 /Address
厦门市湖里区南山冠军路 7 号
No.7, Nanshan Guanjun Road,
Huli District, Xiamen

营业时间 Opening Hours
午餐 Lunch 11:30 – 14:30
晚餐 Dinner 17:30 – 22:00
着装要求 Dress Code
优雅便服 Smart Casual
人均消费 Per Capita Consumption
200 元 200 RMB

乐美中餐厅作为采用独特设计理念的中餐厅，充分彰显当地市场及地区文化特色。客人在欣赏餐厅时尚温馨环境的同时，还能体验到酒店与餐厅高效友好的服务。

Le Mei is a Chinese restaurant with a unique design concept that adapts to the local market and regional culture. Guests will experience efficient and friendly services while enjoy the warm and fashionable environment.

红厝 8 号 · 烧酒配
NO. 8 RED HOUSE

私房菜
Chef Table

2.6 必应搜索热度
Search priority

电话 /Tel
+86 592 5171 333

地址 /Address
厦门市思明区谊爱路 8 号
No.8, Yi'ai Road, Siming District, Xiamen

营业时间 Opening Hours
午餐 Lunch 11:30 – 14:00
晚餐 Dinner 17:30 – 22:00
着装要求 Dress Code
优雅便服 Smart Casual
人均消费 Per Capita Consumption
255 元 255 RMB

极具本土文化气息的名字背后是对闽南传统民俗和美食的传承。漂亮的红砖、精美的石雕、优美的屋脊，再加上美味的菜品，给前来品尝的食客不一样的温馨体验。

Such a local name reveals the heritage of Southern Fujian customs and gourmets. The beautiful red bricks, delicate stone carvings and the impressive ridge with the delicious food must give each diner an extraordinary home-like dining experience.

明阁
Ming Court

无限卡特权

中餐
Chinese Cuisine

必应 搜索热度 Search priority 5.5

电话 /Tel
+86 592 6029 999-8908

地址 /Address
厦门市仙岳路 4668 号厦门朗豪酒店 2 层
2F, Langham Place Xiamen, No.4668, Xianyue Road, Xiamen

营业时间 Opening Hours
午餐 Lunch 11:00 – 14:30
晚餐 Dinner 17:30 – 22:00
着装要求 Casual
整齐休闲 Neat and Casual
人均消费 Per Capita Consumption
150 元 150 RMB

厦门明阁中餐厅秉承香港同名食府的优良传统，带来各种新派粤式经典珍馐佳肴和地道特色美馔，呈现一场艺术与味蕾的盛宴。厨艺精湛的厨师们发挥超凡创意，挑选顶级稀珍食材，精心炮制令人耳目一新的精致新派粤菜。

This restaurant follows the fine traditions of Hong Kong's restaurant with the same name, and brings various new Cantonese classic delicacies and authentic featured dishes to present a feast of art and taste buds. The masterful chefs select the top rare ingredients to make a refreshing new Cantonese cuisine with extraordinary creativity.

黑明餐厅
Hennessy

中餐
Chinese Cuisine

必应 搜索热度 Search priority 8.1

电话 /Tel
+86 592 2221 577

地址 /Address
厦门市湖滨南路 57 号
No.57, Hubin South Road, Xiamen

营业时间 Opening Hours
午餐 Lunch 11:00 – 15:00
晚餐 Dinner 17:00 – 21:00
着装要求 Dress Code
优雅便服 Smart Casual
人均消费 Per Capita Consumption
140 元 140 RMB

黑明餐厅的创始人作为新派厦门菜的代表人，以其好学、质朴、善于钻研的精神，跨地域的烹饪方式和多元化的事业，赢得了业内外的一致好评。餐厅的豪华五星薄饼是一道招牌菜，以其丰富的配料，吸引了无数慕名而来的食客。

As a representative of the new Xiamen cuisine, the founder of this restaurant has earned high praise among the industry for the spirit of learning, purifying and researching, cross-regional cooking methods and diversified careers. Its Luxury Five-star Griddle Cake is a signature dish, which attracts numerous diners with its rich ingredients.

万豪中餐厅
Man Ho

中餐
Chinese Cuisine

4.7 必应搜索热度 Search priority

电话 /Tel
+86 371 8707 8200

地址 /Address
郑州市郑东新区商务中央公园 2 号
郑州绿地 JW 万豪酒店 39 层
39F, JW Marriott Hotel Zhengzhou, No.2, Center Garden, Zhengdong New District, Zhengzhou

营业时间 Opening Hours
午餐 Lunch 11:30 - 14:30
晚餐 Dinner 17:30 - 22:30
着装要求 Dress Code
无特别着装要求 Non-specified
人均消费 Per Capita Consumption
260 元 260 RMB

万豪中餐厅行政总厨带领其厨师团队，融合豫菜精髓烹饪出别具一格的粤菜，还提供川派创新菜式，为食客打造中原盛宴，餐厅还可为宴会设计不同主题的五谷摆台。餐厅服务用心、周到，令食客有一种宾至如归的温暖。

The executive chef of this restaurant, leads the chef team to produce distinctive Cantonese cuisine by integrating essences of Henan cuisine, and also provides innovative Sichuan dishes, bringing a feast of Central Plains to diners. In addition, it can design crops presentation according to different banquets with distinct themes. Its services are thoughtful and considerate, making diners feel at home.

圆顶阁西餐厅
The Dome Brasserie

西餐
Western Cuisine

2.6 必应搜索热度 Search priority

电话 /Tel
+86 371 6555 7820

地址 /Address
郑州市索菲特国际饭店下沉 1 层
Underground, Sofitel Zhengzhou, Zhengzhou

营业时间 Opening Hours
早餐 Breakfast 06:30 - 10:30
（周六、周日 Sat. - Sun. 11:00）
午餐 Lunch 12:00 - 14:30
晚餐 Dinner 18:00 - 21:30
着装要求 Dress Code
优雅便服 Smart Casual
人均消费 Per Capita Consumption
200 元 200 RMB

圆顶阁西餐厅的环境高端大气，装饰布置令人赏心悦目，适合商务宴请、朋友聚餐、情侣约会等场合。餐厅出品正宗西餐，将各式菜肴相结合，给食客耳目一新的用餐体验。餐厅始终致力于将精致美食带给有品位的食客。

It has an elegant and high-end environment with beautiful and pleasant decorations, which is suitable for business banquets, friend gatherings and lovers dating. This restaurant mainly provides authentic Western food and brings diners a refreshing dining experience by combining various dishes. This restaurant has always been committed to bringing delicacies to tasteful diners.

都会尚膳
Zhengzhou Kitchen

自助餐
Buffet

必应 搜索热度 Search priority 2.8

电话 /Tel
+86 371 8707 8220

地址 /Address
郑州市郑东新区商务中央花园 2 号
郑州绿地 JW 万豪酒店 38 层
38F, JW Marriott Hotel Zhengzhou, No.2, Center Garden, Zhengdong New District, Zhengzhou

营业时间 Opening Hours
早餐 Breasfast 6:30 – 10:30
午餐 Lunch 11:30 – 14:00
晚餐 Dinner 17:30 – 21:30
着装要求 Dress Code
奇装异服除外 Except Fancy Dress
人均消费 Per Capita Consumption
250 元 250 RMB

都会尚膳餐厅设有中、西、日式开放式厨房，厨师团队精心烹制，献上丰盛多样的早、中、晚自助餐。餐厅提供质嫩爽口的扇贝、波士顿龙虾、阿拉斯加雪蟹腿、品种丰富的海鲜寿司以及来自各国的季节性美食与餐后甜品。

It is equipped with open kitchens in Chinese, Western and Japanese style, and provides various breakfast, lunch and dinner buffets carefully prepared by its chef team. This restaurant provides tender and refreshing scallops, Boston lobster, Alaska snow crab legs, diversified seafood sushi, as well as seasonal delicacies and desserts of various countries.

烤汇餐厅
The Grill

西餐
Western Cuisine

必应 搜索热度 Search priority 7.4

电话 /Tel
+86 371 8707 8230

地址 /Address
郑州市郑东新区商务中央公园 2 号
郑州绿地 JW 万豪酒店 39 层
39F, JW Marriott Hotel Zhengzhou, No.2, Center Garden, Zhengdong New District, Zhengzhou

营业时间 Opening Hours
晚餐 Dinner 17:30 – 22:30
着装要求 Dress Code
正装 Formal Clothes
人均消费 Per Capita Consumption
500 元 500 RMB

烤汇餐厅格调时尚摩登，拥有专业的烧烤扒房，为宾客提供纯正的澳洲牛扒、海鲜烧烤和飘香四溢的香煎鹅肝等精致的西餐菜品，令人回味。餐厅处于城市高层，像置身于云端之中，可以一边眺望城市夜景，一边品尝佳肴。

With a modern and fashionable style, it has a professional barbecue steak house to provide authentic and exquisite Western dishes for diners, such as Australian Steak, Seafood Barbecue and fragrant Pan Fried Goose Liver, which are memorable. Located at an urban high-rise building, diners can enjoy the night view of city while tasting the food, like looking in the cloud.

品味餐厅
Taste Restaurant

无限卡特权

西餐
Western Cuisine

6.5 必应搜索热度 Search priority

电话 /Tel
+86 731 88708888

地址 /Address
吉首市乾州新区载福西路
凯莱大饭店 B2 层
B2, Gloria Grand Hotel, Zaifu West Road, Qianzhou New District, Jishou

营业时间 Opening Hours
午餐 lunch 11:30-14:30
晚餐 Dinner 17:30-22:00
着装要求 Dress Code
无特别着装要求 Non-specified
人均消费 Per Capita Consumption
168 元 168 RMB

品味餐厅是一个全日制西餐厅，宽敞的用餐空间能满足多人同时就餐。餐厅融合了丰盛的海鲜、亚洲精选美食、中国地方菜肴和各式精致甜品等多种美食，再配以开放式厨房，形成独具特色的餐厅与客人互动的盛宴概念。

It is an all day dining Western restaurant with spacious environment to accommodate many people at the same time. This restaurant provides abundant seafood, Asian selected delicacies, Chinese local dishes and various refined desserts, together with an open kitchen, forming a distinctive feast concept of dining and interacting with diners.

船中餐厅
Sampen

无限卡特权

中餐
Chinese Cuisine

7.0 必应搜索热度 Search priority

电话 /Tel
+86 731 5588 9999-6706

地址 /Address
湘潭市岳塘区福星中路 169 号
福星国际金融中心 E 座福星凯莱酒店 6 层
6F, Gloria Plaza Hotel Xiangtan, Building E, Fuxing International Financial Center, No.169, Fuxing Central Road, Yuetang District, Xiangtan

营业时间 Opening Hours
午餐 Lunch 11:30 - 14:00
晚餐 Dinner 17:00 - 21:00
着装要求 Dress Code
休闲正装 Business Casual
人均消费 Per Capita Consumption
150 元 150 RMB

船中餐厅位于酒店 6 层，是凯莱酒店集团运营多年的一个特色中餐厅品牌，拥有多间装修豪华的包厢。主营湘菜、粤菜、海鲜，华贵的中式格局，经验丰富的厨师，为您奉上精心烹调的菜肴，并充分迎合不同区域顾客的口味。

As a Chinese cuisine restaurant brand operated by the Gloria Hotel for many years, it is situated on the sixth floor of the Hotel and has many luxurious private rooms. It provides Hunan cuisine, Cantonese cuisine, and seafood. Diners from different places will be satisfied with luxurious Chinese style pattern and carefully prepared dishes by experienced chefs.

附 厨师奖

APPENDIX: BEST CHEFS

金强
Jin Qiang

北京东方君悦大酒店
长安壹号
中厨房总厨师长
Made in China, Grand Hyatt Beijing Chinese Chef

金强是地道的北京人，从事烹饪行业至今已有30余年。他善于博采众长和改进创新，为普通家常菜赋予新意。为给宾客带来独特新颖的用餐体验，金强师傅每年至少两次去各地采风，探寻当地风味及特色食材，并将其融合创新。他的足迹已遍及祖国大江南北，也让广大食客通过他的菜品环游舌尖上的中国。

Jin Qiang is a Beijing native and entered culinary field for over 30 years. He is skilled at learning the advantages from others and creating something new. His dishes are always expressing the common home dishes in a creative way. To refresh his diners' palate, he would travel around at least twice a year to look for some regional flavors and ingredients for integration and innovation. His paces have been almost around China, allowing his diners experiencing A Bite of China in palate.

董振祥
Dong Zhenxiang

大董餐厅 主厨
Da Dong Restaurant Chef

董振祥在京城餐饮界被赞为奇才，这不仅是因为他的烤鸭店门庭若市，还因为他在烹饪行业有着很高的声誉与地位，更因为他还是中国餐饮圈内唯一一位获得 MBA 学位的厨师兼餐饮管理者。大董的烤鸭与众不同。大董在烹饪工艺上有了很大的改变，从健康的角度为食客考虑是大董创新的基础，这也是大董烤鸭店生意红火的原因。

Dong Zhenxiang is praised as a talent in the Beijing food industry; it not only because his Roast Duck restaurant is crowded with diners and he has a high reputation and status among the culinary industry, but also because he is the only chef and restaurateur in the Chinese catering industry who has obtained an MBA degree. Different with other roast ducks, Da Dong has made great changes in cooking techniques and innovated dishes based on diners' health which is also the reason for the prosperous business of Da Dong Roast Duck restaurant.

袁超英
Yuan Chaoying

海天阁中餐厅 行政主厨
The Horizon Chinese Restaurant Executive Chef

在中国享誉盛名的烤鸭厨神，同时也是北京嘉里大酒店京菜行政主厨的袁超英，自 1978 年在全聚德的时候起，钻研烤鸭长达 23 年，随后创立了闻名京城的“鸭缘烤鸭餐厅”，众多名人都是他的座上宾。他在 2011 年正式入职北京嘉里大酒店海天阁，继续以他拿手的烤鸭，完美创造肥而不腻的绝佳口感。

Yuan Chaoying is a famous master of Roast Duck and the Executive Chef of Beijing cuisine of The Horizontal Chinese Restaurant. Mr. Yuan's research for cooking roast duck is as long as 23 years since he worked in Quan Ju De, and then he founded the famous Yayuan Roast Duck Restaurant attracting numerous celebrities. Mr. Yuan started to work in The Horizon Chinese Restaurant since 2011 and has been developing his legend of Roast Duck and presenting great taste which is fatty but not greasy.

杨占胜
Yang Zhansheng

和木私厨 主厨
The Home Chef

杨占胜的父亲是厨师，从小的耳濡目染让他对烹饪产生了浓厚的兴趣，20 年来的奋斗让他已然成为国家高级烹饪技师和高级营养师。为了和志同道合的朋友分享美食和烹饪，他在钟楼后的一条老北京胡同里开了私厨。杨占胜选用西餐常用的食材，融合中餐的烹饪手法，推出“中菜西做”的独家特色菜品，将精湛的厨艺淋漓尽致地展示在广大食客面前。

Yang Zhansheng's father was also a chef and his interest in cuisine might root in that. After 20 years of dedicated work, Yang has become a national senior cook technician and nutritionist. To share his love with those having the same belief and understanding in cuisine, he ran a chef-table restaurant in an old Beijing alley behind Zhong Lou. With the ordinary western ingredients and Chinese culinary art, he brings in his feature of Chinese cuisine in a western way and presents exquisite cooking skill to all gourmets.

李冬
Li Dong

北京瑜舍酒店京雅堂
行政总厨

Jing Yaa Tang, The Opposite House, Beijing Executive Chef

李冬曾在任职于嘉里中心大酒店期间负责过两次中国网球公开赛的饮食，同时负责过泰国公主、芬兰总统、马来西亚总理等国外重要人物访华的宴会接待工作。他拥有超过 20 年的餐厅工作经验，擅长使用美食给食客带来独特体验，创作出能取悦最挑剔美食家的作品。

During his career in Beijing Kerry Hotel, Li Dong oversaw the food and beverage for China Open twice and the banquets for receiving the important foreign Politicians, such as Thailand Princess, Finland President and Malaysian Premier. With over 20 years of culinary experience, he is good at bringing unique delicacy experience for diners and his dishes even can please the pickiest gourmets.

保罗 · 派雷特
Pau L Pairet

Ultraviolet by Paul Pairet & Mr & Mrs Bund-Modern Eatery by Paul Pairet
主厨，创办人

Ultraviolet by Paul Pairet & Mr & Mrs Bund-Modern Eatery by Paul Pairet
Chef & Founder

派雷特出生并受训于法国，他摒弃了刻板守旧的烹饪方式，以高度创新的个人风格赢得了全球美食爱好者的心。他“法式又非法式”的独特风格也为他赢得了国际赞誉：“以张扬的高超技术颠覆了食材结构及温度的处理，并且常常出人意料。”

Born and trained in French, Paul gets rid of the stiff and conservative culinary methods and creates his own style which attracts the gourmets across the world. His non-French French style earned international fame for him, with comment like that, "his excellent culinary art overthrows the ingredient structure and renews the temperature usage, and his dishes are always out of expectation."

卢怿明
Tony Lu

福和慧 行政主厨
Fu He Hui
Executive Chef

卢怿明不仅担任福系列餐厅（福和慧、福 1015 等）的行政主厨，还身兼上海文华东方酒店、北京四季酒店、杭州西子湖四季酒店的顾问主厨，并屡次获得国内外大奖。卢怿明被誉为中餐创意先锋，对美食有独到的理解，擅长融合各派所长，比如借鉴粤菜和西餐的食材、搭配与做法，将其融入上海菜中。

Tony Lu, an award-winning chef, is the Executive Chef of Fu He Hui and FU 1015. Besides, he is also the Consultant Chef for Mandarin Oriental Shanghai, Beijing Four Seasons Hotel and Hangzhou Four Seasons Hotel. He is regarded as a pioneer in Chinese cuisine and has his own understanding about delicacy. He's good at blending the advantages of various styles of cuisine. For example, he references the ingredients, food matching and cooking of Cantonese and Western cuisines to his refined Shanghai dishes.

厉晓麟
Li Xiaolin

厉家菜传人
The Family Li's Successor

热爱中华宫廷美食文化的厉晓麟多年来精心研究食材，他创办的厉家菜秉承传统，沿用古法，让食客能够感受百年前御膳房的饮食工艺。他说：“厨师不是一份工作，而是一份热情，热情才能激发内在的动力，为客人创造美味佳肴。”

Li Xiaolin is keen on Chinese Royal Delicacies for years. With elaborated research on ingredients of his family, Li stays true to traditions and adopts the old culinary art to present the hundred-year-ago royal dishes. He said, "chef is not a job but my passion; only passion can inspire a chef to create delicious food."

高晓生
Gao Xiaosheng

桂花楼 主厨
Gui Hua Lou Restaurant Chef

拥有近 30 年淮扬料理烹饪经验的桂花楼行政总厨高晓生师傅热衷于淮扬菜的烹饪。他凭借精湛的厨艺和丰富的烹饪经验，在食材、品质及烹饪方法上进行改进。高师傅率领精英厨师团队不断创新，为食客奉上一系列匠心独具的菜品。其中，红汤蒸鲥鱼、迷你葫芦八宝鸭、一品海鲜狮子头、干煸红袍清远鸡、蟹粉炖狮子头、八珍冬瓜盒等桂花楼招牌菜深受食客喜爱。

With nearly 30 years of Huaiyang cuisine experience, Gao Xiaosheng, as the Executive Chef, always commits to Huaiyang cuisine. He has improved the ingredients, quality and cooking methods based on his excellent culinary arts and rich cooking experience. He leads a team of elite chefs to innovate and provide diners with a series of ingenious dishes. Among those signature dishes, the Red Soup Steamed Shad, Mini Calabash Eight Treasure Duck, High-rank Seafood Large Meatballs, Dry-fried Red Robe Qingyuan Chicken, Crab Meat Braised Large Meatballs, and Eight Treasures Winter Melon are favored by numerous diners.

马里诺 · 安东尼奥
Marino D'Antonio

Frasca
行政总厨

Frasca
Executive Chef

马里诺从小在餐饮世家长大，后来进入圣培露烹饪学院学习深造，之后在欧洲多家知名餐厅工作，学习如何把对菜品的把控做到极致。毫无疑问，他是一个大师级的意大利厨匠，将全部的精力投入到自己所创造的每道菜里，受到很多人的喜欢。

Grown up from a family of chefs, Marino received expert training in S. Pellegrino Cooking School. After graduation, he worked for many European restaurants and learnt how to control the dish making best. Doubtlessly, Marino is an Italian chef master who dedicates to exert all his effort on every cuisine which attracts numerous diners.

梁经伦
Alvin Leung

Bo Innovation
创始人兼总厨

Bo Innovation
Founder & Executive Chef

梁经伦在伦敦出生，在加拿大成长。40 岁才出道的他，很快因其富有想象力和创造性的美食理念而备受关注，被称为“厨魔”。继香港 Bo Innovation 后，之后餐厅的开业，进一步贯彻了梁经伦的“终极中餐”概念——融合各地餐饮文化精髓，又完全以自己独特的方式演绎，带来颠覆性的美味体验。

Born in London and grown up in Canada, Alvin Leung received much attention for his imaginative and creative food belief soon after his debut in his 40s, known as "The Demon Chef". After Bo Innovation in Hong Kong, the others restaurants develop Alvin's concept of utmost Chinese cuisine which combines the food essence from different areas and is presented in Alvin's style to overthrow the mechanical idea about food.

Umberto Bombana
Umberto Bombana

香港 8 ½ Otto e Mezzo BOMBANA 主厨
Hong Kong 8 ½ Otto e Mezzo BOMBANA Chef

Umberto Bombana 在香港开设了 8 ½ Otto e Mezzo BOMBANA 餐厅，用他细腻独特的当代美食创意，激活了无数美食家的胃口。坐落在香港中环的心脏地带，优雅的亚历山大大厦内，这位意大利烹饪大师的新杰作成为香港高端餐饮的瞩目热点。他亲自为餐厅取的这个名字，是向他最喜爱的电影《8 ½》致敬，同时也是对意大利生活风格的致敬，并激发大家对意大利式享乐的探索。

Umberto Bombana has opened 8 ½ Otto e Mezzo BOMBANA in Hong Kong, and inspired numerous foodies with his exquisite and unique contemporary culinary arts. Located at the heart of Hong Kong Central and inside the elegant Alexander Building, this restaurant built by this Italian chef has become a hotspot place for high-end dining in this city. The restaurant is named after his favorite movie 8 ½ and also reflects the Italian way of life, and arouses the exploration of Italian pleasure.

理查德·埃克布鲁斯
Richard Ekkebus

Amber 主厨

Amber
Chef

历经传统法国烹饪的正统熏陶与锤炼，名厨埃克布鲁斯以其优秀的创意、精湛的技艺与可贵的创新精神，成为各界向往的顶级名厨。他十分擅长利用顶级食材与现代手法相融合来烹饪经典菜式，为宾客带来绝佳的餐饮体验。

Thanks to the cultivation and training of the authentic French culinary, Ekkebus became a world-class chef for his excellent innovation, remarkable culinary art and honorable pursue for creation. He is a master in presenting the classic dishes taking use of the top ingredients through modern culinary skills to offer extraordinary dining experience for every diner.

陈恩德
Chan Yan Tak

香港四季酒店龙景轩
行政总厨

Lung King Heen, Four Seasons Hotel Hong Kong
Executive Chef

陈恩德是地地道道的香港人，13岁时为生计走进厨房，从此便与美食结下了不解之缘。龙景轩在他的带领下屡获殊荣，备受食客好评。陈恩德将烹饪视为生活中不可或缺的一部分，认为一个厨师最坏的情况就是拒绝求变，而他每时每刻都在思考新菜式。

Chan Yan Tak is a Hong Kong native, and started his career at 13 years old for living. Under his leadership, Lung King Heen becomes award-winning and highly-appraised Chinese restaurant. Now, cooking has become an indispensable part of his life. He figures out that no changing is the worst status for a chef. Therefore, he never stops attempting to create new dishes.

黄景辉
Huang Jinghui

江 - 由辉师傅主理 主厨
Jiang By Chef Fei
Chef

身为江 - 由辉师傅主理餐厅主厨的黄景辉是中国最备受关注的著名厨师之一。16 岁出道至今共 30 年的丰富厨艺经验，年仅 26 岁当上行政总厨，率领着 20 多位名厨的团队。如今他以创意粤菜而闻名，善于利用独具创意的菜式设计，将简单的食材烹制出令人赞叹的美味。辉师傅的菜单以全新的方式展现粤菜的精致与完美，同时还原传统家庭式的用餐氛围。

As one of famous star chefs in China, he serves as the head chef of this restaurant. He has 30 years cooking experience since working at the age of 16. When he was only 26 years old, he became an executive chef and led a team of more than 20 famous chefs. Today, he is known for his creative Cantonese cuisine which is made with simple ingredients to create amazing dishes through creative designs. Its menu reflects the delicacy and perfection of Cantonese cuisine in a wholly new way, while restoring the traditional family dining atmosphere.

陆章林
Lu Zhanglin

苏浙总会 行政总厨
Jade Mansion Executive Chef

陆章林拥有 31 年专业烹饪经验，主攻淮扬菜，对上海菜、粤菜也颇有研究。他不断追求菜品的创新与融合，专注中华烹饪的传统工艺技巧和饮食文化的传承，致力于将淮扬菜的严谨选料、精细制作、雅丽风格、醇和风味、养生食疗、药膳文化等完整呈现给食客。

With 31-year culinary experience, Lu Zhanglin specializes in Huaiyang cuisine and is also good at Shanghai and Cantonese cuisines. He dedicates to pursuing dish creation and fusion, and focuses on the Chinese traditional culinary art and the heritage of food culture. Through his dishes, you can find the cautious ingredient selection, skillful cooking, elegant style, authentic flavor, healthy diet and Chinese medical diet.

雷威
Wayne Lei

深圳 1949 全鸭季 行政主厨

Duck de Chine by 1949 (Shenzhen) Executive Chef

雷威 1997 年入行，至今已经超过 20 载。和所有的厨师一样，他也经历过迷茫和煎熬，但因为恩师所写的一句李清照的“绿肥红瘦”而开悟，从此开启了不一样的厨师之旅。恩师对技艺的严格要求，对菜品的融合变化，以及他的敬业精神，都在雷威的心上留下了深深的烙印。雷威不仅深深爱着这个行业，更从心里把它当成自己终生奋斗的事业。

It has been over 20 years since 1997 when Wayne Lei started his career. Like all the chefs, he also went through a great many of doubts and frustrations. And the turning point is the piece "flourishing leaves and withering flowers" composed by the ancient Chinese famous poet Li Qingzhao which was written down by his teacher. From then on, he started a different chef exploration trip. His teacher left a great impression on him by his strict requirements, dish creation and the dedication. For Wayne, he not only loves this industry but also regards it as a life-span undertaking.

张韶华
Harris Zhang

钱湖渔港 主厨
Seafood House Chef

张韶华自 1993 年在杭州开始其厨房工作生涯并积累了丰富的工作经验。2016 年 2 月，张韶华获得了由凯悦集团亚太区高级运营总裁 Sara 女士颁发的亚太区专家奖，以表彰他精湛的厨艺和为中餐烹饪方面所做出的杰出贡献。同年张韶华被任命为宁波柏悦酒店行政总厨。张韶华带领他的厨师团队不断将菜肴推陈出新，为酒店赢得了良好的口碑，钱湖渔港餐厅也成了明星餐厅。

Harris Zhang started his chef career in Hangzhou in 1993 and has accumulated rich work experience. In February 2016, he was awarded the Asia Pacific expert award by Ms Sara, senior chief operating officer of Asia Pacific, in recognition of his excellent cooking skills and outstanding contributions to Chinese cuisine. At the same year, he was appointed the Executive Chef of Park Hyatt Ningbo Resort. He leads his chef team to constantly introduce new dishes, win a good reputation for the Hotel, and make this restaurant become famous.

江振诚
Andre Chiang

廊桥 主厨
The Bridge Chef

江振诚先生作为横跨米其林及世界五十佳餐厅评鉴榜单以及全球百大名厨榜中的唯一华人，在国际餐饮舞台上的耀眼成就迄今无人企及。如今，江振诚先生的工作重心逐渐回归故乡，廊桥 The Bridge 是他在中国大陆的第一家餐厅作品。江振诚先生首度推出了川菜国际化的“岁时料理”概念，敢于打破常规，用他独到的国际视野去还原川菜的另一面。

As the only Chinese in the list of Michelin Star restaurants, top 50 restaurants in the world and global top 100 chefs, Mr. Andre Chiang has made great achievements in the international catering industry. Now, he changed his emphasis to his hometown. The Bridge is his first restaurant in mainland China. He first introduced the Sichuan cuisine internationalization concept of "Season Cuisine" to break the routine and restore another aspect of Sichuan cuisine with his unique international vision.

张淙明
Zhang Congming

黑明 · 越界食尚 创办人
Ming's Way Restaurant Founder

"如果不在餐厅，那就是去菜市场了"是张淙明的微博签名，由此可见他对烹饪的热忱。22 年丰富的厨房经验，各地从厨的广阔行业视角，多年来对食材孜孜不倦的深度钻研，以及个人对厨师行业的独到见解，使他成为闽南地区自成一派的闽菜代表人。张淙明制作的菜肴一直将致敬传统与创新意识相结合，赢得了业内外的赞誉。

"If I was not in the restaurant, then I must be on the way to the food market." This is the tag of Zhang Congming's weibo and really testifies his love to cuisine. He has 22 years of culinary background. The working experience in different regions cultivates his grand vision and years of continuous research for ingredients with his understanding of being a chef make him an important spokesman of Fujian cuisine in south Fujian. His dishes always bring a fabulous combination between tradition and creation, earning tons of praises and fame for him.

刘韵棋
Vicky Lau

TATE Dining Room & Bar
创始人兼主厨
TATE Dining Room & Bar
Founder & Executive
Chef

平面设计师的背景，让刘韵棋指导下的餐厅装潢、菜单设计、菜品摆盘都有非常鲜明的艺术特色。精致的菜肴淋漓尽致地彰显着她的美学才华，她的每一份菜单都是一个“可食用的故事”。通过一个主题串连，她发挥天马行空的想象力精心设计每一道佳肴，务求呈现丰富的视觉效果、新颖的味觉体验及非同凡响的食材口感。

With a graphic design knowledge, Vicky Lau presents a vibrant artful style in her restaurant's interior, menu design and plate presentation. The delicate cuisines make a perfect expression of her aesthetic talent and every her menu is an eatable theme story. Her imagination brings out carefully-designed dishes fulfilling a wonderful visual and novel experience as well as extraordinary taste.

郑永麒
Vicky Cheng

VEA Restaurant and Lounge 主厨
VEA Restaurant and Lounge Chef

郑永麒虽然在西方文化下长大，但是不忘他的亚洲血统与传统，他综合了中国菜与法国菜的特色，结合了法国烹饪技术的精确性和技巧，并始终强调使用新鲜、正宗和季节性的食材，其中餐厅的食材选自世界各地，尤其是亚洲地区。在VEA餐厅，精心制作的品尝菜单围绕着一种独特的烹饪理念，就是当食材对香港本地食客散发出怀旧的吸引力时，对于外国食客可能是一种口味上的新发现。

Vicky Cheng grew up in Western culture, but he did not forget his Asian descent and traditions. He combines the characteristics of Chinese cuisine with French food, adopts the accuracy and skills of French culinary arts, and always selects fresh, authentic and seasonal food materials. The ingredients of this restaurant come from all over the world, especially from Asia. At VEA, the elaborate menu displays a unique culinary concept: the ingredients attracts local Hong Kong diners because of nostalgic atmosphere, and may be new flavors for foreign diners.

阿涅罗
Aniello Turco

Mio 餐厅 主厨
Mio Restaurant Chef

阿涅罗 24 岁时便决定启程去探访和了解世界各国美食，开始舌尖上的探索之旅，这段围绕着美食和烹饪所展开的体验，使他树立起自己人生的目标。他认为依靠食物自然转换和发酵，不加任何化学物质的原生态美食将在都会时尚餐饮界独领风骚。

At the age of 24, Aniello decided to start a gourmet trip across the world to explore the global delicacies. He set up his goal of life through this experience about food and cooking. According to him, the original food to be cooked through natural transformation and fermentation without any man-made seasonings can always have its place in the fashion restaurant industry.